W9-ADJ-944

AFFIRMATIVE ACTION

LIBRARY IN A BOOK

AFFIRMATIVE ACTION

Rachel Kranz

☑®
Facts On File, Inc.

AFFIRMATIVE ACTION

Facts On File, Inc.
132 West 31st Street
New York NY 10001

Library of Congress Cataloging-in-Publication Data
Kranz, Rachel.
    Affirmative action / Rachel Kranz.
      p. cm. — (Library in a book)
    Includes bibliographical references and index.
    ISBN 0-8160-4733-2
      1. Affirmative action programs—Law and legislation—United States.
I. Title. II. Series.
    KF3464, K73 2002
    342.73′087—dc21   2001058595

Facts On File books are available at special discounts when purchased in bulk quantities for businesses, associations, institutions, or sales promotions. Please call our Special Sales Department in New York at (212) 967-8800 or (800) 322-8755.

You can find Facts On File on the World Wide Web at http://www.factsonfile.com

Printed in the United States of America

MP Hermitage 10 9 8 7 6 5 4 3 2 1

This book is printed on acid-free paper.

*This book is gratefully dedicated to Gerrie Casey,
from whom I continue to learn so much.*

CONTENTS

PART III
APPENDICES

PART I

OVERVIEW OF THE TOPIC

CHAPTER 1

INTRODUCTION TO AFFIRMATIVE ACTION

We hold these truths to be self-evident, that all men are created equal, that they are endowed by their Creator with certain inalienable Rights, that among these are Life, Liberty, and the pursuit of Happiness.

— Declaration of Independence, *1776*

The migration or importation of such persons as any of the states now existing shall think proper to admit, shall not be prohibited by the Congress prior to the year one thousand eight hundred and eight [1808], but a tax or duty may be imposed on such importation, not exceeding ten dollars for each person.

— U.S. Constitution, *Article I, Section 9, 1787*

No person held to service or labor in one state, under the laws thereof, escaping into another, shall, in consequence of any law or regulation therein, be discharged from such service or labor, but shall be delivered up on claim of the party to whom such service or labor may be due.

— U.S. Constitution, *Article IV, Section 2, 1787*

From the very birth of the United States, the question of slavery and the legal inequality of African Americans was problematic, as was the position of women. Although the statement of "inalienable Rights" in the Declaration of Independence was meant to be universal, it implicitly excluded women, and as the Constitution makes clear, it also excluded "such persons" as might be imported by "any of the states now existing," as well as any "person held to service or labor"—that is, the men and women who had been brutally kidnapped from their homes in Africa and brought to the United States to live in slavery. From the beginning of American political history, the unequal

3

status of African Americans and women has been explicitly written into the highest law of the land, and for almost two centuries, each group has fought to rewrite that law while seeking social, political, and economic equality.

One response to this history of discrimination has been the policy of affirmative action. Affirmative action is literally the practice of "acting affirmatively": taking positive, specific steps to overcome the history and current practice of discrimination by having employers, schools, and government contractors make a special effort to include people of color and women in predominantly white and/or male workforces, student bodies, and businesses receiving government contracts.

For example, employers who practice affirmative action might make special efforts to hire more women and minorities.* They might have a specific goal, such as that minorities should ideally make up the same percentage of the workforce as their percentage in the surrounding population. Or their efforts might center on a particular kind of activity; a law firm, say, might make a special effort to send recruiters to law schools at places such as the historically black Howard University. Affirmative action might also include efforts to promote women and/or minorities to middle or upper management or to keep women and/or minorities from being concentrated in only one or two departments.

Likewise, the affirmative action programs of colleges, universities, and professional schools (law, medicine, business, and the like) might involve setting goals for a certain percentage of minority or female students; including race or gender as one criterion in admissions decisions; recruiting from minority high schools; offering mentoring or tutoring programs; setting up scholarships for women or minorities; or other activities designed to keep student populations from being predominantly white and/or male, as they were for the first two centuries of our nation's history.

Finally, many government programs that involve contracting (awarding contracts to businesses) have required that a certain portion of the contracts must go to firms owned by minorities and/or women. Likewise, the Federal Communications Commission (FCC) has established policies to help minorities obtain the licenses to television and radio stations. Other kinds of government programs are also designed to benefit female- or minority-owned businesses.

---

* The term *minority* to indicate people of color or the so-called ethnic minorities is problematic, as these groups are not necessarily in the minority in many U.S. communities, let alone worldwide. Indeed, the 2000 census revealed that white people are actually a minority in California, where they make up only 47 percent of the population. Because the term appears so often in the legal literature, however, it is used here with the understanding that it is in many ways misleading.

4

WHOM DOES AFFIRMATIVE ACTION INVOLVE?

Historically, affirmative action has focused primarily on women and people of color. While many other groups have fought discrimination, including gays and lesbians, the elderly, and the disabled, these groups have rarely, if ever, been included in affirmative action programs. Discrimination against a particular group may be illegal under federal, state, or local law, but that does not mean that an employer or college will actively try to recruit or promote people from that group or that a government program will set aside part of its budget for businesses owned by members of that group. Race and gender have been the focus of affirmative action, and so this book, too, will focus on race and gender.

Moreover, although affirmative action for women has had a huge impact on the role of women in management and the professions, most of the controversy over affirmative action—the lawsuits, the public debate, the political campaigns—has focused on the issue of race. In the past 25 years, a number of lawsuits have been brought against public colleges, universities, and professional schools, challenging their affirmative action policies. These suits are virtually all brought by white students—both male and female—claiming that the school's special efforts to recruit minority students caused white students to suffer as a consequence. Likewise, most of the landmark affirmative-action cases concerning employment have involved either white or minority employees charging discrimination. As a result, this book, too, will focus primarily on race, although gender will also be discussed.

FROM DRED SCOTT TO JIM CROW

The rationale for affirmative action has always been that a long history of discrimination and legalized inequality makes it necessary to take affirmative, positive action to overcome both past and current discrimination. Supporters of affirmative action argue that discrimination still persists and that special efforts to overcome it are still necessary. Opponents of affirmative action argue either that discrimination no longer exists or that affirmative action programs are not the appropriate remedy for it. To understand these arguments, a historical context is necessary. This overview of affirmative action therefore begins with a look at the legal status of African Americans and women in early U.S. history.

Before the Civil War, many African Americans were legally enslaved, and even free blacks faced a wide variety of legal restrictions in both the North and the South. In 1857, the Supreme Court's ruling on the Dred Scott case clarified the legal status of black Americans, calling them "subordinate and inferior beings" who could not constitutionally be citizens of the United States, whether slave or free, in the North or the South.

Four years later, the Civil War began, and two years after that, President Abraham Lincoln signed the Emancipation Proclamation, freeing the enslaved African Americans in the Confederacy. This action was given constitutional weight in 1865, six months after the Civil War had ended, when the Thirteenth Amendment permanently abolished slavery throughout the United States. In response, the former Confederate states began passing the so-called Black Codes to reestablish a separate legal category for African Americans. Both before and after the Civil War, African Americans were usually unable to testify in court or bring suit against a white person, serve on a jury, or vote, and they were generally barred from public education or shunted off to segregated institutions. Throughout the South, they were expected to ride in separate railway cars and to keep out of "white-only" hotels, restaurants, and other public accommodations. In numerous ways, the law explicitly restricted people of color from a range of opportunities in employment and education.

The Radical Republicans had control of Congress, however, and they were a passionately antislavery group, committed to bringing about full African-American equality. They were infuriated by the South's recalcitrance in granting legal rights to black people and enraged by President Andrew Johnson's veto of the country's first civil rights legislation, which would have used federal power to overcome the states' Black Codes. Thus, the Civil Rights Act of 1866 held that

> *All persons within the jurisdiction of the United States shall have the same right in every State and Territory, to make and enforce contracts, to sue, be parties, give evidence, and to the full and equal benefit of all laws and proceedings for the security of persons and property as is enjoyed by white citizens.*

The Radical Republicans saw to it that Johnson became the first U.S. president in history to face impeachment and trial by the Senate—and he was also the first to have his legislative veto overridden by Congress, which insisted on passing the civil rights laws that Johnson had refused to sign.

In 1866, Congress also passed the Fourteenth Amendment, which certified that all people born in the United States should be considered citizens, and that states had to provide citizens with "equal protection" and "due process" under the law before depriving them of life, liberty, or property. The Fourteenth Amendment was ratified in 1868. (For a constitutional

6

amendment to become law, it must be passed by two-thirds of Congress and ratified by two-thirds of the states.) One year later, Congress passed the Fifteenth Amendment, which guaranteed to every male citizen over 21 years of age the right to vote, "regardless of race, color, creed, national origin, or previous condition of servitude." That amendment was ratified in 1870.

Meanwhile, the Radical Republicans continued to take affirmative steps to involve African Americans in politics, such as engaging in massive voter registration drives throughout the South. The Freedmen's Bureau also provided emergency assistance to displaced Southerners of all races, and special tribunals were installed to settle racial disputes. The enforcement of these reforms depended on the Union army, which was stationed throughout the former Confederacy. Many white Southerners viewed the army with resentment as an occupying force, even as many black Southerners felt that only the army's presence could guarantee their rights.

If the goal of this early "affirmative action" was black political empowerment, it was remarkably successful, for in 1867, more blacks than whites were registered to vote in the 10 states of the old Confederacy. African Americans and Radical Republicans controlled many state legislatures, and a number of new laws were passed.

Soon, however, a backlash developed. In the 1870s, a white-power vigilante group called the Ku Klux Klan joined with former Confederate soldiers and "white leagues" in a campaign of violence and terror against black Southerners. Mob violence and intimidation marked the state and local elections of 1874, and black voting rates declined. Old-line Southern Democrats replaced blacks and Radical Republicans in office, even as Congress passed the Civil Rights Act of 1875, which outlawed discrimination by nongovernmental entities.

Meanwhile, the Radical Republicans were losing control of their party, and in 1876 the Republicans dropped their commitment to civil rights. Their presidential candidate, Rutherford B. Hayes, was involved in a narrowly contested election in which electoral college votes were split and Congress had to choose the president. In the famous Compromise of 1877, Hayes promised to remove the Union army from the South if he were given the presidency. Soon after, in 1883, the Supreme Court struck down the Civil Rights Act of 1875. With this apparent federal permission, many legislatures, especially those in the South, passed a new round of laws instituting segregation (racial separation) in education, employment, and public accommodations. Known as the Jim Crow laws, the new legislation kept people of color out of white schools, jobs, movie theaters, and restaurants, as well as away from the voting booth, off juries, and out of political office.

WOMEN'S FIGHT FOR EQUALITY

During the early history of the United States, even free white women had few legal rights to speak of, for unmarried women came under the guardianship of their fathers or brothers, while married women and their children were under the legal control of their husbands. If a man chose to send his children to the poorhouse, for example, their mother had no legal standing to object. In some communities, however, women were given the right to act as lawyers on their own behalf, suing for property and otherwise representing themselves. In some places, too, married women could own property if their husbands agreed; otherwise, a married woman's property was legally the possession of her husband.

In early-19th-century England, a branch of law known as equity law began to focus on the principle of equal rights, rather than tradition. English law was highly influential on U.S. law and had a liberalizing influence on women's rights. In 1839, for example, the state of Mississippi passed a law enabling a married woman to own property separately from her husband (presuming that neither the woman nor her husband was enslaved), with New York and Massachusetts passing similar legislation in 1848 and 1864, respectively. Even in those states, however, a divorced woman lost all claim to her children (of course, enslaved women had no claim to their children in the first place).

Formal education for free women was far less available than for free men throughout most of the 18th and 19th centuries. White girls in colonial America, for example, did not attend schools with boys, but were taught to read and write at dame schools. They were occasionally allowed to attend master's schools for boys when there was room—usually during the summer months, when the boys were working.

Both African-American and white women played a prominent role in the abolitionist movement to end U.S. slavery, an experience that led to the first stirrings of feminism. In 1848, women and their abolitionist allies gathered at Seneca Falls, New York, to consider their own political situation and to formulate demands for, among other things, the right to vote. The strong coalition between feminists and abolitionists, which reached across race and gender lines, was shaken in the aftermath of the Civil War, however, when the movement split over the right to vote: The Fifteenth Amendment granted suffrage (voting rights) to African-American men, but not to women of any race.

Some white feminists, such as Lucy Stone and Lucretia Mott, supported the Fifteenth Amendment because they had an urgent sense of the need to overcome the effects of slavery. They hoped, too, that the coalition they had

8

helped to form would continue to fight for the rights of women. Other white feminists, such as Susan B. Anthony and Elizabeth Cady Stanton, felt betrayed by abolitionists' acceptance of the vote. They broke away from the coalition and sometimes used racist arguments in their campaigns, such as asking why uneducated black men should be allowed to vote when educated white women were not. The pre–Civil War alliance between abolitionists and feminists was decisively broken, and for nearly 100 years, the feminist movement would be as segregated as all other areas of U.S. society. Black women went on to form their own organizations, both by themselves and with men, while the white suffrage movement took on an increasingly racist and anti-immigrant tone. Women would not gain the vote until 1920, although their political and social condition improved in other ways.

THE SUPREME COURT AND JIM CROW

The Supreme Court's role in race discrimination cases was decidedly mixed. Despite striking down the Civil Rights Act of 1875, the Court often upheld the principles of racial equality. For example, the 1886 case of *Yick Wo v. Hopkins* concerned a San Francisco city ordinance that made it illegal to operate a laundry without the consent of the board of supervisors (city council), unless the laundry was located in a building made of brick or stone. The Chinese resident Yick Wo and his associates were convicted of violating the city ordinance by operating a laundry in a wooden building without the supervisors' consent. Wo took the case to court, charging that his Fourteenth Amendment rights to equal protection under the law had been violated. At this time, San Francisco was home to many Chinese immigrants, among whom laundries were a common business. During the case, it was revealed that the supervisors had denied consent to some 200 Chinese laundry operators, even though at least 80 non-Chinese had been allowed to operate laundries "under the same condition."

In an apparently unanimous decision, the Supreme Court found that the San Francisco law was illegal, for though it seemed to be fair and impartial, it might easily be administered "with an evil eye and an unequal hand." Even if the law did not explicitly discriminate against Chinese immigrants— after all, it did not mention race—it offered too many opportunities for city government "to make unjust and illegal discriminations between persons in similar circumstances," and in fact, the city government had used the law to discriminate against Chinese residents. The *Yick Wo* case would be cited frequently in affirmative action law throughout the 1970s, 1980s, and 1990s.

Yet the Supreme Court also upheld the principle of Jim Crow in the famous 1896 *Plessy v. Ferguson* decision, which involved a black man's lawsuit against segregated railway cars in Louisiana. The Supreme Court upheld the policy of segregation, holding that as long as black facilities were "equal," they might also be "separate" without violating the Fourteenth Amendment. The legal principle of "separate but equal" would reign until 1954.

As *Yick Wo* and *Plessy* make clear, Jim Crow laws were quite common throughout the United States at the beginning of the 20th century—yet there was also some public opposition to racial discrimination. Indeed, some 18 northern and western states had antidiscrimination laws on the books. In the South, however, as in other parts of the country, Jim Crow persisted, along with discrimination against the Chinese, Irish, Italians, Jews, and many other immigrant groups.

THE ROOTS OF THE CIVIL RIGHTS MOVEMENT

Throughout the first half of the 20th century, the African-American civil rights movement persisted in trying to win social, political, and legal equality in the face of numerous local, state, and federal laws that explicitly mentioned race. In 1905, W. E. B. DuBois led the Niagara Movement of African-American intellectuals, calling for equal rights and voting rights. In 1909, the Niagara group joined with white activists to create the National Association for the Advancement of Colored People (NAACP), an influential civil rights group still in existence today.

The Supreme Court may have been affected by the growing strength of the civil rights movement in 1917 when it considered the case of *Buchanan v. Warley*, involving a Louisville, Kentucky, ordinance that prevented any person of color from occupying a house on a predominantly white block. The Court found that

> *This interdiction [prohibition] is based wholly on color; simply that, and nothing more. In effect, premises situated . . . in the so-called white block are effectively debarred [prohibited] from sale to persons of color, because, if sold, they cannot be occupied by the purchaser nor by him sold to another of the same color. This drastic measure is sought to be justified . . . [because] [i]t is said such legislation tends to promote the public peace by preventing racial conflicts; that it tends to maintain racial purity; that it prevents the deterioration of property owned and occupied by white people, which deterioration, it is contended, is sure to follow the occupancy of adjacent premises by persons of color.*

However, the Court pointed out, the Fourteenth Amendment protects life, liberty, and property from invasion by the government; thus, the state

10

cannot simply tell property owners how to use or enjoy their property unless it has a very good reason (what would later be called a "compelling interest"). In the Court's opinion, the reasons given by the state—public safety and the protection of property values—were not nearly compelling enough, for property values could also be hurt if a neighboring property was occupied by "undesirable white neighbors," while the public peace "cannot be accomplished by laws or ordinances which deny rights created or protected by the Federal Constitution." Therefore, the Court struck down the Louisville law, upholding the right of black homeowners to live where they pleased.

Another milestone in the civil rights movement came in 1941, with the efforts of union leader and socialist A. Philip Randolph to create the "Negro March on Washington." Randolph mobilized thousands of black workers who stood ready to pressure President Franklin D. Roosevelt to carry out civil rights reforms. To prevent the march, Roosevelt agreed to sign Executive Order 8802, prohibiting segregation by government defense contractors.

Segregation may have been barred from the defense industry, but not from the U.S. Army, which was not integrated until 1948. That was also the year that the Supreme Court ruled on *Sipuel v. Board of Regents of the University of Oklahoma*, another civil rights case.

Sipuel concerned an African-American woman seeking to enter the University of Oklahoma law school. Oklahoma state law barred all black students from the school—so Sipuel sued. The Supreme Court ordered Sipuel to be admitted, explaining that her Fourteenth Amendment rights had been denied.

A similar case was *Sweatt v. Painter*, a 1950 suit involving a black applicant who was denied admission to the all-white University of Texas law school solely because of his race; in fact, state law explicitly prohibited black students from entering the Texas law school. When the student, Sweatt, brought a successful suit against the school, the University of Texas actually established a second all-black law school to avoid admitting him; however, Sweatt charged that the new school was not on an academic par with the existing all-white law school. The Court agreed. By trying to shunt Sweatt off to an inferior institution, the Court ruled, the state of Texas had violated his Fourteenth Amendment rights to equal protection under the law.

The Court heard *Sweatt* at the same time that it handed down *McLaurin v. Oklahoma State Regents*, concerning G. W. McLaurin, a black man who had applied to the University of Oklahoma to pursue a doctorate in education. Despite *Sipuel*, Oklahoma state law had continued to preserve the University of Oklahoma as an all-white institution, so McLaurin's application was denied solely on the basis of race. When McLaurin filed suit in district court, the court ruled that the state had a constitutional responsibility to provide him with the same education that it made available to everybody else, and it struck down the state law that had kept him out of school.

In response, Oklahoma's legislature amended its laws: African Americans would now be allowed into state institutions of higher education—but only if the courses they sought were not available in the state's all-black schools. Moreover, black students who were admitted to all-white schools were to be taught in a strictly segregated way. McLaurin had to sit in a room that adjoined the classroom; he was not allowed into the actual classroom. He had to sit at a special desk on the library mezzanine instead of using the desks in the regular reading room; and he was given a special lunch hour at the school cafeteria so that he could not eat with any of the other students. McLaurin filed another suit protesting these conditions; but the lower court upheld these "separate but equal" facilities, saying that the Constitution allowed them. The U.S. Supreme Court, however, struck them down.

While both *McLaurin* and *Sweatt* were considered victories for the civil rights movement, the impression they leave of the quality of life for African Americans in the 1950s is bleak indeed. A black law student was so unwelcome at the University of Texas law school that the state was willing to start a whole new law school simply to keep him out. An African-American graduate student in education so disturbed the Oklahoma state legislature that they wrote laws specifying a separate classroom for him. These were the conditions of segregation that would lead some civil rights leaders to call for affirmative action—positive efforts to include African Americans and other people of color in the universities and law schools that had previously gone to such lengths to exclude them.

WOMEN AT WORK AND IN THE PROFESSIONS

Although women had worked on family farms and in family businesses from the beginning of U.S. history, they began working outside the home in large numbers in the 19th century, generally in textile mills and garment shops. Like working-class men, these women labored under difficult conditions: 12-hour days, poorly ventilated rooms, the constant threat of industrial accidents. Women were generally paid less than men, usually because they were segregated into lower-paying jobs, though sometimes women were also paid less for the same jobs. Women and men struggled, side by side and separately, to establish unions and on-the-job protection, working together in the campaign for the eight-hour day and other employment rights.

Sometimes the labor movement was able to win laws restricting the conditions of women's employment, such as establishing an eight-hour day for women, banning them from night work, or prohibiting them from carrying heavy loads. These laws were considered problematic by a later generation of feminists and by middle-class feminists of the time, for the legislation served to keep women out of certain jobs. At the time, however, they were viewed as victories by working-class men and women, who saw women as winning the right to the kind of employment protections that men were seeking as well. Women were also viewed by many in the labor movement as "the weaker sex," so these laws were also seen as protections of their "weakness" from employers who were ready to exploit them to the fullest— just as they exploited men.

In academia and the professions, middle-class women made some small forays into the public sphere. In 1870, about 20 percent of all college and university students were women, in a time when higher education was far less common than it is today. By 1900, more than 33 percent of all higher-education students were women, with women obtaining almost 20 percent of all undergraduate college degrees toward the beginning of the 20th century.

Professional schools were another matter. Most U.S. law and medical schools would not admit women, and the American Medical Association (AMA) barred women from membership. In 1850, however, women had established the Female Medical College of Pennsylvania, where they could obtain M.D. degrees. By 1890, women made up some 5 percent of all U.S. doctors. By the 1910s, they had won admission to many leading "men's" medical schools, and in 1915, the AMA dropped its ban on women members. However, for many decades to come, women made up only a very small percentage of all U.S. doctors.

The women's suffrage movement had never stopped agitating for the vote, and in 1920, it was finally successful. The Nineteenth Amendment to the Constitution guaranteed women's suffrage, although it did not usher in the new age of "women's politics" that its supporters had expected. Women still rarely ran for public office, and the ranks of government were virtually all male. (In the 1920s, they were also virtually all white.)

After the vote was won, the remains of the suffrage movement turned its attention to the Equal Rights Amendment (ERA), which would have written full equality for women into the Constitution. Here, too, the split between middle- and working-class women's perspectives emerged: Since the ERA would have overruled any legal distinctions between women and men, working-class women feared that it would strike down the women's labor laws for which they had fought so hard. Consequently, both working-class women and the labor movement opposed the ERA. The feminist-abolitionist split meant that African-American leaders—both men and women—had little interest in the ERA, either; what good would full constitutional equality for women do for African-American women laboring under Jim Crow laws and other forms of discrimination? With few allies, the suffragists had little hope of winning ratification for the ERA, although a new feminist movement would take up the cause again 50 years later.

Women continued to enter the workforce in ever-increasing numbers in the 1930s and 1940s, primarily in working-class and service-sector jobs. The professions were still almost exclusively male (and white), so that in 1930, for example, only about 2 percent of all U.S. lawyers and judges were women, and there were almost no women engineers. In the 1940s, however, with men away at war, women of all races took over many of their industrial jobs while white women and some women of color gained more access to higher education and the professions. After the war, however, women of all races were often sent back home or to lower-paying "female" jobs to make room for the returning G.I.'s. Except for the old labor laws for factory women, U.S. working women had few legal protections in the 1950s.

CIVIL RIGHTS AND THE BEGINNINGS OF AFFIRMATIVE ACTION

The strict racial segregation experienced by students like Sweatt and McLaurin led the NAACP to launch a campaign against the principle of "separate but equal." In 1952, the group's legal director, Thurgood Marshall, took five consolidated cases on public school segregation to the Supreme Court. (Cases that are considered to raise similar legal issues are often consolidated, or put together, so that the Court can hear and rule on them all at once.) Meanwhile, the notion that the government should take an active, affirmative role in dismantling institutional racism found its first expression in President Harry Truman's Committee on Governmental Contract Compliance. In 1953, this committee urged another federal agency to "act positively and affirmatively to implement the policy of nondiscrimination."

In 1954, the Supreme Court ruled on Marshall's cases, in the famous *Brown v. Board of Education* decision. The Court overturned the notion of "separate but equal" enshrined by *Plessy v. Ferguson* in 1896, finding that "in the field of public education . . . [s]eparate facilities are inherently unequal." The Court ordered the public school systems involved to begin integration "with all deliberate speed." In the coming years, the Court would hand down similar messages regarding segregated public beaches, hospitals, libraries, and parks.

The *Brown* decision had concerned public education not in the South, but in the Midwestern town of Topeka, Kansas. Nevertheless, the most dramatic instances of legal segregation were still concentrated in the South. The civil rights movement of the 1950s and early 1960s, led by such figures

Introduction to Affirmative Action

as Martin Luther King, Jr., and Rosa Parks, represented the concerted effort of African Americans and their white allies to end legal segregation below the Mason-Dixon line.

As the civil rights movement continued, President John F. Kennedy became the first president to use the phrase "affirmative action" when he issued Executive Order 10925, creating the Equal Employment Opportunity Commission (EEOC), a federal agency intended to provide equal employment opportunities for people of color. The 1961 executive order instructed contractors who received federal funds that they must take "affirmative action" to ensure that their workers were employed "without regard to race, creed, color, or national origin." (No mention was made of gender discrimination.)

The southern civil rights struggle had been long, hard, and bloody. Civil rights activists organized boycotts, sit-ins, voter registrations drives, and marches. They were faced with forceful and often violent resistance by individuals, the police, and local sheriffs, resulting in jail, beatings, and in some cases, death. The movement reached new heights on August 27, 1963, when 250,000 Americans of all races joined in a march on Washington for racial justice—the largest demonstration in U.S. history at the time.

Pressure was mounting on Congress to take decisive action. In 1964, under the leadership of President Lyndon B. Johnson, Congress passed the Civil Rights Act of 1964, a set of laws banning discrimination in public accommodations involved in interstate commerce; in federally funded programs; and in employment by federal employers and by private employers who received federal funds or who were involved in interstate commerce. (Supreme Court cases of the time had restricted congressional enforcement of the Fourteenth Amendment to government entities and businesses involved in interstate commerce; later, laws were also passed to outlaw some kinds of private discrimination.)

The Civil Rights Act was followed by the 1965 Voting Rights Act, which gave the U.S. Department of Justice power to enforce the Fifteenth Amendment's guarantee of voting rights to all Americans. Also in 1965, President Lyndon B. Johnson issued Executive Order 11246, giving the Department of Labor responsibility for enforcing affirmative action and calling on the Department's Office of Federal Contract Compliance (OFCC) to develop regulations requiring contractors to submit affirmative action plans. At the time, the construction industry was virtually all-white, so Johnson's order was intended to open up construction jobs for people of color. Businesses that received government funds were supposed to analyze their existing workforces, comparing their ratio of minority hires with the percentage of minorities in the surrounding population. They were also supposed to indicate proactive measures that they would take to end employment discrimination by increasing the number of minorities hired. For

15

example, a business might promise to advertise jobs in minority publications or plan to train personnel managers in discrimination law.

On June 4, 1965, President Johnson spoke to the graduating class of Howard University, explaining the reasoning behind affirmative action programs:

> . . . *[F]reedom is not enough. You do not wipe away the scars of centuries by saying, Now, you are free to go where you want, do as you desire, and choose the leaders you please. You do not take a man who for years has been hobbled by chains, liberate him, bring him to the starting line of a race, saying, "You are free to compete with all the others," and still justly believe you have been completely fair. Thus it is not enough to open the gates of opportunity. All our citizens must have the ability to walk through those gates. This is the next and more profound stage of the battle for civil rights. We seek not just freedom but opportunity—not just legal equity but human ability—not just equality as a right and a theory, but equality as a fact and as a result.*

PRESIDENT NIXON AND THE PHILADELPHIA PLAN

The civil rights movement received a blow in 1968, when Martin Luther King, Jr., was assassinated. One week later, however, Congress passed the nation's first open housing law, the Civil Rights Act of 1968, while the Supreme Court handed down decisions upholding the Civil Rights Act of 1964 and similar legislation.

When President Richard M. Nixon took office in January 1969, few viewed the Republican leader as a potential champion of civil rights. Yet it was under President Nixon that affirmative action became even more entrenched in federal civil rights policy, particularly after the 1970 Philadelphia Plan authored by Nixon's assistant secretary of labor, Arthur Fletcher. Fletcher conducted an experiment with the traditionally all-white craft unions and construction industry responsible for building the Philadelphia-area portion of the new interstate highway system. The unions and contractors would be subject to Labor Department Order No. 4, which required them to engage in extensive affirmative action efforts to hire more minority workers. The order was revised in 1971 to include women.

Also in 1971, the U.S. Commission on Civil Rights released a report criticizing various federal equal opportunity programs for doing too little to achieve equality. In response, Congress passed the Equal Employment Opportunity Act of 1972, which extended the EEOC's jurisdiction to employ-

16

ers with more than 15 employees, unions with more than 15 members, and federal employment activity at all levels. The new act also made it easier to bring a class-action suit charging race or sex discrimination in hiring, promotion, wages, benefits, and working conditions.

Nixon's initial support of affirmative action may have surprised people on all sides of the issue—but by the end of his term, the president was advocating a constitutional amendment that would have banned busing as a means for achieving desegregation in the public schools. Nixon's final attitude toward affirmative action helped set the stage for the backlash that was to follow.

FEMINISM AND AFFIRMATIVE ACTION

Just as women's involvement in abolitionism had helped spur the first wave of feminism, women's participation in the civil rights movement helped give birth to feminism's second wave. The 1970s saw the beginning of the modern women's movement, along with an unprecedented influx of women into the workforce, higher education, and the professions. Changes in the labor market, new political visions, and the influence of the civil rights movement combined to produce a large, vocal, and influential feminist movement whose goals included affirmative action in education and employment.

In 1972, Congress passed the Education Amendments, including Title IX, a provision banning sex discrimination at all schools that receive federal funding. Suddenly, affirmative action for women had a legal foundation, leading to a dramatic increase in the number of women in law schools, medical schools, and other areas of higher education—though women were still vastly underrepresented in graduate schools of all types.

Affirmative action also enabled women to rise to the ranks of middle and sometimes upper management in the business world. Women were still paid far less than men—in 1972, they earned only 59 cents for every dollar that a man took home, and that figure had risen to only about 71 cents a quarter-century later. But they were beginning to establish the principle of "equal pay for equal work"—that a woman doing the same job as a man deserved the same pay. Activists were also developing the concept of pay equity—the notion that when jobs traditionally held by women were comparable to those traditionally held by men in terms of skill and responsibility, women and men should be paid at the same rate, so that secretaries, for example, should earn as much as janitors.

Questions of race continued to plague the modern women's movement, which included women of color to some extent, but which was often accused of replicating the racism in the larger society. On the one hand, white women could see that they had a common interest both in joining with women of color on women's issues and in joining with the African-American, Latino, Asian, and Native American communities in the fight to end discrimination of all types and to support affirmative action. On the other hand, white women, especially from the middle and upper classes, were far more able than people of color to take advantage of affirmative action programs that helped them enter professional schools and the ranks of management. Once again, tensions arose between potential allies who enjoyed widely varying access to power and privilege.

BACKLASH: FROM BAKKE TO BUSH

Despite potential or actual conflicts, affirmative action for both women and minorities seemed to be in full swing in the late 1970s. Women of all races were beginning to enter professional schools, management, and the political arena, while African Americans had won several lawsuits upholding their right to be hired at formerly all-white companies and to have a fair promotions system (see chapter 2).

Then a rejected white applicant to the University of California, Davis (UC Davis) medical school named Allan Bakke filed a suit challenging the medical school's affirmative action program. Every year, the school set aside 16 of the 100 places in its entering class for "special admissions": people of color and economically disadvantaged white people. For two years in a row, the special admissions program had admitted people of color whose grades and test scores were lower than Bakke's, so Bakke—who had been rejected by 10 other medical schools—argued that UC Davis had violated the Fourteenth Amendment by depriving him of equal protection under the law on account of his race.

In 1978, the Supreme Court ruled that Bakke was right: UC Davis's affirmative action program was unacceptable. All of the justices agreed that the particular details of the program rendered it unconstitutional. (For more detail, see chapter 2.) However, a majority of the Court agreed that, at least in theory, race might be an acceptable factor in college admissions programs that were better designed than the one at Davis.

Usually, in Supreme Court cases, a majority of justices joins in a particular opinion, which makes clear the way that the Court intends all other courts to interpret the laws. But in *Bakke*, there was no majority opinion. There were many different opinions, which added up to a rejection of the UC Davis program. The reasoning behind the opinions, however, varied from justice to justice. Thus, it was unclear just what lesson lower courts were supposed to draw from *Bakke*. How were they supposed to rule on affirmative action programs that avoided the particular flaws of the one at UC Davis? Courts have struggled with this question for the past quarter-century. Despite the confusion, three points have emerged:

1) **Compelling Interest.** The Court established that any government agency or publicly funded school with an affirmative action program would have to demonstrate a "compelling interest" in the goals that the program was meant to achieve. Affirmative action programs were a form of depriving white people of life, liberty, or property on the basis of their race. The government had to demonstrate a compelling interest that would justify taking such a step. In the case of *Yick Wo v. Hopkins*, for example, the city of San Francisco had not been able to demonstrate a compelling interest for requiring laundry operators to get permission from the city. In *Bakke*, on the other hand, the medical school had shown a compelling interest—the state's interest in training more minority doctors, who were expected to go on to serve minority communities desperately in need of health care. The Court agreed this was a compelling interest—but that alone was not sufficient to make the program constitutional.

2) **Strict Scrutiny.** Once a compelling interest could be demonstrated, then "strict scrutiny" had to be used to determine whether the affirmative action program in question was the only possible way to fulfill that interest. While the Court thought that training more minority doctors was a laudable goal, it did not agree that the only way to achieve that goal was by violating Allan Bakke's constitutional rights. The Court held that there were other ways to recruit minority doctors that would not involve discriminating against Bakke on racial grounds. So the affirmative action program at UC Davis medical school failed the strict scrutiny test.

The liberal justices on the Court—Thurgood Marshall, William Brennan, and Harry Blackmun—disagreed with the application of strict scrutiny to affirmative action programs. They argued instead for the "rational basis" test, sometimes colloquially referred to as "intermediate scrutiny." The liberal justices felt that affirmative action programs could be justified as having a "rational basis"—that they might reasonably be expected to fulfill the state's compelling interest. They did not have to be strictly scrutinized to see whether they were the *only* way of fulfilling that interest.

Debates over the appropriate level of scrutiny for affirmative action cases would continue throughout the next two decades. Over time, the conservative "strict scrutiny" approach won out, but some decisions in the 1980s and 1990s appeared to contradict this trend.

3) **Educational Diversity.** Justice Lewis Powell wrote an opinion in which he suggested that educational diversity might be the kind of compelling interest that would allow an affirmative action program to pass the strict scrutiny test. If the university had argued that it wished to have a diverse student body to enhance the education of all students, then racial diversity would be essential to its educational mission. In that case, an affirmative action program designed to achieve such diversity would indeed be a compelling interest that would pass the strict scrutiny test. The college would in effect be saying that the only way it could properly educate all its students would be to make sure that a certain percentage of people of color were admitted.

Unfortunately for the university, it had not made that argument, and its program was considered flawed for other reasons. But Powell's suggestion that affirmative action to achieve educational diversity was "constitutionally permissible" had established the cornerstone of affirmative action law. For the next 25 years, every court brief defending affirmative action at state colleges and universities would invoke the notion of "educational diversity."

The *Bakke* decision began a backlash against affirmative action as numerous people complained that they had faced discrimination because of being white and/or male and began bringing suits challenging the affirmative action policies of schools, employers, and federal agencies. *Bakke* seemed to suggest that affirmative action's day was over, that the notions of backlash and reverse discrimination were now more resonant with the American majority than the notions of fairness, diversity, and equality.

Indeed, two years after the *Bakke* decision, President Ronald Reagan was elected on a conservative platform that promised, among other things, to overturn affirmative action. When Reagan took office in 1981, he immediately began to fill key positions in his administration with opponents of affirmative action, including Clarence Thomas, the conservative African-American jurist whom Reagan put in charge of the EEOC. When Supreme Court vacancies opened up, Reagan nominated Antonin Scalia and Anthony Kennedy, both staunch foes of affirmative action and of civil rights in general. He also nominated Sandra Day O'Connor, who went on to write some of the landmark opinions opposing affirmative action, as well as appointing numerous federal judges opposed to affirmative action. During his two terms in office, he cut the funding of the EEOC and other civil rights agencies and frequently criticized affirmative action as a program of "racial quotas" and "reverse discrimination." Reagan was also an opponent of feminism who criticized gender-based affirmative action while opposing other demands of the women's movement. Perhaps ironically, he appointed the first female Supreme Court justice—but

O'Connor herself was critical of the women's movement and a staunch opponent of most of its demands.

When Reagan's vice president, George H. W. Bush, was elected president in 1988, he took a far more moderate position on affirmative action than Reagan had. Nevertheless, Bush, too, opposed the policy, and his Supreme Court appointee Clarence Thomas has ruled against virtually every affirmative action program that has come before him. Throughout the 1980s, as conservative justices replaced liberal ones, the Court moved slowly but surely toward the principle of applying "strict scrutiny" with ever more rigor.

Moreover, in *Ward's Cove v. Antonio* (1989; see chapter 2), the Court made a historic shift. Previously, if employees could demonstrate statistically that discrimination existed—say, by proving that no black people had ever been promoted, or by showing that all the black workers at a company were stuck in its lowest-paying department—then it was up to the employer to justify the apparent discrimination. The company was given the chance to show that the situation was in fact the result of a "business necessity," rather than institutional racism or systemic discrimination. If the company could not meet that burden of proof, it was required to change whatever practices had led to the racially unbalanced workforce.

Ward's Cove changed all that in 1989. Now it was the employees' responsibility to demonstrate that an employer had intended to discriminate. Even if all the high-paid employees at a company were white and all the low-paid employees were people of color, as happened in the *Ward's Cove* case, the burden was on the employees to prove that this apparent discrimination was intentional rather than accidental. After *Ward's Cove*, it became far harder to bring a class-action suit charging either race or gender discrimination—although such suits continued to be brought, and won.

AFFIRMATIVE ACTION: THE CLINTON YEARS

Civil rights supporters greeted the election of President Bill Clinton with high hopes, while conservatives watched him take office with despair. Clinton did make two liberal appointments to the Supreme Court, Justices Ruth Bader Ginsburg and Stephen Breyer, and he did assert several times during his term in office that affirmative action was a necessary and useful program. However, the president could do little to stop the ever more conservative cast of the Supreme Court's decisions. He seemed equally helpless before the conservative onslaught of 1994, in which newly elected House Speaker Newt Gingrich led right-wing Republican members of

Congress in advocating the Contract with America, a new approach to government that included the abolition of affirmative action.

Although Gingrich's legislative efforts to end affirmative action were unsuccessful, he did succeed in fanning the flames of discontent. Nor was dissatisfaction confined to Washington, D.C. In 1995, conservative African-American businessman Ward Connerly, a member of the University of California Board of Regents, successfully lobbied for the university to drop its affirmative action programs. Connerly also campaigned to put an anti–affirmative action initiative called Proposition 209 on the California ballot. The measure passed in 1996, ending affirmative action in the state. Connerly launched a similar campaign in Washington State for Initiative 200, which was passed in 1998. Although he was unsuccessful in getting a similar measure on the ballot in Florida, he has vowed to take his message to all 50 states.

The Clinton years also featured a number of suits that successfully ended affirmative action in several state university systems. For example, a young woman called Cheryl Hopwood brought suit against the University of Texas law school, claiming that she and another rejected applicant had been discriminated against because they were white. *Hopwood v. Texas* was decided by the Fifth Circuit Court of Appeals in 1996, with the court ruling that any race-based system of college admissions was unconstitutional and ordering the University of Texas to scrap the program. Hopwood's suit had been conducted by the Center for Individual Rights (CIR), a conservative Washington, D.C., public-policy law firm that actively seeks rejected white applicants to represent pro bono (for free). Thus the CIR was involved in 1997 and 1998 suits against the Universities of Washington and Michigan. A similar anti–affirmative action lawsuit was brought in 1999 by another law firm in Georgia. In all but one case, courts have found for the plaintiff, leading to the end of affirmative action in higher education in Georgia, Texas, and Washington; the Michigan case is still pending.

THE FUTURE OF AFFIRMATIVE ACTION

As George W. Bush completes the early years of his presidency, the present and future status of affirmative action is unclear. Bush, like his father, has taken a moderate position on affirmative action and nominated even more women and people of color to his cabinet than the liberal civil rights supporter President Clinton. Yet his choice of Attorney General John Ashcroft and Health and Human Services Secretary Tommy Thompson—

both longtime foes of affirmative action—suggest that his actual policy is far more conservative than his public statements indicate.

On the other hand, when a federal program guaranteeing set-asides for women- and minority-owned businesses was challenged in a Supreme Court suit (see the discussion of the *Adarand* case in chapter 2), President Bush's Justice Department filed a brief defending the federal program. (A set-aside is a portion of federal funds literally set aside, or reserved, for a particular purpose.) Bush was careful to clarify that the Justice Department was moved by the principle of upholding federal law rather than by any preference for affirmative action. As a result, both conservatives and liberals have charged that Bush's position is unclear. Given the appointments of Ashcroft and Thompson, however, it seems likely that Bush's choice for a Supreme Court nominee, if he has the chance to make one, will be another strong opponent of affirmative action.

Even without a new nominee, the current Supreme Court has at least five justices who have consistently ruled against affirmative action programs: Chief Justice Rehnquist and Justices Kennedy, O'Connor, Scalia, and Thomas. As of this writing, the Court has decisively taken the conservative position of requiring strict scrutiny for all affirmative action cases, rather than the "moderate scrutiny" that liberal justices would prefer. However, this principle has not yet been applied to affirmative action in educational admissions, as the last Supreme Court decision in that realm remains the 1978 *Bakke* decision. The Court has agreed to hear some education cases in its 2001–02 term, and observers expect that a new ruling—probably far more conservative than *Bakke*—will finally clarify that portion of the law. If the decision is as conservative as other kinds of affirmative action decisions have been, the future of affirmative action at all state-funded institutions is likely to be in jeopardy.

Meanwhile, Ward Connerly and others continue their campaigns to get anti–affirmative action campaigns on state ballots. As of this writing, Connerly is working for a 2002 ballot measure in California that would outlaw all public record keeping based on race. Should the new measure prove successful, affirmative action at all levels in California would grind to a halt, for employers and schools would lack the means to track the numbers of minorities in their ranks or to evaluate whether minorities were being promoted, paid, and otherwise treated equally to white men.

Yet even as Connerly and others have fought to end affirmative action, a growing movement emerges to defend it. Although the University of California regents voted to end affirmative action in 1995, they elected to reinstate it in 2000, despite the statewide ban on the program resulting from Proposition 209. A large and vocal organization known as By Any Means Necessary has arisen in California and Michigan to protest the threats to affirmative action at those state's university systems.

EVALUATING AFFIRMATIVE ACTION

A number of studies have emerged suggesting that affirmative action has had a positive impact on women, minorities, and society as a whole. For example, a 1998 study conducted by two former presidents of Ivy League universities, political scientist Derek Bok of Harvard and economist William Bowen of Princeton, concluded that the affirmative action of the past 20 years had played a central role in the creation of the African-American middle class and helped show white students the value of integration. Published in book form as *The Shape of the River: Long-Term Consequences of Considering Race in College and University Admissions*, the study surveyed more than 60,000 white and African-American students from the classes of 1976 and 1989. Black students accepted into colleges were able to rise above their backgrounds in income and status, while white students described their contact with people of color as enriching and enlightening.

A 1998 report from the Association of American Medical Colleges revealed that the number of women in U.S. medical schools had grown steadily over the past two decades (although the study concluded that the figure had now reached a plateau). While the study did not specifically examine the results of affirmative action programs, it seemed clear that the growing number of women in medicine had resulted at least in part from a concerted effort on the part of medical schools to make room for them.

In October 2000, another landmark study appeared in the *Journal of Economic Literature*, in which economists Harry Holzer of Georgetown University and David Neumark of Michigan State University reviewed more than 200 scientific studies of affirmative action. The researchers discovered that affirmative action offered concrete benefits for the economy as a whole, as well as for the women and minorities it was specifically intended to benefit.

A September/October 2001 article in the *Journal of Education*, by Patrick T. Terenzini and colleagues, reviewed the studies on the impact of diversity on a student's experience of education. The authors concluded that

> *The evidence is almost uniformly consistent in indicating that students in a racial/ethnically or gender-diverse community, or engaged in a diversity-related activity, reap a wide array of positive educational benefits. "Diversity" in its various forms has been linked to such outcomes as higher minority student retention [keeping more minority students in school] . . . greater cognitive development . . . and positive gains on a wide range of measures of interpersonal and psychosocial developmental changes, including increased openness to diversity and challenge . . . greater racial/cultural*

24

knowledge, and understanding and commitment to social justice . . . more positive academic and social self-concepts . . . more complex civic-related attitudes and values . . . and greater involvement in civic and community-service behaviors.

On a more anecdotal note, an article in the May 26, 1998, *Los Angeles Times* by Peter Y. Hong found that businesses such as a Toyota dealership in southern California benefited from diverse employment because sales agents from different ethnic backgrounds could appeal to a wider range of customers. Higher up the corporate ladder, Microsoft entrepreneur Bill Gates is a strong supporter of affirmative action on the grounds that it better enables U.S. corporations to deal with an increasingly complex and diverse domestic and global market. Gates was joined by more than 20 major corporations in supporting the affirmative action program at the University of Michigan (see chapter 2).

Yet despite the contribution of affirmative action to creating a black middle class, black Americans' income per capita is only 59 percent of that for white Americans—the same ratio that economists Richard Vedder, Lowell Gallaway, and David C. Klingaman estimate was the case in 1880. Studies conducted in the 1990s by the Urban Institute in Chicago, San Diego, and Washington, D.C., and by the Fair Employment Council of Greater Washington Inc. in the Washington metropolitan area show that black and Latino job applicants still face significant levels of discrimination. According to economists William Darity, Jr., and Patrick Mason, black men have earned 12 to 15 percent less than white men over the past 25 years. (Darity reported these results in an article in the December 1, 2000, issue of *The Chronicle of Higher Education.*)

Moreover, when Darity joined with researchers Jason Dietrich and David Guilkey to study census data from 1880 to 1990, controlling for variables such as age, years of schooling, marital status, and country of origin, they found that there was a strong correlation between the kind of job a person was doing in 1980 and 1990, and the kind of discrimination that his or her racial/ethnic group had experienced a century ago. (Results of their research were published in *The American Journal of Economics and Sociology.*)

In the same vein, when Ngina Chiteji and Frank Stafford examined studies of wealth for an article published in the May 1999 issue of *American Economic Review*, they discovered that the median white household wealth is greater than $10,000, while median black household wealth was near zero. Even if a white and a black household enjoy a similar income, the disparity in wealth—total assets minus debt—reveals a huge gap that many argue dates back to the days of slavery and Jim Crow. Since African Americans were not allowed to own property for so long, and since they were legally excluded from education and employment opportunities, they never had the chance to accumulate the kind of assets that even moderate-income white Americans were able to pass down to their families. Indeed, some observers argue that if college affirmative action programs were simply conducted on the basis of wealth (not income), minorities would be at least as well represented in student bodies as they are now.

Certainly the abolishment of affirmative action at state colleges and universities has led to drastic declines in the percentage of minority students, particularly at the most prestigious schools. Although many schools seek alternate means of recruiting minorities, and although minority enrollment does tend to recover somewhat after an initial drop, no school that has scrapped its affirmative action program has seen minority enrollment return fully to affirmative action levels. Even when affirmative action was in place, minority students tended to be underrepresented at state schools based on their share of the state's population. Without affirmative action, the question of how to provide truly equal access to education becomes even more difficult.

Opponents of affirmative action—including many conservative African Americans, Latinos, and women of all races—argue that the program has promoted dissension between races, that it casts doubt on the real achievements of people of color and women, that it is insulting and condescending to people of all races, and that it brings race as a category back into the U.S. legal system, whereas the goal of the civil rights movement should have been to remove race as any kind of meaningful basis for awarding jobs, education, or other benefits. Some opponents feel that affirmative action was once necessary but that it has outlived its usefulness; others argue that it was never necessary or never the right way to achieve otherwise important goals.

Supporters of affirmative action maintain that the program actually benefits everyone, not only minorities and women. When a society is diverse and well-integrated, they argue, everyone's experience of life is richer and more meaningful—and when no one category of worker is underpaid or mistreated, everyone's wages and working conditions improve. Affirmative action supporters also argue that the historic effects of racism cannot be overcome in one or two generations, that racism does not belong solely to slavery or the 1950s but continues into the present as an active force shaping where people live, work, and go to school; how much money they earn; the kind of health care they receive; and numerous other factors that profoundly affect their lives.

It seems clear that some form of affirmative action will continue, at least for the next few years. Even if the Supreme Court rules against affirmative action for state schools, some private colleges and universities will

26

probably continue to focus on including people of color in their student bodies, while unions will persist in fighting for equal representation for all their members, including minorities and women. The future status of affirmative action, however, and the role it plays in the shape of the United States, remains to be seen.

CHAPTER 2

THE LAW OF
AFFIRMATIVE ACTION

CONSTITUTIONAL AMENDMENTS

THIRTEENTH AMENDMENT

The Thirteenth Amendment to the U.S. Constitution was passed by Congress in 1865 and ratified on December 6, 1865. It abolished slavery as a legal institution. The Constitution does not mention slavery by name, but it does refer to slaves as "such persons" in Article I, Section 9 and refers to "a person held to service or labor" in Article IV, Section 2. The Thirteenth Amendment, in direct terminology, puts an end to slavery. (See chapter 8 for the relevant text of all the amendments discussed in this section.)

In response to the Thirteenth Amendment, many formerly slave states began to enact the so-called Black Codes, designed to limit the rights of former slaves (and other people of color) in various ways. The Radical Republicans' outrage at the Black Codes led to the passage of the Fourteenth Amendment, the cornerstone of the affirmative action law.

FOURTEENTH AMENDMENT

The Fourteenth Amendment was passed in 1868. It has five sections, each designed to protect the rights of the newly freed slaves and other people of color, and to establish the political defeat of the Confederacy. The first section, known as the equal protection clause, is key to affirmative action law. It holds that all people born or naturalized in the United States are citizens, and that no state can make any law abridging the "privileges or immunities" of citizens; deprive any person of life, liberty, or property without due process of law; or deny to any person the equal protection of the law. Both people of color and

28

women, alleging historic discrimination, and white people and men, alleging reverse discrimination, have invoked the Fourteenth Amendment in virtually all of the affirmative action cases under consideration here.

Also important to affirmative action law is the Fourteenth Amendment's Section 5, which gives Congress the power to pass any laws needed for its enforcement.

FIFTEENTH AMENDMENT

The Fifteenth Amendment was passed in 1869 and ratified in 1870. It establishes that voting rights for citizens shall not be "denied or abridged" by either the federal government or the states "on account of race, color, or previous condition of servitude." While this amendment is not specifically invoked in most affirmative action cases, it forms part of the larger body of law designed to overcome the legal inequality of African Americans.

NINETEENTH AMENDMENT

The Nineteenth Amendment guarantees women's right to vote. Passed in 1920 after nearly 75 years of agitation and protest on the part of women's groups, it remains the only constitutional reference to women's legal status.

TWENTY-FOURTH AMENDMENT

While not directly involved in affirmative action law, the Twenty-Fourth Amendment is important to gaining an understanding of the larger context within which affirmative action debates play out. Passed by Congress on August 27, 1962, and ratified on January 23, 1964, it bans the use of the poll tax in presidential and congressional elections. The poll tax was a fee for voting that five states—Alabama, Arkansas, Mississippi, Texas, and Virginia—had implemented to circumvent black voting rights under the Fourteenth Amendment. In *Harper v. Virginia State Board of Elections* (1966), the Supreme Court ruled that the tax was also unconstitutional in state elections, as it violated the Fourteenth Amendment's guarantee of equal protection under the law. Partly as a result of the Twenty-Fourth Amendment, the 1965 Voting Rights Act was passed.

EQUAL RIGHTS AMENDMENT

The Equal Rights Amendment (ERA) was intended to guarantee women's equality under the law. It holds simply that "Equality of rights under the law shall not be denied or abridged by the United States or by any state on account of sex." First proposed by Congress in 1923, the Equal Rights Amendment met with little support among the states, but a resurgence of feminist activism in the 1970s led many observers to believe that the ERA would soon be passed. However, the amendment has been ratified by only 35 of the necessary 38 states, with little immediate prospect of more support, despite the formation in 1996 of a nationwide coalition of women's groups to press for its ratification. Should the ERA pass, it would become the Twenty-Eighth Amendment.

CIVIL RIGHTS ACTS DURING RECONSTRUCTION

The first set of civil rights acts came in the 1860s, in response to the efforts of Southern legislatures to reinstate the subordinate status of African Americans after the Civil War. The 1866 Civil Rights Act guaranteed every citizen "the same right to make and enforce contracts . . . as is enjoyed by white citizens. . . ." The principles behind this act were soon written into the Constitution as the Fourteenth Amendment.

During the Reconstruction era after the Civil War, numerous other civil rights laws were passed, many of which are still in force today. These laws were intended to protect individuals from discrimination and from being deprived of their civil rights. For example, Section 1981 of Title 42 (Equal Rights under the Law) protects individuals from discrimination based on race in making and enforcing contracts, participating in lawsuits, and giving evidence. Other similar statutes include Civil Action for Deprivation of Rights, Conspiracies to Interfere with Civil Rights, Conspiracy against Rights of Citizens, Deprivation of Rights under Color of Law, Jurisdictional Statute for Civil Rights Cases, and Peonage Abolished.

THE CIVIL RIGHTS ACT OF 1964

The most significant civil rights legislation since Reconstruction is the Civil Rights Act of 1964, a piece of legislation that outlawed discrimination based on "race, color, religion, or national origin" in public establishments that had a connection to interstate commerce or that were supported by the government. Such establishments include places of public accommodation, such as hotels, motels, and trailer parks; restaurants, gas stations, bars, taverns, and places of entertainment. The Civil Rights Act of 1964 also declared Congress's intent to bar discrimination in public schools and colleges, as these institutions receive public funds.

The reason that the act was restricted to publicly funded businesses and to firms connected with interstate commerce was that Supreme

Court decisions of the time had limited Congress's enforcement of the Fourteenth Amendment to actions taken by the government. In order to affect the actions of individuals, Congress had to rely on its right to regulate matters involving interstate commerce and federal funds. (Since 1964, the Supreme Court has expanded the reach of the Fourteenth Amendment to apply to private individual discrimination in some cases.)

Key portions of the 1964 Civil Rights Act include Title II, barring discrimination in public accommodations; Title VI, banning discrimination in federally funded programs; and Title VII, prohibiting employment discrimination when the employer is involved in interstate commerce. Title VII also established the Equal Employment Opportunity Commission (EEOC) to enforce its provisions.

The Civil Rights Act of 1964 was later amended to include a ban on discrimination based on gender. Numerous class-action lawsuits against employers relied upon the protections in this act. The act was also the topic of many Supreme Court cases that helped to shape civil rights and affirmative action policy.

OTHER EMPLOYMENT DISCRIMINATION LAW

The Fifth and Fourteenth Amendments have been the basis of much law in the field of employment discrimination. These amendments limit the power of state and federal governments to discriminate against their employees, since their due process and equal protection clauses require that the state treat all citizens equally. Discrimination in the private sector is not prohibited by the Constitution, but a growing body of federal and state statutes have sought to limit it.

In 1963, the Equal Pay Act amended the Fair Labor Standards Act. The Equal Pay Act does not prohibit discrimination in hiring, but it does outlaw unequal payment of wages based on sex. It also holds that if workers perform equal work in jobs requiring "equal skill, effort, and responsibility and performed under similar working conditions," they must receive equal pay. The Fair Labor Standards Act protects employees of businesses engaged in interstate commerce.

The Equal Employment Opportunity Act of 1972 extended the EEOC's jurisdiction to employers with more than 15 employees, unions with more than 15 members, and federal employment activity at all levels. The new act also made it easier to bring a class-action suit.

The Age Discrimination in Employment Act (ADEA) of 1967 bans discrimination on the basis of age, using language nearly identical to Title VII.

Employees are protected from age discrimination once they reach the age of 40. The ADEA also contains explicit guidelines for benefit, pension, and retirement plans.

The goal of the Rehabilitation Act of 1973 is to "promote and expand employment opportunities in the public and private sectors for handicapped individuals" through antidiscrimination practices and some forms of affirmative action. The act covers federal government agencies and employers receiving more than $2,500 in federal funds. The Department of Labor enforces the portion of the act that applies to federal employees via the EEOC, while the Department of Justice monitors conditions in private employment.

The Americans with Disabilities Act (ADA) of 1990 also bans discrimination against the disabled by state governments and employers engaged in interstate commerce. Again, the language of Title VII is the model for this law, which is enforced by the EEOC.

The Black Lung Act of 1969 prohibits discrimination against miners who suffer from pneumoconiosis, known as "black lung."

Various nineteenth-century civil rights acts, amended in 1993, guarantee all people equal rights under the law and outline the damages available to those who bring lawsuits under the Civil Rights Act of 1964, Title VII; the Americans with Disabilities Act of 1990; and the Rehabilitation Act of 1973.

State statutes also provide various types of protection from discrimination at work.

EXECUTIVE ORDERS AND RELATED ORDERS

Executive Order 10925 (1961) established the President's Committee on Equal Employment Opportunity, with a mission of ending discrimination in employment by government and its contractors. The order calls upon contractors to

> *take affirmative action, to ensure that applicants are employed, and that employees are treated during employment, without regard to their race, creed, color, or national origin.*

Executive Order 11246, issued in 1965 and amended in 1967, bans discrimination in government employment and in employment activities of contractors doing business with government funds. While engaged in government business, the contractor agrees not to *discriminate against any employee or applicant for employment because of race, color, religion, sex, or national origin. The contractor will take affirmative action to ensure that applicants are employed and that employees are treated during employment, without regard to their race, color, religion, sex, or national origin.*

Executive Order 11478, issued in August 1969, amended Executive Order 10925 to include age and handicap as protected categories. It requires department and agency heads in federal government to provide resources for the equal employment and recruitment of various types of employees.

In 1970, the Department of Labor issued Revised Order No. 4, requiring all contractors to develop "an acceptable affirmative action program" to further the hiring and equal treatment of minority groups, defined as "Negroes, American Indians, Orientals, and Spanish Surnamed Americans." In 1971, the order was amended to include women.

LAWS AFFECTING AFFIRMATIVE ACTION IN EDUCATIONAL INSTITUTIONS

Affirmative action programs operate under a complicated system of overlapping laws, some of which have already been discussed. Here is a brief overview of laws that affect affirmative action in colleges and universities:

- Title VI of the Civil Rights Act of 1964 prohibits race discrimination in any program that receives federal funds; it covers both admissions and employment.

- Title VII of the Civil Rights Act of 1964, as amended, bans discrimination based on race, color, religion, or national origin by any employer with 15 or more employees; as amended in 1972 it applies to public and private educational institutions as well.

- Title IX of the Education Amendments of 1972 bans sex discrimination at all schools that receive federal funding; it applies to both employment and admissions.

- Executive Order 11246 (1965), as amended by Executive Order 11375 (1967) requires federal contractors to adopt and implement "affirmative action programs" to promote the attainment of "equal employment" objectives; it bans the use of quotas but allows the use of "goals." It applies to discrimination based on race, religion, color, national origin, and sex.

- State laws also affect public and private educational institutions.

SUPREME COURT CASES

GRIGGS V. DUKE POWER CO.
401 U.S. 424 (1971)

Background

The Duke Power Company's Dan River plant, a power-generating facility located in Draper, North Carolina, had a policy whereby African Americans were employed in only one of its five departments, the one known as Labor. This was the poorest-paid department, whose highest-paid jobs paid less than the lowest-paid jobs in the other four departments: Coal Handling, Operations, Maintenance, and Laboratory and Test. In 1955, the company began to require a high school education for anyone hired in the four "white" departments, and for transfer from Coal Handling to the other three departments. However, people who had been employed at the company before 1955 without high school diplomas were kept on and even promoted.

Then, in 1964, Congress passed the Civil Rights Act, whose Title VII prohibited employment discrimination on the basis of race. So in 1965, the company abandoned its formal policy of restricting black workers to the Labor Department. Instead, it added a new apparently race-neutral requirement: Anyone wishing to transfer from Labor to the other departments needed to have a high school diploma. However, many white employees who had been hired before the new requirements continued to work and get promoted in other departments.

The company added another requirement on July 2, 1965, the day on which Title VII became effective. For any job except those in the Labor Department, an applicant had to score well on two aptitude tests, for general intelligence and mechanical ability. Neither test was specifically created in response to the requirements of working at Duke Power.

Title VII includes a provision for bringing class-action suits—suits brought by a group of people claiming that they have all been affected by the same problem. So 13 of the 14 African Americans working at the Dan River plant brought a class-action suit in district court, claiming that the company was discriminating against them through the tests and the high school diploma requirement. (One of the employees was named Griggs, giving the case its name.) They claimed that these requirements had nothing to do with whether a worker could perform a job at the plant but were simply ways of keeping African Americans segregated in the lowest-paying department.

Legal Issues

At issue in *Griggs* was a key point in affirmative action law: the question of intent. Had the company intended to discriminate by instituting the diploma and testing requirements, and did it matter if it had? Could an employer discriminate without intending to do so? Was such "unintentional" discrimination still illegal under Title VII?

The district court found that while the company had indeed followed a policy of overt racial discrimination before the Civil Rights Act had been passed, that policy had ended. The district court also believed that Title VII was only intended to prevent future injustices, not to correct past ones. True, because of prior discrimination, there were many white people in the higher-paid departments who had not finished high school and had never taken the tests. But the policy under which they had been hired was in the past and so beyond the reach of Title VII. At this point, all the workers at Duke Power had to meet the same requirements, regardless of race. Therefore, the district court found that the diploma and testing requirements were acceptable under Title VII.

The court of appeals agreed that Duke Power Company was not in violation of Title VII, stressing that a "subjective test" of the employer's intent should be the deciding factor. Clearly, said the court of appeals, the new requirements had not been intended to discriminate, for they applied equally to both African Americans and white people. Indeed, the company was even willing to finance two-thirds of the cost of getting a high school diploma. In the absence of "a discriminatory purpose," the company's actions were legal—even if they had a discriminatory result.

Decision

The Supreme Court overturned the appeals court decision, ruling unanimously (with Justice William Brennan taking no part in the case) that Duke Power Company's actions were in fact illegal under Title VII. Chief Justice Warren Burger, writing the sole opinion in the case, explained:

> *The objective of Congress [in writing Title VII] . . . is plain. . . . It was to achieve equality of employment opportunities and remove barriers that have operated in the past to favor an identifiable group of white employees over other employees. Under the Act, practices, procedures, or tests neutral on their face, and even neutral in terms of intent, cannot be maintained if they operate to "freeze" the status quo of prior discriminatory employment practices.*

In explaining the decision, Burger cited the fable of the fox and the stork. When the fox invited the stork to dinner, he served the food in a shallow bowl. The stork, with his long bill, was unable to eat the food that was offered. In the same way, Burger said, employment policies had to genuinely offer equality of opportunity. They could not pretend to offer opportunity in a form that made it impossible for a whole class of people to accept. Burger cited previous court cases establishing that African Americans in the South had "long received inferior education in segregated schools." Therefore, they were likely to do less well on standardized tests. This did not necessarily mean that they could not do well at a particular job. Any test that an employer instituted had to be shown to be directly related to the job in question; a general test offered too many opportunities for discrimination. "The touchstone is business necessity," Burger wrote. "If an employment practice which operates to exclude Negroes cannot be shown to be related to job performance, the practice is prohibited," even if there was nothing inherently discriminatory about the practice itself.

Burger stressed that in employment discrimination cases, the burden of proof was on the employer to show why a particular test or requirement was needed. If a high school diploma was needed to do a particular job, and there was a shortage of African Americans with high school diplomas, that was not the employer's problem. But if a high school diploma was not needed, and if having such a requirement prevented African Americans from being hired, then the requirement was illegal under Title VII. Whether or not discrimination was intended, it had occurred—and it was against the law.

Impact

The decision in *Griggs* was a milestone in affirmative action history, for it established the precedent that employers were responsible for discrimination in their workplaces whether or not they had consciously intended such results. This was what President Johnson had meant by the phrase "affirmative action": An employer could not simply coast on past practices or carelessly adopt new practices that would perpetuate an old, perhaps unnoticed, pattern of discrimination. Rather, employers had to think actively and affirmatively about whether people of color could be integrated into their workforces. They had to at least consider the possibility that if their workforces were disproportionately white, discrimination was occurring, even if no one had consciously intended it.

Civil rights activists were pleased with the *Griggs* decision, for it fit with their own view of how racism worked. Sometimes people acted in overtly and deliberately racist ways, with the conscious intention of keeping people of color out of particular jobs or schools. Often, though, once a discriminatory system was set up, it could continue to produce discriminatory results "on its own." From a civil rights point of view, it was not enough for someone to simply avoid obvious acts of discrimination. People had to look at discriminatory results, think about what might be causing them, and take steps to change the situation. This was the worldview suggested by *Griggs*, and it was all the more remarkable because the justice who wrote the opinion, Warren Burger, was known as a conservative who had been appointed by Republican president Richard M. Nixon. The fact that both conservatives and liberals on the Court were unanimous in their support of the *Griggs* decision suggested that a new day had indeed dawned for the civil rights movement.

As a result of *Griggs*, employers were forced to become far more careful about their employment requirements and to look closely at racial imbalances at all levels of their workforce. *Griggs* is still cited today by people working in personnel and human resource departments to warn employers that they must make sure there is a "business necessity" for every job requirement.

However, the era of *Griggs* ended in 1989 with another Supreme Court case: *Ward's Cove Packing Co., Inc. v. Antonio*. In that case, the burden of proof was shifted from employers to employees, who were now required to demonstrate an employer's discriminatory intent. *Ward's Cove* is the standard in use today, making it much more difficult for employees to bring class-action suits protesting discrimination. From 1971 through 1989, however, many class-action suits were brought—and many more precluded by employers' own efforts to end discrimination in their companies.

DEFUNIS V. ODEGAARD
416 U.S. 312 (1974)

Background

Marco DeFunis, a rejected candidate at the University of Washington law school, brought a suit claiming that he was the victim of affirmative action policies that had discriminated against him as a white person. The school had made an effort to save 15 to 20 percent of the places in its entering class for African Americans, Chicanos, Filipinos, or American Indians, and DeFunis charged that some of the students admitted under this program were less qualified than he was. However, under order of the trial court, DeFunis was admitted to the law school and was about to graduate when his case reached the U.S. Supreme Court. (Odegaard was an administrator at the law school, giving the case its name.)

Legal Issues

At issue was the question of whether educational diversity was a worthy enough goal to warrant a school excluding some white students who might otherwise be admitted. As supporters of affirmative action had frequently argued, strict consideration of merit had never been the grounds for all college admissions. Geographic diversity, ensuring a range of interests among the student body, respect for alumni, and a host of other subjective factors had always been involved in a school's choices about whom to admit. Why then should a law school not attempt to fill 15 to 20 percent of its slots with minority students in the name of educational diversity?

In addition to "a diverse student body," the Washington State Supreme Court cited two other issues as "compelling state interests": "promoting integration in public education" and "alleviating the shortage of minority attorneys, prosecutors, judges, and public officials."

DeFunis, on the other hand, argued that his Fourteenth Amendment rights had been violated.

Decision

Because DeFunis's own situation had been resolved, the Supreme Court dismissed the case. However, Justice William O. Douglas dissented from the dismissal, arguing that the kinds of arguments presented in *DeFunis* would be heard again, so the Court should deal with them now. In Douglas's view, there was a clear distinction between making an active effort to include people of color in a school and simply trying not to discriminate against them. The first policy was racially motivated and unacceptable; the second was an attempt to overcome racial bias and so was acceptable. In an opinion that would be heard again in *Bakke*, Douglas objected to the university's setting aside a fixed number of places for minority students, which meant that it had to consider white and minority applications separately. In Douglas's view, this constituted a quota system that unfairly limited the number of spots available to DeFunis solely on the basis of his race.

Impact

Although the Supreme Court did not rule on the merits of DeFunis's suit, Douglas's arguments would be an important precedent for the 1978 *Bakke* case, in which Allan Bakke would likewise claim that a university's affirmative action program had violated his rights as a white person. As Douglas had suggested, quotas and separate admissions procedures for minority and white applicants would soon be at issue again.

ALBEMARLE PAPER CO. V. MOODY
422 U.S. 405 (1975)

Background

Present and former African-American employees (one of whom was named Moody) of Albemarle Paper Company brought a suit against their employer and their union, claiming that they had been discriminated against under Title VII of the Civil Rights Act of 1964, as amended by the Equal Employment Opportunity Act of 1972. By the time the case reached the Supreme Court, the major issues were the plant's seniority system, its program of employee testing, and back pay awards that employees were requesting to compensate for the alleged discrimination.

Legal Issues

The district court found that black employees had been "'locked' in the lower-paying job classifications" and ordered the company to implement a seniority system. But the court refused to order back pay that might compensate the employees for the money they would have gotten had they been paid fairly. They had two reasons for refusal: 1) the company's breach of Title VII had not been done in "bad faith," and 2) the workers had waited too long to ask for the back pay. The court also refused to enjoin or limit Albemarle's testing program, saying that "personnel tests administered at the plant have undergone validation studies and have been proven to be job related." The court of appeals reversed the district court's judgment.

Decision

The Supreme Court upheld the court of appeals, ordering that the testing program be ended and that the district court figure out a fair policy of awarding back pay to employees. As in *Griggs*, which Justice Potter Stewart's majority opinion frequently cited, the Court held that the employer's "discriminatory intent" or "bad faith" was irrelevant. Title VII was not intended to be a punishment for an employer's "moral turpitude" but rather to be a system of fairness for workers. Whether unfair treatment was intentional or unintentional, Title VII was there to provide a remedy, which in this case should take the form of back pay.

Moreover, as in *Griggs*, the Court found that job tests had to be very strictly correlated to actual job requirements if they were to be permitted by the Court. Even though Albemarle had employed a psychologist to show that many people who scored well on the tests also did well at their jobs, the Court found that was not enough. The psychologist's tests had dealt with only three of the eight job categories at the plant, and they had focused on top-performing senior employees, not on entry-level workers seeking promotion. Stewart's opinion reiterated the language from *Griggs*: "such tests are impermissible unless shown, by professionally acceptable methods, to be 'predictive of or significantly correlated with important elements of work behavior which comprise or are relevant to the job or jobs for which candidates are being evaluated."

39

Impact

Albemarle Paper Company served to reinforce the message of *Griggs:* Employers were responsible for the racial fairness of their workplaces, and workers were entitled to ask for compensation or relief on the basis of actual discrimination, if it could be proven, without needing to show an employer's intent. Until the *Ward's Cove* decision of 1989, this would be the controlling standard in affirmative action cases, and it led to many similar class-action suits. It also led to many efforts by employers to preclude such suits by eliminating various conditions that helped create discrimination and engaging in affirmative action programs for hiring and promotion.

FRANKS V. BOWMAN TRANSPORTATION CO.
424 U.S. 747 (1976)

Background

A group of African Americans (one of whom was named Franks) brought a class action against Bowman Transportation Company and a number of labor unions, alleging that the employer and unions had violated Title VII of the Civil Rights Act of 1964 in failing to hire black applicants as over-the-road (OTR) truck drivers. Title VII guarantees equal opportunity in employment without regard to race or color (and, as amended in 1972, sex).

Legal Issues

The district court enjoined the company and the unions to stop discriminating and ordered the employer to notify the members of the class that they had priority consideration for OTR driver jobs in the future. However, the district court would not grant back pay or retroactive seniority to any member of the class.

Seniority is usually figured from the date of employment, and greater seniority usually carries with it greater privileges with regard to pay, vacation time, overtime, and other benefits. The African Americans who had not been hired because of discrimination were claiming that they should be given seniority dating back to the time that, had there been no discrimination, they would have been hired. They also wanted back pay dating back to that time.

The court of appeals agreed with the class about back pay but agreed with the lower court about seniority. The appeals court believed that section 703(h) of Title VII allowed employers to apply different conditions of employment as part of a seniority system; for example, a part-time employee might not get the same kind of seniority as a full-time worker.

However, the workers saw it differently. They felt they were entitled to jobs, back pay, and seniority, because, they argued, it was only due to discrimination that they had not gotten these things. The Supreme Court agreed to hear their case.

Decision

The Supreme Court agreed with the workers. An important aspect of Title VII, the Court held, is that an employer guilty of discrimination is required to "make whole" the workers who had suffered as a result. Making whole in this case involved remedying the entire ill by restoring all the benefits that workers would have enjoyed had there been no discrimination in the first place, including a high seniority status. Otherwise, workers who had to start earning seniority from the day of the court decision, rather than from the day they would have been hired, were still being penalized for the discrimination.

The Court pointed out that the workers were not asking Bowman Transportation to modify its seniority system in any way, merely to apply the benefits of that system to them as if they had been hired when they should have been hired.

The decision was written by Justice John Brennan, joined by Justices Potter Stewart, Byron White, Thurgood Marshall, and Walter Blackman; Justice Lewis Powell joined in part of the decision. Chief Justice Warren Burger filed an opinion concurring in part and dissenting in part, which Justice William Rehnquist joined. Justice John Paul Stevens took no part in the consideration or decision of the case.

Impact

Franks v. Bowman is typical of the early days of affirmative action decisions, when the Court tended to support claims of discrimination and call for significant remedies. As in other early decisions, the burden is on the employer to justify or explain apparent discrimination, and if the employer cannot do so, he or she is liable for back pay and the restoration of benefits. In this and other cases of the late 1970s and early 1980s, the Court saw Title VII's intent as being a total end to discrimination in the workplace, a goal that should be achieved by making employers clearly responsible for integrating their workforces, with significant penalties if they did not. The result was a number of class-action suits nationwide, as workers sought to overcome discrimination. Perhaps even more significant was the number of employers who voluntarily changed their practices, either due to the actual threat of a lawsuit or out of fear that they might someday face such a threat. The Supreme Court decision in *Franks* and similar cases was a way to put employers on notice: The 1964 Civil Rights Act had called for sweeping changes in "business as usual" and employers were expected to take vigorous and "affirmative" responsibility for helping to end discrimination.

HAZELWOOD SCHOOL DISTRICT V. UNITED STATES
433 U.S. 299 (1977)

Background

The school district of Hazelwood, Missouri, in St. Louis County, was accused by the U.S. government of engaging in a "pattern or practice" of discrimination against black teachers under Title VII of the Civil Rights Act of 1964 (as amended). The federal government based its claim on the low percentage of African-American teachers in the district.

Legal Issues

The district court found that the U.S. government had failed to establish a "pattern or practice" of discrimination. When the court compared the percentage of black teachers and black students in Hazelwood, it seemed that Hazelwood had hired "enough" black teachers.

The appeals court disagreed. In its view, the relevant basis for comparison was not between Hazelwood's black teachers and black pupils, but between Hazelwood's black teachers and the black teachers in the surrounding area. Since 15.4 percent of the teachers in St. Louis County and the City of St. Louis were African American, while only 1.4 and 1.8 percent of Hazelwood's teachers were black, in 1972–73 and 1973–74, respectively, there was clearly a prima facie case of discrimination. The appeals court also cited Hazelwood's discriminatory hiring procedures.

Decision

The Supreme Court agreed with the appeals court that "the proper comparison was between the racial composition of Hazelwood's teaching staff and the racial composition of the qualified public school teacher population in the relevant labor market." However, the Court found, the appeals court had erred in not sending the case back to the district court so that more statistical evidence could be gathered, since Hazelwood's hiring practices might have changed after the 1964 Civil Rights Act had been passed. The true test of discrimination would be "the number of Negroes hired compared to the total number of Negro applicants," for once a prima facie case of discrimination had been established by the use of statistics, "the employer must be given an opportunity to show that "the claimed discriminatory pattern is a product of pre-Act hiring rather than unlawful post-Act discrimination": Hazelwood could not be penalized for discrimination that had taken place before discrimination was illegal.

In fact, the record showed—but the court of appeals had ignored— that for the two-year period 1972–74, 3.7 percent of the new teachers hired in Hazelwood were black. When compared with St. Louis County as a whole, where 5.7 percent of the new teachers hired during the same period were black, Hazelwood seemed to be doing pretty well. On the other hand, in the city of St. Louis, the rate of black teachers hired was far higher, for the city sought to maintain a teaching staff that was 50 percent black. Should Hazelwood be compared to the city and county together, or just to the county alone? The appeals court should have sent the case back to the district court to find out. Therefore, the Supreme Court vacated the appeals court decision and itself sent the case back to district court for a new trial.

Impact

The significance of *Hazelwood* lies in the Supreme Court's acceptance of prima facie evidence. The Court was far less interested in intent or employment practices than in statistics. If "not enough" black teachers were being hired, discrimination was taking place and ought to be remedied, and the main legal question was simply "What counts as 'enough'?" The Court felt that this question had not been sufficiently addressed at trial, so it sent the case back to a lower court where more evidence could be gathered. But it had also sent a powerful message to school districts and other employers across the country: They would be judged by results, not intentions; results that could be measured in clear, objective ways. Once again, the burden would be on an employer to show why a clear statistical imbalance was not discrimination, rather than asking employees or the U.S. government to prove that discrimination had been intended or was the inevitable result of certain practices.

On the other hand, employers could not be penalized for the results of actions taken before 1964. The Supreme Court recognized that it might take a while before the effects of pre-1964 discrimination could be overcome. As long as an employer was hiring fairly *now*, the law was being upheld.

The decision was delivered by Justice Potter Stewart, joined by Chief Justice Warren Burger and Justices John Brennan, Byron White, Thurgood Marshall, Harry Blackmun, Lewis Powell, and William Rehnquist. Justices Brennan and White filed concurring opinions, while Justice John Paul Stevens filed a dissenting opinion.

Affirmative Action

REGENTS OF THE UNIVERSITY OF CALIFORNIA V. BAKKE
438 U.S. 265 (1978)

Background

The 1970s were a time of general concern about the lack of minorities in the legal, medical, and other professions. In an effort to become more diverse, colleges and universities across the nation adopted various affirmative action guidelines. A set of guidelines that was to prove particularly controversial was adopted by the medical school of the University of California, Davis (UC Davis).

The UC Davis medical school accepted 100 students in each entering class. These 100 seats were divided into two groups: 84 went to students who applied through the regular admissions program, and 16 were reserved for those applying through a special admissions program. Each program had its own admissions committee, with primarily minority members on the special admissions committee.

In many ways, the admissions criteria for both programs were the same: Each committee considered overall grade point averages (GPAs), science GPAs, Medical College Admissions Test (MCAT) scores, interviewers' ratings, letters of recommendation, extracurricular activities, and other biographical data, and then combined them all into a total benchmark score. However, the general admissions committee would not even consider students whose GPA was below 2.5 (on a 4.0 scale), while the special admissions program had no such cutoff. To be considered for special admissions, a candidate simply had to say on the admissions form that he or she wanted to be considered as "economically and/or educationally disadvantaged" and/or as a member of a minority group: African American, Chicano, Asian, or American Indian. Candidates in the special admissions program were ranked only against each other, not against candidates in the general program. Although many disadvantaged white students applied under the special program, none was ever admitted.

Allan Bakke, a white man, applied under the general admissions program in 1973 and 1974 and was rejected both times. In 1973, his benchmark score was 468 points out of a possible 500—but he filed his application late, and by the time the general admissions committee received it, they were no longer taking students with scores of less than 470 for the general program. In 1974, Bakke applied early, and his score was 549 out of a possible 600. Once again, he was rejected. In neither year was he put on the waiting list. In both years, many special applicants with scores significantly lower than Bakke's were admitted.

After being turned down the second time, Bakke filed suit in state court. Although he had been rejected by 10 other medical schools, he claimed that Davis had rejected him because of his race.

The Law of Affirmative Action

Legal Issues

Bakke claimed that by excluding him on the basis of race, the UC Davis medical school had violated the equal protection clause of the Fourteenth Amendment, which guarantees equal protection under the law to all citizens, regardless of race. Bakke also alleged that the UC Davis program had violated the California State Constitution and Section 601 of Title VI of the Civil Rights Act of 1964, which provides that no person can be excluded on the grounds of race from a program that receives federal funding.

The trial court ruled in Bakke's favor, finding that the UC Davis special admissions program operated as a racial quota, in which minority applicants competed only against each other, with a fixed number of seats always reserved for them. Thus, the trial court found, the UC Davis special admissions program violated the federal and state constitutions as well as Title VI. However, the court stopped short of ordering the UC Davis medical school to admit Bakke, because Bakke had not proved that he would have been admitted if the special program had not existed.

The California Supreme Court agreed that the state had a "compelling interest" in integrating the medical profession and increasing the number of doctors willing to serve minority patients. But the court chose to apply a "strict scrutiny standard," finding that UC Davis had not chosen the "least intrusive" method of achieving its goals. (For further explanation of "compelling interest" and standards of scrutiny, see chapter 1.) The State Supreme Court chose not to rule on state constitutional grounds or with regard to Title VI, finding simply that the UC Davis program had violated the equal protection clause of the Fourteenth Amendment. Since UC Davis could not show that, without the special program, Bakke would *not* have been admitted, the State Supreme Court ordered that Bakke be accepted into the medical school.

Decision

The entire Supreme Court agreed that the UC Davis special admissions program violated the equal protection clause of the Fourteenth Amendment and that Bakke should be admitted to the UC Davis medical school. However, the court voted 5-4 to reverse the portion of the California Supreme Court's decision that suggested race could never be a factor in college admissions. Unfortunately for future litigation, the Court did not make its position clear by handing down a majority decision. Instead, several different decisions were written, none of which commanded a majority.

One of the most important decisions in *Bakke* was written by Justice Lewis Powell, who affirmed that the goal of achieving a diverse student body was indeed compelling enough to justify taking race into consideration under some circumstances. Perhaps ironically, although Powell had voted to strike down the affirmative action program at UC Davis, his reference to "educational diversity" would be cited many times in defense of affirmative action.

Powell's decision is invoked even today, so it is worth a closer look. Contrary to the view of the California Supreme Court, he wrote, race could be a factor in admissions policy, for Title VI did not prohibit all racial classifications—only those that violated the equal protection clause. However, in his view, the UC Davis special admissions program had violated the equal protection clause because it had foreclosed whole categories of students from being considered. Moreover, Powell concluded, since UC Davis could not prove that Bakke would have been turned down even without a special admissions program, he had to be admitted to the program.

Justices William Brennan, Byron White, Thurgood Marshall, and Harry Blackmun wrote their own opinion, emphasizing their passionate conviction that race should be able to be used as a factor in university admissions. Justice John Paul Stevens wrote yet another opinion, joined by Chief Justice Warren Burger and Justices Potter Stewart and William Rehnquist. These four justices withheld their opinions on whether race could ever be a factor in college admissions, but agreed that in this case, the UC Davis policy had violated Title VI and that Bakke should be admitted to Davis.

Impact

The *Bakke* decision might easily be the most influential affirmative action decision in modern history, for it helped to turn the tide against affirmative action and opened the door to numerous similar suits by white men and women claiming reverse discrimination. Yet Justice Lewis Powell's opinion in *Bakke* did affirm race as a constitutionally permissible factor in college admissions if the goal was to achieve "educational diversity"—and that opinion was to be the major legal precedent cited by anyone who wished to defend affirmative action in education in the coming decades. As of spring 2002, *Bakke* was the last Supreme Court decision on affirmative action in educational admissions, and so Powell's affirmation of educational diversity has been enormously influential.

Perhaps ironically, given its influence, the *Bakke* decision itself was a limited and qualified one. It addressed only one particular special admissions program, which even defenders of affirmative action agreed was particularly clumsy and heavy-handed, and a majority of the Court specifically found that race *could* be used as a factor in college admissions—and, implicitly, in employment. Moreover, the *Bakke* majority stressed that Title VI did not prohibit all forms of race-based consideration, only those that violated the equal protection clause.

Nevertheless, *Bakke* seemed to suggest that affirmative action's day was over, that the notions of backlash and reverse discrimination were now more resonant with the U.S. majority than the notions of fairness, diversity, and equality. *Bakke* also established the standard of "strict scrutiny" as the appropriate one in affirmative action cases. Not all the justices agreed with the application of this standard, and it would not be uniformly applied in all affirmative action cases in the 1980s and 1990s. *Bakke*, however, was influential in establishing the use of this standard—even as the case also provided the major source of support for those who wished to defend affirmative action in education.

UNITED STEELWORKERS OF AMERICA, AFL-CIO-CLC
V. WEBER
433 U.S. 193 (1979)

Background

In 1974, the skilled craft workers at the Kaiser Aluminum and Chemical Corporation were almost exclusively white, especially in Kaiser's southern plants. At the Kaiser plant in Gramercy, Louisiana, for example, only 1.83 percent of craft workers—5 out of 173—were African American, even though the work force in the Gramercy area was approximately 39 percent black.

The racial imbalance at Kaiser was the result of years of racial discrimination. Until 1974, the Kaiser plant in Gramercy had hired only experienced craft workers. But because African Americans had been excluded from certain unions for so long, they had never been able to become craft workers, and so they had no experience, creating a vicious cycle that seemed likely to exclude them permanently from the more highly skilled—and better paid—positions.

To remedy the situation, Kaiser and the steelworkers union, United Steelworkers of America (USWA), negotiated a special agreement. Kaiser would establish a training program for unskilled production workers so that they could become skilled craft workers. Production workers would be eligible for the training program based on seniority (how long they had worked at the plant) with one exception: until the percentage of black craft workers at the Gramercy plant matched the percentage of black people in the Gramercy workforce, at least 50 percent of the workers admitted into the training program were to be black.

In 1974, the first year of the Kaiser-USWA affirmative action plan, 13 craft trainees were chosen from among Gramercy's production workers—seven black and six white. Although the workers were chosen according to seniority within their racial categories, some of the black workers who were chosen had less seniority than some of the white workers who were passed over. One of those white workers, Brian Weber, brought a class action in U.S. District Court for the Eastern District of Louisiana, charging that the training program was discriminatory and in violation of Title VII of the 1964 Civil Rights Act.

Legal Issues

The 1964 Civil Rights Act was intended to prevent discrimination on the basis of race; Title VII specifically prohibited job discrimination. Weber's suit was based on Title VII's Section 703(d):

> *It shall be an unlawful employment practice for any employer, labor organization, or joint labor-management committee controlling apprenticeship or other training or retraining, including on-the-job-training programs to discriminate against any individual because of his race, color, religion, sex, or national origin in admission to, or employment in, any program established to provide apprenticeship or other training.*

Normally, in most union contracts, seniority is the basis for deciding how rewards and privileges will be allocated. The seniority system is intended to ensure fairness and prevent favoritism, so that an employer cannot award benefits based on personal preference. Weber argued that by making race more important than seniority, the training program was discriminating on the basis of race, putting the agreement in violation of Title VII.

The district court agreed with Weber and granted a permanent injunction to prohibit Kaiser from granting slots in the training program on the basis of race. The Fifth Circuit Court of Appeals agreed with the lower court's decision, finding that the race-based preferences in the plan violated Title VII.

The steelworkers' union took the case to the Supreme Court, arguing that race-conscious measures were needed to overcome years of race-based discrimination against African-American workers. Moreover, the USWA argued, Title VII did not cover voluntary agreements made between an employer and a union.

Decision

Writing the majority decision for the Court, Justice William Brennan reversed the lower court's decision and held that Title VII does not prohibit race-conscious affirmative action plans. Brennan wrote:

The Law of Affirmative Action

It would be ironic indeed if a law triggered by a Nation's concern over centuries of racial injustice and intended to improve the lot of those who had "been excluded from the American dream for so long," . . . constituted the first legislative prohibition of all voluntary, private, race-conscious efforts to abolish traditional patterns of racial segregation and hierarchy.

In other words, Brennan was saying, the whole point of Title VII and the 1964 Civil Rights Act had been to abolish racial discrimination—and that was also the point of the Kaiser-USWA training plan. How could the Court use an antiracist law to prohibit an antiracist program?

However, Brennan wrote, "We emphasize at the outset the narrowness of our inquiry." The Court was not offering a sweeping endorsement of all race-based programs, only this particular plan. First of all, the Kaiser program was voluntary and did not involve state action, so it did not constitute a violation of the Fourteenth Amendment's equal protection clause. The equal protection clause guarantees that all citizens are entitled to the government's equal protection—but the government was not involved in a private, voluntary agreement.

Second, in Brennan's view, the Kaiser-USWA training plan did not "unnecessarily trammel the interests of the white employees": No white employees were fired to make room for black ones, nor were white workers barred absolutely from the training program. Moreover, the training program was only a temporary measure; as soon as the workforce at the Gramercy plant reflected the workforce in the area as a whole, the racial requirements of the training program would cease. The program, wrote Brennan, was "not intended to maintain racial balance but simply to eliminate a manifest racial imbalance."

Brennan acknowledged that Title VII could not be used to *require* an employer to grant preferential treatment to any racial group. However, he wrote, Title VII did *allow* an employer to grant preferential treatment, as long as the goal of that treatment was "to correct racial imbalances."

Justice William Rehnquist wrote the minority dissenting opinion, joined by Chief Justice Warren Burger. "Today's decision represents a dramatic and . . . unremarked switch in the Court's interpretation of Title VII," Rehnquist wrote angrily. In all previous decisions, the Court had found that Title VII's intent was

to provide an equal opportunity for each applicant regardless of race, without regard to whether members of the applicant's race are already proportionately represented in the work force . . . Today, however, the Court behaves . . . as if it had been handed a note indicating that Title VII would lead to a result unacceptable to the Court if interpreted here as it was in our prior decisions.

As a result, Rehnquist wrote, the majority was simply coming up with a whole new interpretation of Title VII, one that was in no way justified either by the language of the law or by the intent of Congress.

Rehnquist's opinion takes up the theme of quotas that had previously been raised in *Bakke:*

> *There is perhaps no device more destructive to the notion of equality than the numerus clausus—the quota. Whether described as "benign discrimination" or "affirmative action," the racial quota is nonetheless a creator of castes, a two-edged sword that must demean one in order to prefer another.*

Rehnquist believed that the confusion created by the majority decision would have serious consequences for future court decisions. "By going not merely beyond, but directly against Title VII's language and legislative history, the Court has sown the wind," he wrote. "Later courts will face the impossible task of reaping the whirlwind."

Impact

Although *Weber* came out squarely in favor of the Kaiser-USWA affirmative action plan, it actually became part of the anti–affirmative action backlash of the 1980s. Simply by bringing a suit on the grounds of reverse discrimination, Brian Weber had made it easier for other white men to charge that they, too, were being passed over in favor of African Americans and/or women and to use the very laws intended to prevent discrimination as their grounds for charging reverse discrimination.

Weber also had important consequences for the role of U.S. unions in affirmative action. Historically, U.S. unions had had a mixed history with regard to racial discrimination. While industrial unions (unions that organized an entire industry) such as the USWA were often in the forefront of fighting employment discrimination, craft unions (unions organized on the basis of a particular craft or skill) had frequently been explicitly racist and anti-immigrant, barring membership to any worker who was not white or native-born. Moreover, even when unions officially supported antiracist efforts, they often faced a struggle within their own ranks, because many white workers feared that their own gains might be threatened by minority workers. The fact that Brian Weber brought a suit against his own union showed that unions would have to work hard to win some of their members to the idea that racism was an injury to all workers. Knowing that supporting affirmative action might open the door to lawsuits like *Weber* definitely had a chilling effect on the labor movement's commitment to programs such as the one the USWA had negotiated with Kaiser.

The Law of Affirmative Action

FULLILOVE V. KLUTZNICK
448 U.S. 448 (1980)

Background

Minority-owned small businesses were a significant focus in the affirmative action debate, since many civil rights activists believed that such enterprises represented an important means of advancement for individual people of color and for minority communities as a whole. In response to this concern, Congress included a provision in the Public Works Employment Act of May 1977 (PWEA) authorizing an additional $4 billion for local public works projects. Section 103(f)2, the minority business enterprise (MBE) provision of the act, required that at least 10 percent of that money had to go to minority business enterprises, which were defined as companies in which at least 50 percent of the stock was owned by "citizens of the United States who are Negroes, Spanish-speaking, Orientals, Indians, Eskimos, and Aleuts."

The PWEA focused on people working in the construction industry, which in the United States had traditionally been virtually all-white. Thus, reserving a certain amount of federal business for minority contractors and subcontractors was a potentially significant change.

On November 30, 1977, a group of white contractors and subcontractors (including a Mr. Fullilove) filed a complaint in the U.S. District Court for the Southern District of New York, seeking an injunction to stop the MBE provision, claiming that they had "sustained economic injury" as a result and charging that the MBE violated the Fourteenth Amendment's equal protection clause, the Fifth Amendment's due process clause, and other laws against discrimination. (Among those named in the suit was U.S. Secretary of Commerce Klutznick). They claimed that the provision had kept them from competing equally for federal contracts simply because they were white.

The contractors' efforts met little success. The district court refused to issue the injunction and eventually upheld the MBE program. The Second Circuit Court of Appeals found that "even under the most exacting standard of review the MBE provision passes constitutional muster." The case eventually came before the Supreme Court.

Legal Issues

At issue in *Fullilove* was the question of whether any race-based factors could be taken into consideration when awarding federal construction grants. Defenders of the MBE provision pointed out that in fiscal year 1978, less than 1 percent of all federal procurement (federal efforts to obtain goods and services) involved minority-owned businesses, even though minorities comprised 15 to 18 percent of the U.S. population. Supporters of

51

the provision believed that the government had to take some kind of positive remedial action to remedy the imbalance.

Those who opposed the MBE provision argued that any use of race-based considerations constituted a violation of every citizen's right to due process—the principle that the law should work in exactly the same way for every citizen. Those who brought suit in *Fullilove* claimed that by setting aside a certain percentage of federal funds for minority-owned businesses, the federal government had denied equal protection to white business owners.

Decision

The Supreme Court upheld the MBE provision, with Chief Justice Warren Burger writing the decision, joined by Justices Byron White and Lewis Powell. Burger wrote that the MBE provision was justified because before it had been passed, virtually no minority-owned businesses had been awarded federal construction contracts. Congress had been responding to "a long history of marked disparity [inequality] in the percentage of public contracts awarded to minority business enterprises," Burger wrote, a disparity that had not resulted from

> *any lack of capable and qualified minority businesses, but from the existence and maintenance of barriers to competitive access which had their roots in racial and ethnic discrimination, and which continue today, even absent any intentional discrimination or other unlawful conduct.*

Therefore, Burger wrote, to accomplish the "plainly constitutional objectives" of changing an existing pattern of discrimination, "Congress may use racial and ethnic criteria, in [a] limited way." Burger agreed that the greatest care had to be taken to avoid violating the due process clause of the Fifth Amendment, and he stressed that any use of racial or ethnic criteria had to be "narrowly tailored" to achieve a specific objective. However, Burger wrote, the MBE provision in question was indeed a "strictly remedial measure," and well within the authority of Congress. "[W]e reject the contention that in the remedial context the Congress must act in a wholly 'color-blind' fashion," he wrote. A careful use of race-based criteria could indeed be constitutional.

Burger also dealt with the accusation that nonminority businesses were being unfairly deprived of opportunity by the provision. He agreed that some white business owners might fail to get business that they otherwise would have gotten, but he pointed out that this was an "incidental consequence of the program, not part of its objective." Just as white business owners now felt that the MBE provision deprived them of a few government contracts, he explained, so had minority business owners felt that "business as usual" deprived them of virtually all government contracts. "The Congress has not sought to give select minority groups a preferred standing in the construction industry," he wrote, "but has embarked on a remedial program to place them on a more equitable footing with respect to public contracting opportunities." In contrast to the medical school program in *Bakke*, which Burger believed had given special privileges to minorities, the MBE provision was simply trying to remedy a long history of discrimination; no special privilege was involved.

In a concurring opinion, Justice Lewis Powell pointed out that the set-aside would reserve only a tiny portion of federal money to minority-owned businesses. Only 0.25 percent of all U.S. construction funds expended each year were being reserved for minority contractors, who made up about 4 percent of the nation's contractors. "The set-aside would have no effect on the ability of the remaining 96 percent of contractors to compete for 99.75 percent of construction funds," Powell wrote.

A dissenting opinion in *Fullilove* was written by Justice Potter Stewart, joined by Justice William Rehnquist. This opinion stressed the need for absolute color-blindness on the part of the government, no matter what the issue; anything else, Stewart wrote, was a violation of both the Fifth and the Fourteenth Amendments. Stewart cited the famous *Plessy v. Ferguson* case which in 1896 had established the infamous principle that "separate but equal" accommodations for different races was acceptable under the Constitution. Dissenting from that decision had been Justice John Harlan, who had written, "Our Constitution is color-blind, and neither knows nor tolerates classes among citizens. . . . The Law regards man as man, and takes no account of his surroundings or his color." Just as Harlan was correct in 1896, Stewart wrote, the principle of color-blindness was correct today— and that principle was violated by the MBE provision.

Stewart had several other objections to the MBE provision:

1) It would require the law to include a definition of race;
2) It might reinforce the stereotype that certain groups could not achieve success without special help;
3) It meant that government was once again teaching the public that rewards and penalties should be given out according to race rather than according to merit, encouraging people to view themselves and others in terms of racial characteristics.

Justice John Paul Stevens also wrote a dissenting view, on narrower grounds than Stewart's opinion. He felt that the MBE provision had raised far too many questions that Congress had failed to answer or even address. In his view, the provision posed the risk that stereotypes, rather than actual analysis, would be used to make decisions and that minorities would be simply assumed to be in need of special help that perhaps they did not actually need.

Impact

The impact of *Fullilove* was twofold. On the one hand, the Court had upheld the constitutionality of setting aside a certain percentage of federal funds for minority-owned businesses. Such set-asides continue as a feature of federal policy to this day, although, as in *Fullilove*, they remain the subject of some controversy.

On the other hand, the dissenting arguments against *Fullilove*—that race-based considerations were demeaning to people of all races; that no government program should ever mention race, for any reason—were the arguments that would come to dominate the debate in the 1980s. Although *Fullilove* itself was a victory for affirmative action forces, the dissenting opinions represented a backlash movement that would become far more powerful: in the Reagan and G. H. W. Bush administrations, among black conservatives, and, to some extent, in public opinion.

MISSISSIPPI UNIVERSITY FOR WOMEN V. HOGAN
458 U.S. 718 (1982)

Background

In 1982, the Mississippi University for Women (MUW) was the oldest state-supported all-female college in the United States. In 1974, MUW had established a four-year nursing program that offered a baccalaureate (four-year bachelor's) degree. As with all MUW programs, the nursing program was open only to women.

Joe Hogan was a registered nurse who held only a two-year degree. Since 1974, he had been working as a nursing supervisor in Columbus, the Mississippi city where MUW was located. In 1979, he applied to MUW's four-year program and was told that, although he was otherwise qualified, he could not enter the school because he was a man. School officials told him that he could audit courses but could not enroll for credit.

Hogan filed suit in the U.S. District Court for the Northern District of Mississippi, claiming that MUW's single-sex admission policy violated the equal protection clause of the Fourteenth Amendment. The case eventually made its way to the Supreme Court.

Legal Issues

The main legal question in *Hogan* was whether the potential educational benefits of single-sex education to women outweighed Hogan's right to be treated without regard to gender. Title IX of the Education Amendments of 1972 had banned gender discrimination in any institution receiving federal funds—but it had also expressly exempted private undergraduate schools that had traditionally used single-sex admissions policies. Thus, traditionally all-male colleges such as Harvard and all-female colleges such as Radcliffe were not considered to be in violation of Title IX. The state of Mississippi argued that MUW should receive a similar exemption from Title IX, on the grounds that women deserved the chance to study in an all-female environment if they chose. Moreover, the state argued, Hogan could attend other four-year nursing programs in Mississippi, although they were not as conveniently located for him as MUW. Still, he could not claim that he was being deprived of an educational opportunity.

Hogan's claim, however, did not rest on Title IX, but on the equal protection clause of the Fourteenth Amendment. Through all the various rehearings and appeals that his case underwent, he argued that being excluded from a school on the grounds of his sex deprived him of equal protection under the law.

Decision

The majority opinion of the Court was written by the Court's first female justice, Sandra Day O'Connor, who found that MUW's single-sex admissions policy did indeed violate the equal protection clause of the Fourteenth Amendment. Any time a statute classified individuals on the basis of gender, O'Connor wrote, it carried the burden of showing an "exceedingly persuasive justification" for that classification. The reasoning behind gender-based choices had to be

> *free of fixed notions concerning the roles and abilities of males and females. [Thus,] if the statutory object is to exclude or "protect" members of one gender because they are presumed to suffer from an inherent handicap or to be innately inferior, the objective itself is illegitimate.*

Moreover, O'Connor wrote, the means the state chose to employ had to bear a "direct, substantial relationship" to its objective. Gender classification could not be based on "the mechanical application of traditional, often inaccurate, assumptions about the proper roles of men and women." Instead, it had to be based on "reasoned analysis."

The state, O'Connor pointed out, had argued for the single-sex admissions policy on the grounds that it compensated for discrimination against women and therefore constituted a form of "educational affirmative action." But, she argued, Mississippi had not shown that women lacked opportunities to study or practice nursing; indeed, nursing was traditionally a female profession. In 1970, the year before MUW's nursing school had opened, women had earned 94 percent of the bachelor's degrees in nursing in Mississippi and 98.6 percent of the degrees nationwide. "Rather than compensate for discriminatory barriers faced by women," O'Connor wrote, "MUW's [policy] tends to perpetuate the stereotyped view of nursing as an exclusively woman's job."

Dissenting from the majority were Justices Lewis Powell and William Rehnquist, along with Chief Justice Warren Burger. Powell wrote that the majority decision "frustrates the liberating spirit of the Equal Protection Clause. It forbids the States from providing women with an opportunity to choose the type of university they prefer." Burger added his own dissenting opinion, pointing out that O'Connor had relied heavily on the argument that women had traditionally dominated the nursing profession and so did not need an all-female nursing school. Burger felt that such an argument "suggests that a State might well be justified in maintaining, for example, the option of an all-women's business school or liberal arts program."

Impact

Hogan is one of the few affirmative action cases that involve gender rather than race. Although this case involved the frustration of a man denied access to an all-female school, it became an important precedent in *United States v. Virginia* (1996), which concerned the right of women to attend Virginia Military Institute, an all-male military school. It also served as a strong warning to both traditional institutions and feminists that all-female programs would face stern scrutiny from U.S. courts.

Hogan addresses one of the more complicated problems of the feminist movement in the 1970s and 1980s: Did women want equal participation in a mixed-gender world, or did they want the right to their own all-female institutions—or both? And if they did support the need for women's spaces where girls and women could be free of the pressures of competing with or trying to impress men, could not then men argue for the very types of all-male clubs and men's spaces that the feminist movement had been trying to integrate? *Hogan* did not resolve this dilemma, but it does offer a fascinating look at the complicated issues that arise from it.

WYGANT ET AL. V. JACKSON BOARD OF EDUCATION ET AL. 476 U.S. 267 (1986)

Background

In 1972, the board of education in Jackson, Michigan, and the teachers union agreed to a new provision in their collective bargaining agreement. In the Jackson school system, as in most unionized places of business, laid-off employees were released in order of seniority: "last hired, first fired." In 1972, though, minorities tended to be more recent hires in the system. Relying entirely on seniority to make layoffs would drastically reduce the proportion of minority teachers.

Because of racial tension in the community, therefore, the parties agreed that "at no time will there be a greater percentage of minority personnel laid off than the current percentage of minority personnel employed at the time of the layoff." In other words, some white teachers with more seniority might be fired before less-senior minority teachers, so that the proportion of white and minority teachers could be maintained. When teachers were called back, the same rule would apply: senior teachers would be given preference, except that less-senior minority teachers might be hired back out of seniority order in order to maintain racial balance. Minorities were defined as "Black, American Indian, Oriental, or of Spanish descendancy."

In 1974, layoffs became necessary in the Jackson school system, but the Jackson Board of Education failed to comply with the contract; instead, they laid off the less-senior minority teachers while keeping the senior white faculty. The teachers union, along with two laid-off minority teachers, brought suit in state court. That court found that the union contract had been breached, so the board reversed its position and followed the contract.

In 1976–77 and in 1981–82, layoffs were again necessary, and again, senior white teachers were laid off while minority teachers with less seniority were retained. Now it was the laid-off white teachers' turn to bring suit, this time in federal district court. (One of the white teachers was named Wygant.)

Legal Issues

At issue was the Fourteenth Amendment's equal protection clause. Had the board violated the white teachers' right to equal protection under the law by laying them off for race-based reasons? The district court did not think so. It found that the racial preferences granted by the board were an attempt to remedy "societal discrimination" by providing "role models" for minority children in the district. The federal court of appeals upheld the lower court's decision.

Decision

The Supreme Court decision in *Wygant* was quite complicated. Five justices wanted to overturn the lower court decision, but for somewhat different reasons. Justice Lewis Powell wrote the plurality decision, joined by Chief Justice Warren Burger and Justice William Rehnquist. Justice Sandra

Day O'Connor joined that decision on most points and wrote her own concurring decision as well. Justice Byron White concurred but did not join in the decision.

The plurality (Powell, Burger, Rehnquist, and O'Connor) represented the most recently appointed and the most conservative justices on the Court. They overturned the lower court decision, finding that the contract had indeed violated the Fourteenth Amendment's equal protection clause. Justice Powell's opinion cited two reasons:

1) The board had not convincingly shown that it had engaged in discriminatory hiring practices against minorities. In *Hazelwood School District v. United States*, he wrote, there had been compelling statistical evidence of past discrimination; not so in *Wygant*. And race-based preferences could be used only to correct previous discrimination by a particular employer, not to achieve some general goal of racial equality. If, as in *Hazelwood*, the board had hired a disproportionate number of white teachers for several years, it might compensate for that error by making a special effort to hire minority teachers for a while. But the Jackson school board had not shown evidence of such discrimination.

2) The layoff provision in the contract was not sufficiently narrowly tailored. The concept of "narrowly tailored" was very important to Powell and the other conservatives (although O'Connor did not join this part of the decision). Since they saw race-based criteria as posing such a grave threat of violating the Fourteenth Amendment, they wanted all race-based factors to be very narrowly constructed so as only to remedy a particular ill; race-based criteria could not be used as a scattershot, general approach to overcoming racial discrimination. As Powell's decision put it, citing *Fullilove v. Klutznick* (1980), "Any preference based on racial or ethnic criteria must necessarily receive a most searching examination to make sure that it does not conflict with constitutional guarantees."

The liberal justices—Thurgood Marshall, William Brennan, and Harry Blackmun—joined in a dissenting opinion, written by Justice Marshall. These justices wanted the case to be sent back to the trial court (the district court), so that more facts could be developed. The case record, they said, was informal and incomplete, and the district court had acted too quickly.

More importantly, the dissenters claimed that previous Supreme Court decisions had not required the strict scrutiny that was now being called for. Justice Marshall pointed out that the Court had never yet been able to agree upon a way of applying the equal protection clause in affirmative action decisions. This had been particularly true, he wrote, in *Bakke* and *Fullilove*. The liberal justices thought that the plurality was wrong to ask for "strict scrutiny." Rather, Marshall wrote, when the goal was to eliminate the effects of discrimination, the

> *remedial use of race is permissible if it serves "important governmental objectives" and is "substantially related to achievement of those objectives." . . . [There is] a wealth of plausible evidence supporting the Board's position that [the layoff provision] was a legitimate and necessary response both to racial discrimination and to educational imperatives. To attempt to resolve the constitutional issue either with no historical context whatever, as the plurality has done, or on the basis of a record devoid of established facts is to do a grave injustice . . . to individuals and governments committed to the goal of eliminating all traces of segregation throughout the country. Most of all, it does an injustice to the aspirations embodied in the Fourteenth Amendment itself.*

Justice John Paul Stevens also dissented, but on different grounds: In his view, it was not necessary to find that the board had been guilty of past racial discrimination; the board had only to show "that it has a legitimate interest in employing more black teachers in the future." He wrote:

> *Rather than analyzing a case of this kind by asking whether minority teachers have some sort of special entitlement to jobs as a remedy for sins that were committed in the past, I believe that we should first ask whether the Board's action advances the public interest in educating children for the future. . . . I am persuaded that the decision to include more minority teachers in the Jackson, Michigan, school system served a valid public purpose, that it was adopted with fair procedures and given a narrow breadth, that it transcends the harm to petitioners [the laid-off teachers bringing the suit], and that it is a step toward that ultimate goal of eliminating entirely from governmental decisionmaking such irrelevant factors as a human being's race.*

Therefore, Stevens wrote, he would have upheld the lower court's decision.

Impact

Wygant was an extremely important decision, for it was a key step in the Supreme Court's growing effort to require "strict scrutiny" and "narrow tailoring" in all affirmative action decisions. As is clear from comparing the plurality and the dissenting decisions, the Court was in transition. The liberal members of the Court—Brennan, Marshall, and Blackmun—were deeply committed to ending segregation, and they were more lenient about when race could be a factor in the decisions of a school, employer, or government agency. If there was an "important governmental objective" at stake, and if the remedy was "substantially related" to achieving it, then a race-based measure was not only constitutional, it was in the very spirit of equal protection promised by the Fourteenth Amendment.

But the conservatives—who were growing in number on the Court—had quite a different point of view. Their primary concern was that government should not overstep its bounds. Unlike the more liberal judges, they were less interested in what Marshall had called "historical context" or "established facts." Rather, they relied upon a literal and absolutist reading of the Fourteenth Amendment—that race should never be a reason to deny someone equal protection. The question of whether someone was being denied equal protection could not be resolved by looking at history, a child's need for role models, the potential for racial tension within a school system, or the possibility that Jackson, Michigan, might end up with an all-white faculty teaching a multiracial student body. The question could only be settled by "strict scrutiny": After the most rigorous examination, was a policy so necessary to overcome a problem, and so narrowly tailored to that problem, that it overcame the dangers of violating constitutional guarantees of color-blindness? To the liberal justices, being conscious of race in order to overcome racial discrimination made sense. The more conservative justices wanted to look only at the letter of the law, which was supposed to be color-blind.

History was on the side of the conservatives, for over the next several years, the Court tended more and more to apply the standards of "strict scrutiny" and "narrow tailoring" to affirmative action cases, sharply curtailing the role of affirmative action in schools, employment, and government activity.

FIREFIGHTERS V. CLEVELAND
478 U.S. 501 (1986)

Background

In Cleveland, Ohio, a group of black and Latino firefighters known as the Vanguards filed a class-action suit in federal district court alleging that the city and various city officials had discriminated on the basis of race and national origin with regard to hiring, assigning, and promoting firefighters, putting them in violation of Title VII of the Civil Rights Act of 1964.

The labor union that represented all Cleveland firefighters, Local 93, International Association of Firefighters, petitioned to intervene. The union claimed that all its members would be affected by any decision that was made, so its point of view should be taken into account. The court allowed Local 93 to join the suit as a party-plaintiff.

Historically, the firefighters union had represented an all-white work-force, although there were now black and Latino members. The fact that minorities had formed their own organization, however, showed that they did not trust the union to protect their interests. And indeed, the union was to argue for a different outcome to this case than the Vanguards wanted.

LEGAL ISSUES

The federal court sought to resolve the case by having the Vanguards and the city of Cleveland sign a consent decree arranging for more black and Latino firefighters to be promoted. A consent decree is a kind of contract between the parties in a suit, in which a defendant voluntarily agrees to correct the situation that the plaintiff claims is illegal. However, no fault is found and no punishment or sentencing is involved.

In this case, however, the union objected to the decree, arguing that all race-based criteria, including those mentioned in the consent decree, were illegal under Title VII of the 1964 Civil Rights Act. Moreover, the union said, a general plan providing for more minority promotions would benefit some people who had not yet been discriminated against. Thus the consent decree exceeded the measures allowed by Title VII, which was only intended to protect workers from actual discrimination, not to indiscriminately benefit racial minorities.

The court of appeals upheld the consent decree, finding against the union.

Decision

The Supreme Court also upheld the consent decree. Congress wanted Title VII to be fulfilled through "voluntary compliance," and what could be more voluntary than a consent decree? The government was not stepping in and forcing anyone to hire more people of color. Rather, the city and the Vanguards were figuring out together how they could rectify a discriminatory situation. Contrary to what the firefighters union claimed, this was perfectly legal. The Court referred to *Steelworkers v. Weber* (1979), saying, "Voluntary action available to employers and unions seeking to eradicate race discrimination may include reasonable race-conscious relief that benefits individuals who are not actual victims of that discrimination."

Moreover, the Court said, the union's agreement to the consent decree was not necessary. True, the union had been allowed to intervene. But there was no legal obligation on the part of the court to satisfy the union. If the union believed that some of its members' rights had been violated under Title VII or under the Fourteenth Amendment (which guarantees every citizen equal protection under the law), it was free to make such claims in district court.

The opinion was delivered by Justice John Brennan, joined by Justices Thurgood Marshall, Harry Blackmun, Lewis Powell, John Paul Stevens, and Sandra Day O'Connor, who filed a concurring opinion. Justice Byron White filed a dissenting opinion, as did Justice William Rehnquist; Chief Justice Warren Burger joined in the Rehnquist dissent.

Impact

Firefighters v. Cleveland is significant on two counts: First, it reinforces the notion that, as late as 1986, race-based criteria were considered constitutional under some circumstances. As the Supreme Court became more conservative, it would become increasingly suspicious of any use of race in decision making.

Second, *Firefighters* speaks to the role of the craft unions, which had historically been all white and which tended to view affirmative action as a threat to their white members. Thus, the case pitted a group of minority union members against the union membership as a whole, in a kind of racial division that was to become increasingly common throughout the 1980s and 1990s. Many unions, particularly the industrial unions, had been in the forefront of fighting for affirmative action and against discrimination (see *Weber v. Steelworkers*, 1979), on the grounds that improving the lot of any workers improved the conditions for all workers. But cases like *Firefighters* spoke to another perception: that the gains of minority and women workers came at the expense of white men, and that affirmative action was simply a new form of discrimination. This tension between white and minority, male and female workers, was played out in a number of political arenas, and it continues as a source of tension within the labor, civil rights, and feminist movements today.

UNITED STATES V. PARADISE ET AL.
480 U.S. 149 (1987)

Background

In 1972, the National Association for the Advancement of Colored People (NAACP), a civil rights group, brought a suit to the 11th district court charging the Alabama Department of Public Safety with having systematically excluded African Americans from employment as state troopers, a violation of the Fourteenth Amendment. The district court agreed that there had been a "blatant and continuous pattern and practice of discrimination." In the 37 years the department had existed, there had never been a black trooper, which was "unquestionably a violation of the Fourteenth Amendment."

The district court therefore enjoined the department to hire one black trooper for each new white trooper that it hired, until there were approximately 25 percent black troopers. The department was also enjoined from engaging in any kind of discriminatory practices in recruitment, testing, appointment, training, or promotion. The department appealed the decision and a long legal battle followed. Some black troopers were hired. But despite the various court rulings in favor of the plaintiffs, by 1979, there were still no African Americans who had been promoted. The court therefore approved a partial consent decree in which the department agreed to develop within a year a procedure for promotion to the rank of corporal that would not discriminate against black candidates and that would comply with the Uniform Guidelines on Employee Selection Procedures under the 1964 Civil Rights Act.

In 1981, however, more than a year after the deadline for the previous decree, there were still no black troopers among the 232 officers at the rank of corporal or above. The court then approved a second consent degree: 1) The department's proposed test for promotion to corporal would be given to applicants; 2) The results would be reviewed to see if they discriminated against African Americans; 3) If the plaintiffs and the department could not agree on a promotion procedure, the court itself would develop one; 4) No promotions would occur until either the parties or the court came up with a fair system.

The department's test was administered to 262 applicants, of whom 60 (23 percent) were African Americans. The applicants were ranked on a list, with only five (8.3 percent) black troopers making it to the top half of the list; the highest black scorer was rated number 80. The department announced that it needed eight to 10 new corporals right away and said that it was going to promote 16 to 20 people before constructing a new promotions list.

By this point the U.S. government was involved in the suit as well. The Justice Department objected to any rank-ordered use of the promotions list, saying that it "would result in substantial adverse impact against black applicants"; in other words, using the list would once again mean that no black troopers were promoted. The United States suggested that the department submit an alternative proposal that complied with the consent decrees. (A department official was named Paradise, giving the case its name.)

The department did not submit a new proposal; nor did it make any new promotions in the next nine months. In 1983, the plaintiffs returned to district court. They had a suggestion: Until the department complied with the two consent decrees it was currently violating, it should be forced to promote one black trooper for every white trooper it promoted. This "one-for-one" hiring plan would be in effect until the department came up with a promotion procedure that was truly fair. This, said the plaintiffs, would "encourage defendants to develop a valid promotional procedure as soon as possible" and would "help to alleviate the gross underrepresentation of blacks in the supervisory ranks of the department," since that underrepresentation had been caused by past discrimination and made worse by the department's continual refusal to come up with a fair procedure. The United States opposed the "one-for-one" promotion requirement, though it did agree that the consent decrees should be enforced.

The district court did not immediately act on the plaintiff's request. Instead, in a 1983 order, it found that the test used by the department did indeed have "an adverse effect" on black people. Even if 79 corporals were promoted, the district court said, instead of the 15 that the department wanted to promote, none of the new corporals would be black. "Short of outright exclusion based on race," the court wrote, "it is hard to conceive of a selection procedure which would have a greater discriminatory impact." It ordered the department to submit a plan to promote at least 15 qualified candidates to corporal in a manner "that would not have an adverse racial impact."

The department offered to promote four black troopers among the 15 new corporals, and asked for more time to develop a new procedure. The United States did not oppose this proposal, but the plaintiffs did. They argued that the department's plan "totally disregards the injury plaintiffs have suffered due to the defendants' four-and-a-half year delay [since the 1979 decree] and fails to provide any mechanism that will insure the present scenario will not reoccur."

The court rejected the department's proposal. It pointed out that almost 12 years had passed "since this court condemned the racially discriminatory policies and practices of the Alabama Department of Public Safety. Nevertheless, the effects of these policies and practices remain pervasive and conspicuous at all ranks above the entry-level position." There were no black majors, captains, or sergeants, the court noted, and of the 66 corporals, only four were black. "Thus the department still operates an upper rank structure in which almost every trooper obtained his position through procedures that totally excluded black persons," and the department still had not developed procedures to rectify the situation.

In response, the court decided to put the one-for-one hiring plan into effect, so long as qualified black candidates were available. As soon as the upper ranks of the department were integrated, or as soon as the department had come up with fair promotion policies, the one-for-one hiring requirement would cease. The department was also ordered to submit a realistic promotion schedule.

Again, a long legal battle followed, with the department making several motions for the court to reconsider or amend its order. Finally, in February 1984, the department promoted eight black troopers and eight white ones. Four months later, it submitted a new promotions procedure, which the court provisionally approved, eventually suspending the one-for-one rule.

Meanwhile, the United States had appealed the district court's one-for-one order, claiming that it violated the Fourteenth Amendment's guarantee of equal protection and had discriminated against the white officers who had been passed over for promotion. But the appeals court upheld the lower court's decision. The case then went to the Supreme Court.

Legal Issues

At issue was the question of what measures could be taken to rectify what the lower court identified as an egregious case of discrimination. Everyone agreed that the relief prescribed by that court—promoting one black officer for every white officer promoted—was "race conscious" and extreme. The question was, could those measures be justified given the situation?

Decision

Justice William Brennan wrote for a plurality that included Justices Thurgood Marshall, Harry Blackmun, and Lewis Powell. Powell also filed a concurring opinion, as did Justice John Paul Stevens. In the plurality's view, "The race-conscious relief ordered by the District Court is justified by a compelling governmental interest in eradicating the Department's pervasive, systematic, and obstinate discriminatory exclusion of blacks." An argument could be made that the promotion relief was not justified, because the established discrimination committed by the department had been in the area of hiring, not promotion. But, Brennan wrote, that contention was "without merit," because promotion had also been an ongoing concern of the district court. If the department had hired enough black people in the first place, it would have had more black people competing for promotion. Besides, the department's promotional procedure was itself discriminatory, resulting as it had in "an upper rank structure that totally excludes blacks."

Moreover, Brennan wrote, the district court's order was also supported by society's interest in people complying with federal court judgments. Given how long the department had resisted compliance, the court was justified in taking strong measures.

Perhaps most importantly, the one-for-one requirement was "narrowly tailored" to serve its purposes. Extreme measures were clearly needed to eliminate the department's "long-term, open, and pervasive discrimination" and to force the department to live up to the consent decrees that it had violated for many years. The one-for-one requirement did not require "gratuitous" promotions, and it could be waived if there were no qualified black troopers. In fact, no black troopers were qualified for the ranks of lieutenant and captain, so the requirement had duly been waived for those ranks. And the requirement was temporary; as soon as the department had "valid promotional procedures," the one-for-one plan would be dropped.

Nor did the one-for-one requirement impose "an unacceptable burden on innocent white promotion applicants," Brennan wrote. "It does not bar, but simply postpones, advancement by some whites," and it did not require any white people to be discharged or laid off; nor did it require that unqualified blacks be promoted over qualified whites.

Justice Stevens wrote that because the record revealed "an egregious violation of the Equal Protection Clause," the district court had "broad and flexible authority to fashion race-conscious relief." Therefore he, too, upheld the order.

Justice O'Connor wrote a dissenting opinion in which Chief Justice Warren Burger and Justice Antonin Scalia joined; Justice Byron White wrote that he agreed with much of it. O'Connor referred back to *Wygant v. Jackson Board of Education* (1986) and that case's use of strict scrutiny. In *Wygant*, she wrote, "we concluded that the level of Fourteenth Amendment 'scrutiny does not change merely because the challenged classification operates against a group that historically has not been subject to governmental discrimination.'" In other words, even though white people had not been discriminated against in the past, that did not mean they had no rights under the Fourteenth Amendment. Courts still needed to look very carefully at race-conscious measures that might discriminate against white people.

Of course, O'Connor agreed, "One cannot read the record in this case without concluding that the Alabama Department of Public Safety had undertaken a course that amounted to 'pervasive, systematic, and obstinate discriminatory conduct.'" And, she agreed, the federal government certainly had a "compelling interest" in remedying past and present discrimination by the department. However, the district court had not fashioned a remedy that was "narrowly tailored to accomplish this purpose." O'Connor chastised the plurality, saying that though they claimed to apply "strict scrutiny," they had not in fact done so. Indeed, the Court had adopted a "standardless view of 'narrowly tailored' far less stringent than that required by strict scrutiny."

O'Connor's main objection was to the notion of "rigid quotas," which she believed could never exactly measure "the precise extent to which past discrimination has lingering effects." Even more flexible "goals" could be dangerous: Since no one could predict the future, it was hard to know just what requirements might be needed on an ongoing basis. Such flexible remedies, she wrote, "also may trammel unnecessarily the rights of nonminorities." Thus, "the creation of racial preferences by courts, even in the more limited form of goals rather than quotas, must be done sparingly and only where manifestly necessary"—and in this case, O'Connor believed, the one-for-one hiring was *not* "manifestly necessary":

> *[T]here is no evidence in the record that such an extreme quota was necessary to eradicate the effects of the Department's delay. The plurality attempts to defend this one-for-one promotion quota as merely affecting the speed by which the Department attains the goal of 25% black representation in the upper ranks. Such a justification, however, necessarily eviscerates any notion of "narrowly tailored" because it has no stopping point; even a 100% quota could be defended on the ground that it merely "determined how quickly the Department progressed toward" some ultimate goal.*

O'Connor agreed that the "recalcitrance of the Department of Public Safety . . . was reprehensible," and she found the lower court's frustration "understandable." Still, because the court had not even considered the available alternatives to a one-for-one promotion quota, O'Connor and her fellow judges dissented.

Impact

The impact of the *Paradise* decision was mixed. On the one hand, the Court had taken a strong stand against egregious cases of discrimination and had set a precedent allowing strong measures to be implemented in such cases. On the other hand, the narrowness of the decision, with four justices dissenting, made it clear that the liberal-conservative split so evident in *Wygant* was stronger than ever. Moreover, the liberal justices were older and their retirement was imminent. Just one more conservative justice would tip the balance against affirmative action and toward the notions of "strict scrutiny" and "narrow tailoring" that O'Connor and her colleagues favored.

CITY OF RICHMOND V. J. A. CROSON CO.
488 U.S. 469 (1989)

Background

The construction industry works through a series of contracts and subcontracts. Several contractors bid for a single job, each saying what price it will charge. A government agency normally gives the job to the contractor with the lowest bid. The contractor then uses that money to hire and supervise other, smaller firms—subcontractors—who supply the materials and do the actual work. If the subcontractors end up charging more than the contractor expects, then the contractor must absorb the costs, for it gets only the money requested in the original bid.

On April 11, 1983, the city council of Richmond, Virginia, adopted a plan intended to support minority-owned businesses. The plan required that contractors doing business with the city subcontract at least 30 percent of the dollar amount of each city contract to minority business enterprises (MBEs), which were defined as businesses that were at least 51 percent owned and controlled by U.S. citizens who were "Blacks, Spanish-speaking, Orientals, Indians, Eskimos, or Aleuts." If a company had shown that "every feasible attempt" had been made to comply but that qualified MBEs were "unavailable, or unwilling to participate," then the contractor might be granted a waiver. The entire plan was due to expire in about five years, on June 30, 1988.

The plan had been justified on the grounds that 50 percent of Richmond's population was black, but only 0.67 percent of the city's prime construction contracts had gone to minority businesses in the past five years. Moreover, virtually no minority businesses belonged to local contractors' associations, suggesting a pattern of racial exclusion. A city councillor added some additional information:

> *I have been practicing law in this community since 1961, and I am familiar with the practices in the construction industry in this area, in the State, and around the nation. And I can say without equivocation that the general conduct of the construction industry in this area, and the State, and around the nation, is one in which race discrimination and exclusion on the basis of race is widespread.*

On September 6, 1983, the city issued an invitation to contractors to bid on the installations of steel urinals and water closets in the city jail, specifying that the products of two particular manufacturers would have to be used. On September 30, the J. A. Croson Company began to prepare its bid. To meet the 30 percent MBE requirement, a minority contractor would have to supply the fixtures, since they would constitute 75 percent of the total contract price.

Croson contacted several MBEs, but none were interested. Finally, Croson found a local firm that was interested. That firm then started looking for suppliers of the fixtures. One supplier had already quoted a price directly to Croson and refused to quote it again to the MBE. The MBE also contacted an agent for the manufacturer of the fixtures, but the agent said that it would need 30 days to do a credit check on the MBE.

Meanwhile, Croson had submitted the lowest bid on the job, approximately $126,000, and so was awarded the contract. Croson had still not gotten a bid from the MBE, so it requested a waiver from the MBE requirement. Meanwhile, the MBE did bid on the subcontracting job, but it quoted Croson a price for the fixtures that was 7 percent higher than the market price. With other costs, the MBE's bid would have added over $7,600 to the cost of the project—a cost that Croson would have had to absorb.

On November 2, the city denied Croson's request for a waiver. On November 8, Croson wrote the city, explaining that the local MBE was not an authorized supplier of the fixtures, that its quotation was subject to credit approval, and that its bids were higher than any other quotation that Croson had received. In addition, Croson claimed, the MBE's bid had been submitted 21 days late. In a second letter, Croson laid out the additional costs involved in using the MBE and asked that the contract price be adjusted accordingly.

The city denied both Croson's request for a waiver and its request for a higher price. Instead, it reopened the bidding process. On December 9, Croson's attorney asked the city to review that decision, but he was told that there was no appeal. Croson took the city to court, claiming that the company's Fourteenth Amendment rights to equal protection under the law had been violated by the Richmond plan.

Legal Issues

The federal district court upheld the City of Richmond's plan, as did the court of appeals, citing *Fullilove*. Richmond had also cited *Fullilove* when it first established the plan. *Fullilove* had claimed that, in light of Congress's findings of past societal discrimination, a 10 percent minority set-aside for certain federal construction grants did not violate the Fifth Amendment's guarantee of equal protection. Therefore, the lower courts said, Richmond's plan was constitutional.

Would the Supreme Court agree? At issue were three questions: 1) What kinds of past discrimination can the government attempt to remedy? 2) What kinds of remedies are legally available? 3) Do the same rules apply to federal, state, and city government?

Decision

Although the justices took various positions, basically, a majority voted to overturn the appeals court decision, ruling that the Richmond plan had indeed violated the Constitution. The plan had not been justified by "compelling governmental interest," in the majority's opinion, and the 30 percent set-aside had not been "narrowly tailored" to accomplish the remedy that was intended.

With regard to "compelling interest," the Court held that Richmond had overstepped its bounds. The city was not acting to remedy its own practices of discrimination, but simply to overcome a general problem—a general problem that might or might not be caused by racial discrimination. The fact that there were so few minority-owned businesses in the Richmond area did not necessarily mean that racial discrimination had occurred. Certainly it did not mean that the city had practiced discrimination, or that individual contractors had. When the city had adopted its plan, it had spoken only in general terms of the need for helping minority businesses; it had not demonstrated that there was a specific practice of discrimination that this plan was intended to remedy.

Even if there had been a specific pattern of discrimination, the Richmond plan was not "narrowly tailored" to address it. The list of minorities eligible for set-asides under the plan was not limited to African Americans, but included minorities who did not even live in the area. There was no justification for the 30 percent figure, or for the provision that allowed contracts to go to MBEs outside the local area.

Moreover, just because Congress had the right to call for minority set-asides, as *Fullilove* had established, that did not give city and local governments the same right. Richmond could regulate its own procurement policies and could take action to correct its own mistakes. But whereas Congress could take action intended to change the racial climate in the whole country, the city did not have similar latitude. It could take "affirmative steps" to dismantle an unfair system in which it had participated, but not to generally support minority businesses.

The majority opinion was written by Justice Sandra Day O'Connor and was joined or concurred with in various ways by Chief Justice William Rehnquist and Justices Byron White, John Paul Stevens, Anthony Kennedy, and Antonin Scalia. Dissenting were Justices Thurgood Marshall, William Brennan, and Harry Blackmun, who joined in an opinion written by Marshall.

Marshall claimed that the Court had now begun using new standards to determine the kinds of affirmative action that were permissible under the Constitution. The city of Richmond, Marshall wrote, had indeed offered evidence to show a history of past discrimination, providing statistics to show how few minority contractors there were and offering the testimony of the city councillor who had asserted that prejudice was rampant in the construction industry. "These are precisely the types of statistical and testimonial evidence which, until today, this Court had credited in cases approving of race-conscious measure designed to remedy past discrimination," Marshall wrote. Moreover, Richmond had two powerful interests in this case: to eradicate the effects of past discrimination, and to prevent the city's own spending decisions from reinforcing and perpetuating the exclusionary effects of past discrimination. In Marshall's view, the Richmond program was strikingly similar to the one the Court had approved in *Fullilove*. Moreover, the Richmond plan was time-limited, had provisions for a waiver, and would have only a minimal impact on innocent third parties. Based on all the Supreme Court's past affirmative action decisions, the Richmond plan should have been accepted.

Justice Harry Blackmun wrote his own dissenting opinion, joined by Justice Brennan. Blackmun felt that the majority had erred in discounting the notions of history and context. Facts could not be looked upon in isolation, Blackmun wrote; the Court had to look at the "big picture":

> *I never thought that I would live to see the day when the city of Richmond, Virginia, the cradle of the Old Confederacy, sought on its own, within a narrow confine, to lessen the stark impact of persistent discrimination. But Richmond, to its great credit, acted. Yet this Court, the supposed bastion of equality, strikes down Richmond's efforts as though discrimination had never existed or was not demonstrated in this particular litigation. . . . History is irrefutable, even though one might sympathize with those who—though possibly innocent in themselves—benefit from the wrongs of past decades.*

> *So the Court today regresses. I am confident, however, that, given time, it one day again will do its best to fulfill the great promises of the Constitution's Preamble and of the guarantees embodied in the Bill of Rights—a fulfillment that would make this Nation very special.*

Impact

Croson made it clear that the liberal-conservative balance on the Court had now shifted decisively in favor of the conservatives. Although they were citing precedent to justify their decision, the conservatives seemed to be departing from the previous pro–affirmative action tendencies of the Court. In *Fullilove*, general statistics had been considered sufficient evidence to demonstrate discrimination. In *Croson*, though, the majority was calling for "strict scrutiny" and "narrow tailoring"; they wanted specific evidence of a particular problem that an affirmative action remedy would narrowly address, not general evidence of an overall problem that an affirmative action program would address in a general way. Despite the protests of the minority that this represented a change in the Court's direction, the views that prevailed in *Croson* would generally continue to prevail over the next decade.

Affirmative Action

WARD'S COVE PACKING CO., INC. V. ANTONIO
490 U.S. 642 (1989)

Background

Two salmon canneries in remote and widely separated areas of Alaska operated only during the salmon runs of the summer months. The canneries offered two types of jobs: cannery jobs, which were unskilled, low-paying, and
filled primarily by Filipinos and Alaska natives from the surrounding region;
and noncannery jobs, which were both skilled and unskilled, and which
were filled primarily by white workers, recruited by the companies' offices
in Washington and Oregon. Virtually all of the noncannery jobs paid more
than cannery positions. The cannery and noncannery workers lived in separate dormitories and ate in separate mess halls.

A group of nonwhite cannery workers (one of whom was named Antonio) filed suit in 9th district court under Title VII of the Civil Rights Act of
1964, claiming that the hiring and promotion practices of the factories were
responsible for the workforce's racial stratification and charging that they
had been denied the better-paying noncannery jobs on the basis of race.
The district court rejected their claims, but the court of appeals upheld
them. The appeals court found that the workers had indeed made a prima
facie case of "disparate [unequal] impact in hiring," that is, discrimination.
The court of appeals relied entirely on the workers' statistics, concluding
that when such clear statistical evidence existed, the burden shifted to the
employer to prove that the apparently discriminatory conditions described
were in fact the result of business necessity.

Legal Issues

At issue was the question of discriminatory intent and burden of proof. If
workers could paint a clear statistical picture of discrimination, on whom
did the burden of proof then fall: on workers, to show discriminatory intent,
or on employers, to show that the apparent discrimination was, in fact, business necessity?

Decision

The Supreme Court voted 5-4 to overturn the appeals court decision and
find for the employer. Justice Byron White wrote the majority decision,
joined by Chief Justice William Rehnquist and Justices Sandra Day O'Connor, Antonin Scalia, and Anthony Kennedy.

White wrote that the appeals court had erred by comparing the racial composition of cannery and noncannery workers. Rather, he wrote, as *Hazelwood*

v. *U.S.* (1977) had shown, the proper comparison was between the racial composition of the jobs at issue and the racial composition of the qualified workers in the relevant labor market.

Considering the skilled noncannery jobs, White wrote that perhaps the employers had not been able to find enough skilled minorities to hire. This was not necessarily the employers' fault, nor did it necessarily reflect discrimination. Considering the unskilled noncannery jobs (which paid more than the cannery jobs and were filled primarily by white workers), White still failed to find discrimination on the employer's part. Rather, he wrote, as long as there were "no barriers" actively keeping nonwhites from applying, and as long as the employer was hiring nonwhite workers in roughly the same proportion that they applied, the employer was within the law.

White and his colleagues warned of the dangers of the court of appeals' approach, which had called upon the statistical unbalance of the labor force to justify a claim of discrimination. Under that system, White wrote,

> *any employer having a racially imbalanced segment of its workforce could be haled into court and made to undertake the expensive and time-consuming task of defending the business necessity of its selection methods. For many employers, the only practicable option would be the adoption of racial quotas, which has been rejected by this Court and by Congress in drafting Title VII.*

White stated in no uncertain terms the Court's current thinking on using statistics to make a prima facie case of discrimination:

> *[A] mere showing that nonwhites are underrepresented in the at-issue jobs . . . will not alone suffice. Rather, the courts . . . must also require, as part of the . . . prima facie case, a demonstration that the statistical disparity complained of is the result of one or more of the employment practices respondents are attacking . . . specifically showing that each challenged practice has a significantly disparate impact on employment opportunities for whites and nonwhites.*

Not only did workers have to show that employers' specific practices were discriminatory, they had to take on each of these practices separately in making their case.

A dissenting opinion was filed by Justice Harry Blackmun, joined by Justices William Brennan and Thurgood Marshall. Justice John Paul Stevens also filed a dissenting opinion, joined by Justices Brennan, Marshall, and Blackmun. Blackmun wrote:

> *Today a bare majority of the Court takes three major strides backwards in the battle against race discrimination . . . thereby upsetting the longstanding*

distribution of burdens of proof in Title VII disparate impact cases. . . . The salmon industry as described by this record takes us back to a kind of overt and institutionalized discrimination we have not dealt with in years, a total residential and work environment organized on principles of racial stratification and segregation, which, as Justice Stevens points out [in his dissent], resembles a plantation economy. This industry has long been characterized by a taste for discrimination of the old-fashioned sort: a preference for hiring nonwhites to fill its lowest level positions, on the condition that they stay there. The majority's legal rulings essentially immunize these practices from attack under a Title VII disparate impact analysis.

Sadly, this comes as no surprise. One wonders whether the majority still believes that race discrimination—or, more accurately, race discrimination against nonwhites—is a problem in our society, or even remembers that it ever was. [See] Richmond v. J. A. Croson Co. (1989).

Justice Stevens's decision focused on the question of employer intent, citing the opinion in *Griggs v. Duke Power Co.* (1971). In that case, Stevens wrote, the Court had clearly found that employer intent was irrelevant; if statistics showed that discrimination existed, the employer was responsible for remedying it, or else for showing that business necessity prevented a remedy. "Regrettably," he wrote, "the Court retreats from these efforts . . . [in a] facile treatment of settled law. . . ." *Griggs* had made it clear that even a neutral practice that excluded minorities should be considered discriminatory unless the employer could show a "business necessity" for it. "[I]ntent plays no role in the disparate impact inquiry," Stevens wrote. "The question, rather, is whether an employment practice has a significant adverse effect on an identifiable class of workers—regardless of the cause or motive for the practice."

Impact

Ward's Cove represented a clear shift in Supreme Court practice: from *Griggs*, where statistical proof of discrimination was accepted by the Court, to *Ward's Cove*, where it was not. The decision in *Ward's Cove* made it far more difficult to win a discrimination suit against an employer, and tended to discourage employees from bringing such suits.

Ward's Cove, and the attitudes it represented, also signified a general turn against affirmative action on the part of the U.S. government at all levels. Lower courts, employers, government agencies, schools, and individual citizens were being given the message that the Supreme Court looked askance at affirmative action and was unlikely to rule in its favor. Coupled with the outspoken opposition to affirmative action from the

Reagan and Bush administrations, this helped to create a climate in which affirmative action was viewed increasingly with suspicion as a tool of reverse discrimination, as opposed to the early-1970s view of it as a proactive means of overcoming discrimination.

METRO BROADCASTING, INC. V. FEDERAL COMMUNICATIONS COMMISSION
497 U.S. 547 (1990)

Background

In the Communications Act of 1934, Congress authorized the Federal Communications Commission (FCC) to license radio (and later television) stations based on "public convenience, interest, or necessity." Periodically, FCC licenses come up for renewal, and recipients have to demonstrate that they are still worthy to operate the radio or TV station in question. To protect the airwaves and facilitate clear transmission, the FCC gives out only a limited number of licenses in any one geographic area. Historically, if a company wanted to operate a TV or radio station, it either had to ask the FCC to open up an entirely new slot in the airwaves or apply for the license of an existing broadcasting facility that was being revoked or renewed.

In response to the civil rights movement, Congress acknowledged that there was insufficient diversity in broadcast content and that minorities' views were insufficiently represented, a situation that Congress considered harmful both to minorities and to the viewing/listening public as a whole. With the goal of increasing diversity in broadcast content, the FCC established two new minority ownership policies: 1) It would give extra weight to minority owners when awarding new licenses; 2) It set up a "distress sale" policy, whereby a station that was going out of business, losing its license, or in the process of renewing its license, could reassign its license to a minority-owned business rather than simply returning it to the FCC.

The *Metro Broadcasting* decision involved two cases: one brought by Metro Broadcasting, Inc., concerning the FCC's preferential treatment of a 90-per-cent-Latino-owned business that was applying for a new license; the other involving a television station that had attempted to reassign its license to a minority-owned business. Shurberg Broadcasting, Inc., an applicant for a new station in the same geographic area, wanted instead for the license to revert to the FCC, so that all applicants could compete for it on an equal basis.

Legal Issues

The legal question in both cases was whether the FCC policies violated the Fifth Amendment's guarantee of due process to all citizens. A related issue was the question of what level of scrutiny to apply. In previous cases, the conservative justices had called for "strict scrutiny" of race-conscious affirmative action policies, meaning that such policies had to be looked at as closely as possible to ensure that they were narrowly tailored to fit exactly the evil they were designed to remedy. The liberal justices had called for "intermediate scrutiny," a looser interpretation of the law that would permit policies with more general aims. Finally, *Metro Broadcasting* involved a debate about whether city programs, such as the one in *City of Richmond v. Croson* (1989), required the same level of scrutiny as actions taken by Congress, such as the one at issue in *Fullilove v. Klutznick* (1980).

Decision

The majority opinion was delivered by Justice William Brennan, joined by Justices Byron White, Thurgood Marshall, Harry Blackmun, and John Paul Stevens. They held that the "benign" race-conscious measures that Congress had called for were indeed constitutional because they served important governmental objectives that were within the power of Congress.

Brennan acknowledged that the race-conscious measures in *Metro Broadcasting* were not technically "remedial," in the sense of being designed to compensate particular people who had suffered from governmental injustice. Unlike, say, class-action suits, in which the people asking for relief were the ones who had faced discrimination, no one was claiming that the minority-owned businesses seeking FCC licenses had previously faced discrimination from the FCC. Instead, the policies were Congress's way of remedying what it perceived as a larger social injustice: the lack of minority voices in the broadcast media.

Brennan had to explain why the minority set-aside program in *Croson* (1989) had been ruled unconstitutional, while the minority set-aside program in *Metro Broadcasting* was now being permitted. The difference, he wrote, was that *Croson* had concerned the actions of a city, whereas *Metro Broadcasting* concerned congressional actions. Hence, the correct precedent was *Fullilove*, which had also involved congressional actions. *Fullilove* had not called for "strict scrutiny"—so, clearly, the policies at issue in *Metro Broadcasting* did not require strict scrutiny either.

Brennan's decision stressed that broadcast diversity was the key issue in this case. He cited the *Bakke* decision's affirmation that a university's effort to seek "a diverse student body" was "a constitutionally permissible goal." So, too, was the FCC's effort to seek diverse broadcast programming. Indeed, Brennan pointed out, although at least 20 percent of the U.S. population were members of minority groups, minorities in 1971 had owned only 10 of about 7,500 U.S. radio stations and none of the

1,000 or more U.S. television stations, while in 1986, minorities owned only 2.1 percent of 11,000 radio and TV stations. An FCC study had concluded that minorities trying to become station owners faced a lack of adequate financing, insufficient information about when licenses were available, and inexperience in the broadcast field. These problems, Congress said, were the result of past racial and ethnic discrimination, leading to the current "severe" underrepresentation of minorities in the broadcast media.

In a concurring opinion, Justice John Paul Stevens referred to his dissent in *Wygant.* In both cases, Stevens wrote, "I endorse this [racial] focus [based] on the future benefit, rather than the remedial justification, of the decision." In other words, Stevens was saying, the FCC policies at issue in *Metro Broadcasting* were justified not on the grounds that minorities had suffered in the past, but on the grounds that they—and the nation as a whole—would benefit from their future inclusion in the broadcast media.

Justice Sandra Day O'Connor wrote a dissenting opinion, joined by Chief Justice William Rehnquist and Justices Antonin Scalia and Anthony Kennedy. As in *Croson,* these justices insisted on the need for strict scrutiny in any case involving race-based preferences. The need for strict scrutiny, O'Connor wrote, applied just as much to Congress and the federal government as it did to any state or municipality.

Moreover, O'Connor wrote, in order to act in a race-based way, government needed a "compelling interest":

> *Modern equal protection doctrine has recognized only one such interest: remedying the effects of racial discrimination The interest in increasing the diversity of broadcast viewpoints is clearly not a compelling interest. It is simply too amorphous, too insubstantial, and too unrelated to any legitimate basis for employing racial classifications.*

Instead, the dissenting justices wanted Congress and the FCC to adopt race-neutral measures, such as requiring station owners to provide diverse programming or favoring applicants with a particular background that might add diversity to the airwaves.

Justice Kennedy wrote an additional dissenting opinion, referring to the infamous "separate but equal" case of *Plessy v. Ferguson* (1896), in which the Court had permitted African Americans to be segregated into separate railway cars:

> *The Plessy Court concluded that the "race-conscious measures" it reviewed were reasonable because they served the governmental interest of increasing the riding pleasure of railroad passengers. . . . The interest the Court accepts*

[today] to uphold the [FCC's] race-conscious measures is "broadcast diversity."
Furthering that interest, we are told, is worth the cost of discriminating
among citizens on the basis of race because it will increase the listening plea-
sure of media audiences.

Impact

The immediate impact of *Metro Broadcasting* was to continue support for the
FCC's policies on minority ownership, which were part of a larger effort
among radio and TV broadcasters to provide diverse representation on the
air and minority-related public-interest programming. Had the FCC's policies been overturned, that might have had a chilling effect on a whole range
of minority-related policies in broadcasting.

In a larger sense, though, the significance of *Metro Broadcasting* lies in what
it reveals about the Supreme Court's response to affirmative action. Clearly, a
battle between the liberal and conservative justices had been going on for some
time, with each side seeking precedents to justify its approach. The liberal justices invoked *Fullilove;* the conservatives called on *Croson.* The liberal justices
called for a looser standard of review, being generally more tolerant of programs designed to remedy racial injustice in a general way, while the conservatives wanted to restrict race-conscious remedies as narrowly as possible.

Yet the *Metro Broadcasting* decision was a kind of anomaly, for when the
next major affirmative action case came before the Court in 1995, most of
the liberal justices were gone. Justice Brennan retired in 1990, Marshall in
1991, and Blackmun in 1994. Justice White, who was not generally considered a liberal but who had voted with the majority in *Metro Broadcasting*, retired in 1993. By 1995, the dissenters in *Metro Broadcasting*—O'Connor,
Scalia, Kennedy, and Rehnquist—would be joined by the conservative
Clarence Thomas, tipping the balance of the Court decisively in favor of the
justices who generally opposed affirmative action and favored strict scrutiny.
And indeed, when Justice O'Connor wrote the majority decision in 1995 for
the landmark affirmative action case *Adarand Constructors, Inc. v. Pena*, she
would be explicit in her effort to dismantle *Metro Broadcasting*.

UNITED STATES V. VIRGINIA
518 U.S. 515 (1996)

Background

In 1996, Virginia Military Institute (VMI) was the only single-sex school
among the 15 public colleges and universities of Virginia. Founded in
1839, this rigorous military school was intended to produce citizen soldiers

through a grueling process of education and personal training, with a focus on instilling physical and mental discipline and imparting a strong moral code. VMI considered itself a training ground for leaders, and its alumni included generals, members of Congress, and business executives. Indeed, despite its name, only about 15 percent of VMI graduates chose careers in the military.

In 1990, a female high school student complained to the U.S. Attorney General that she was not allowed to enter VMI. As a result, the United States sued the Commonwealth of Virginia, alleging that VMI's all-male admissions policy violated the equal protection clause of the Fourteenth Amendment. By the time the case was brought to trial, some 347 women had sent inquiries to VMI, but none had received a reply.

The case was only the beginning of a long and complicated set of proceedings. The district court initially ruled in favor of VMI, but that decision was overturned by the Fourth Circuit Court of Appeals. In response to the Fourth Circuit Court's ruling, Virginia proposed a parallel program for women, Virginia Women's Institute for Leadership (VWIL), a state-sponsored undergraduate program to be located at Mary Baldwin College, a private liberal arts school for women. VWIL was to share VMI's mission of producing citizen soldiers, but its program was to be substantially different in academic offerings, methods of education, and financial resources. The average combined SAT score of Mary Baldwin's entering class was about 100 points lower than the VMI freshmen score, and Mary Baldwin's faculty held "significantly fewer Ph.D.'s" and received "significantly lower salaries" than the VMI faculty.

The district court approved the plan for VWIL, however, anticipating that both VMI and VWIL would "achieve substantially similar outcomes." But VWIL was not acceptable to the attorney general, who continued to appeal the case. Eventually, it reached the Supreme Court.

Legal Issues

There were two key issues in the *Virginia* case: Did Virginia's exclusion of women from VMI deny women the equal protection guaranteed by the Fourteenth Amendment? And if VMI's unique situation as the only single-sex public college in Virginia was indeed unconstitutional, what was the appropriate remedy?

Throughout the legal proceedings, courts had cited *Mississippi University for Women v. Hogan* (1982) as its guide. That case had established that a single-sex admissions policy was unacceptable unless there was "exceedingly persuasive justification" for it. Was there an "exceedingly persuasive justification" for keeping VMI an all-male school?

Affirmative Action

Decision

The Supreme Court ruled that there was not. In a majority decision written by Justice Ruth Bader Ginsburg, the Court found that since there were many women who could meet the requirements of VMI, and since the kind of education available at VMI was offered nowhere else, the school's all-male policy was a form of discrimination against women. The supposedly parallel program, VWIL, did not in fact provide equal opportunity, since the two schools were not equal. Therefore, eligible women had to be admitted to VMI.

Virginia had argued that VMI served a useful purpose in providing "diversity" in education: Both co-ed and single-sex educational opportunities should be available. But, Ginsburg wrote, "educational diversity" was not the real reason for VMI's single-sex policy. Rather, that policy was a holdover from the days in which all higher public education in Virginia had been restricted to men. Ginsburg even cited a 1929 history of women's education which stated, "[N]o struggle for the admission of women to a state university was longer drawn out, or developed more bitterness, than that at the University of Virginia." Although Virginia did have some all-female seminaries and colleges, women were not admitted to the University of Virginia until 1970.

Ginsburg cited *Mississippi University for Women v. Hogan* as her precedent. In that decision, the Court found, Mississippi had given a spurious reason for maintaining an all-female school: that single-sex education compensated for discrimination against women and therefore constituted a form of "educational affirmative action." The Court did not find this persuasive, however, pointing out that women had plenty of opportunities to practice and study nursing. By the same token, Virginia was now claiming that VMI was all-male in order to promote educational diversity. Ginsburg did not find this persuasive either, holding that traditional discrimination against women was the real reason that VMI had remained all-male.

Many supporters of VMI's policies had claimed that admitting women to the school would result in a lowering of standards and a weakening of the rigorous system on which the school was based. That notion, Ginsburg wrote, was "hardly proved,' and she pointed out that "When women first sought admission to the bar and access to legal education, concerns of the same order were expressed." Indeed, she wrote, such concerns were "once routinely used to deny rights or opportunities" of all kinds. Therefore, women had to be accepted into VMI.

Chief Justice William Rehnquist wrote a concurring decision, saying that he agreed with the Court's conclusion but not with its analysis. Ginsburg had written that there was no way a new institution for women could be considered "equal" to VMI, which had been founded in 1839 and had an enormous base of alumni support, tradition, and reputation that no new institution could ever hope to match. Therefore, to offer women equal educational opportunity, Ginsburg gave Virginia two choices: admit women to VMI, or scrap VMI and start two new single-sex schools on an equal footing.

Rehnquist found those alternatives too limited. "Had Virginia made a genuine effort to devote comparable public resources to a facility for women, and followed through on such a plan, it might well have avoided an equal protection violation," he wrote. "I do not believe the State was faced with the stark choice of either admitting women to VMI . . . or abandoning VMI and starting from scratch. . . . " Even if the new women's school could not match VMI right away, it might eventually have achieved that goal, allowing the venerable VMI to be preserved. However, he wrote, Virginia had not in fact made a genuine effort to start a comparable women's institution, and so he supported the majority decision.

Justice Antonin Scalia wrote a dissenting decision, claiming that Ginsburg was applying her own modern ideas about women's education to the U.S. Constitution. The Constitution, wrote Scalia, had left U.S. citizens free to create whatever kinds of educational institutions they chose. The people of Virginia had chosen to create an all-male school, and since there were a variety of other public schools that women in Virginia might attend, the Court had no right to impose its own views in the name of the Constitution.

Scalia ended his dissent by citing "The Code of a Gentleman," which was included in a booklet that first-year VMI students were required to have with them at all times. The code included such provisions as "A Gentleman . . . Does not discuss his family affairs in public or with acquaintances; Does not speak more than casually about his girl friend; Does not go to a lady's house if he is affected by alcohol . . . ; Does not lose his temper; nor exhibit anger, fear, hate, embarrassment, ardor, or hilarity in public . . . Does not slap strangers on the back nor so much as lay a finger on a lady. . . . A Gentleman can become what he wills to be."

"I do not know whether the men of VMI lived by this Code; perhaps not," wrote Scalia. "But it is powerfully impressive that a public institution of higher education still in existence sought to have them do so. I do not think any of us, women included, will be better off for its destruction."

Impact

After 157 years as an all-male institution, VMI admitted its first female cadets in 1997. Although 30 women were admitted that fall, only 23 were still enrolled by the following spring. However, of the 430 men admitted as first-year students, only 361 remained. Observers insisted that the first-year program at VMI, which included virtually nonstop intensive hazing, was difficult for students of both genders. Indeed, when the hazing period formally ended in March, the remaining women attested that they had been treated the same way as the men. Moreover, according to a March 18, 1998, article by Peter Finn in the *Houston Chronicle*, the first-year students of both genders who had survived the arduous initiation period had formed strong bonds with one another.

Nevertheless, problems associated with the presence of women continued to arise throughout the first year: A female cadet was suspended for striking a male student, and a male and female student were found having sexual contact in the barracks. Similar problems persisted over the years, including allegations that a top cadet had used his position to extort sexual favors, an incident of a cadet becoming pregnant, and other difficulties. Women's involvement in VMI proceeded slowly: By spring 2001, when the school's first class of women to spend four years at VMI was ready to graduate, only 58 of the school's 1,300 students were women.

The VMI case helped encourage other all-male military institutions to open their doors to women. Among them was the Citadel, a traditionally all-male military school in South Carolina, whose transition to coeducation was also rocky and also resulted from a lengthy court battle. Under the supervision of the U.S. Department of Justice, the Citadel made several sweeping changes, including the addition of a female dean of women, recruitment officer, and assistant commandant of cadets. The school also agreed to work with an outside gender consultant who would help design sensitivity training programs. Other changes at the Citadel included increased counseling for female students, clearer policies on sexual harassment, hiring a full-time ombudsman to handle confidential student complaints, more careful selection of cadet leadership, and full-time faculty supervision in the barracks.

VMI also made efforts to help both male and female cadets adjust to the new coeducational environment, though its efforts were less extensive than the Citadel's. Still, in December 2001, a federal judge agreed to end the U.S. Justice Department lawsuit that had forced VMI to admit women in the first place. Both government officials and the VMI praised the judge's decision, with VMI's superintendent, Maj. Gen. Josiah Bunting III, calling it "a vindication of many years of dedication and hard work." Bunting, who had said in 1998 that women did not belong at VMI, acknowledged as he retired in December 2001 that his initial opposition to coeducation may have been mistaken.

According to Laura Brodie, author of *Breaking Out: VMI and the Coming of Women*, Bunting "set the right tone in those early years." But, added

Brodie, citing the school's low percentage of female students, "no one can claim that coeducation is successful at VMI now."

Clearly, turning all-male schools into coeducational institutions can be a difficult process that proceeds unevenly. Yet the VMI decision and its aftermath seems to indicate that the trend is definitely toward coeducation—and, however slowly, toward the acceptance of groups by institutions that had previously excluded them.

ADARAND CONSTRUCTORS, INC. V. PENA
515 U.S. 200 (1995)
ADARAND CONSTRUCTORS, INC. V. SLATER
528 U.S. 116 (2000)
ADARAND CONSTRUCTORS, INC. V. MINETA
532 U.S. 941 (2001)

Background

The *Adarand* case is one of the longest, most complicated, and potentially most significant cases in the history of affirmative action law. The case has gone to the Supreme Court three times, with three different names, through three presidential administrations, and a great many changes in the particular affirmative action policy that was originally challenged. (The names Pena, Slater, and Mineta refer to the various U.S. secretaries of transportation at the time each suit was brought.) As *Adarand v. Pena*, the case was enormously influential, for reasons that will be discussed below. Although many observers hoped that *Adarand v. Mineta* would be equally influential, bringing much-needed clarity to the Supreme Court's position on affirmative action, the Court decided in November 2001 to dismiss *Adarand* on the grounds that the case was far too muddled procedurally.

The *Adarand* case began with the small Colorado Springs company of Adarand Constructors, Inc., run by Randy Vech, a white man. In 1989, Adarand submitted a bid to a local contractor, Mountain Gravel & Construction Company, to install the guardrails on 4.7 miles of highway in the San Juan National Forest in southwest Colorado. Mountain Gravel had received its contract from a subdivision of the U.S. Department of Transportation (USDOT), which had a minority set-aside program: The agency offered a cash bonus to any contractor that hired a disadvantaged business enterprise (DBE). DBEs had to be certified by a government agency, with the agency instructed to "presume" disadvantage if the owner of a company was black, Latino, Asian Pacific, subcontinental Asian, Native American, or a member of any other group designated by the Small Business Administration. Businesses owned by people who were not members of those categories could apply for DBE status.

In order to get the bonus, Mountain Gravel decided to give the subcontract for the guardrails to Gonzales Construction Company, a DBE, even though Adarand's bid had been the lowest—so the company decided to sue. In 1992, Adarand went to 10th district court, claiming that its Fifth Amendment rights of equal access to due process had been violated.

Legal Issues

Adarand claimed that the racial preferences in the USDOT's set-aside program were unconstitutional, as had already been established in *City of Richmond v. Croson*. Adarand pointed out that *Croson* had called for "strict scrutiny" in determining the constitutionality of any affirmative action program, a scrutiny that the USDOT program could not withstand. In her *Croson* decision, Justice O'Connor had called the city of Richmond's minority set-aside program both too broad and too narrow: it offered special governmental help to businesses that might not actually be disadvantaged, and it denied special help to businesses that might be. Adarand argued that the same was true for the USDOT program: Racial classifications in and of themselves could not reveal whether a particular business was disadvantaged and so should not be the basis for governmental action.

Moreover, Adarand argued, *Croson* had shown that the only reason for a governmental affirmative action program was to remedy a particular wrong taken by the government. No one had accused the city of Richmond of racially discriminating against minority business enterprises; nor had anyone accused the USDOT of doing so. Therefore, neither governmental body was justified in giving MBEs or DBEs special help on the basis of race, even if those groups had faced other kinds of discrimination.

The district court disagreed. Rather than using the strict scrutiny proposed under *Croson*, the court said, the appropriate standard was the "intermediate scrutiny" required in *Fullilove* and *Metro Broadcasting*—and under that standard, the USDOT program of minority set-asides was indeed constitutional.

The Tenth Circuit Court of Appeals agreed that the program was constitutional, but on different grounds than those of the district court. Adarand then took the case to the Supreme Court, which overturned the appeals court. In the landmark 1995 decision, *Adarand v. Pena*, the Supreme Court sent the case back to district court, asking it to review the case again under the standard of strict scrutiny.

The Court's reasoning in the 1995 *Adarand* decision is worth repeating, for it influenced numerous affirmative action cases that came after, including *Hopwood v. Texas* (2001) (see below). Justice Sandra Day O'Connor wrote the majority opinion, joined (with some minor discrepancies) by

The Law of Affirmative Action

Chief Justice William Rehnquist and Justices Anthony Kennedy, Antonin Scalia, and Clarence Thomas. O'Connor laid out three major principles that should determine any use of race in government programs:

1) Skepticism: O'Connor cited the decision in *Wygant:* "'[a]ny preference based on racial or ethnic criteria must necessarily receive a most searching examination.'"
2) Consistency: Here she cited *Croson:* "the standard of review under the Equal Protection Clause is not dependent on the race of those burdened or benefited by a particular classification." In other words, white people, minorities, men, women—all deserved the same equal protection under the law. The same standards for a law that barred black people from a public railway car should be applied to a law that gave special help to minority-owned businesses.
3) Congruence: Any standard that applied to city and local agencies should also apply to federal law. Just because Congress was supposed to set social policy in ways that went beyond the mission of state or local governments, did not give Congress the right to use race-based criteria more freely than lower levels of government.

O'Connor acknowledged that her opinion might seem to contradict the majority decision in *Metro Broadcasting* (1990). Nevertheless, she wrote,

all racial classifications, imposed by whatever federal, state, or local governmental actor, must be analyzed by a reviewing court under strict scrutiny. In other words, such classifications are constitutional only if they are narrowly tailored measures that further compelling governmental interests. To the extent that Metro Broadcasting is inconsistent with that holding, it is overruled.

To make absolutely sure there was no room for error, O'Connor also specified that *Adarand* overruled *Fullilove:*

Of course, it follows that to the extent (if any) that Fullilove held federal racial classifications to be subject to a less rigorous standard, it is no longer controlling.

The other four justices strongly dissented. Justice John Paul Stevens, joined by Justice Ruth Bader Ginsburg, argued that the Court was now departing from the precedent set by *Fullilove* and *Metro Broadcasting*, in which "intermediate scrutiny" had been acceptable. In this way, he wrote, the majority had breached its own principle of "consistency." He also took issue with the notion that a law intended to impose racial discrimination was to be viewed in the same light as a law intended to overcome discrimination. Finally, he challenged the assertion that Congress had no more power than local governments to create social policy:

> *The majority's concept of "consistency" ignores a difference, fundamental to the idea of equal protection, between oppression and assistance. The majority's concept of "congruence" ignores a difference, fundamental to our constitutional system, between the Federal Government and the States.*

Yet, wrote Stevens, the *Croson* decision, which had been joined by four of the five justices writing the majority in this decision, had stressed the difference between federal and state government to explain why *Croson* had departed from *Fullilove*.

Justice Ginsburg also wrote a dissenting opinion, joined by Justice Stephen Breyer. She took issue with the majority's apparent disregard of contemporary racial discrimination:

> *Job applicants with identical resumes, qualifications, and interview styles still experience different receptions, depending on their race. White and African-American consumers still encounter different deals. People of color looking for housing still face discriminatory treatment by landlords, real estate agents, and mortgage lenders. Minority entrepreneurs sometimes fail to gain contracts though they are the low bidders, and they are sometimes refused work even after winning contracts. Bias both conscious and unconscious, reflecting traditional and unexamined habits of thought, keeps up barriers that must come down if equal opportunity and nondiscrimination are ever genuinely to become this country's law and practice.*

Impact

The 1995 decision had a huge impact on affirmative action law, for as a result, strict scrutiny was the new standard by which all affirmative action programs had to be judged. Scores of other cases, including *Hopwood, Smith v. Washington* (2000), and *Grutter v. Bollinger* (2000) (see below) cited this standard as a reason for overturning an affirmative action program.

But the *Adarand* story did not end here. The Supreme Court had sent the case back to district court, so that the lower court could review the matter under the new "strict scrutiny" standard. Under that standard, the district court found that the DBE program was not constitutional, for it was not narrowly tailored: it offered relief to groups that were not disadvantaged (such as, say, wealthy members of minority groups) and it failed to offer relief to groups that were (such as, say, poor white people). The Department of Transportation appealed this decision back to the 10th Court of Appeals.

While the USDOT's appeal was pending, Adarand filed a second suit in district court, asking Colorado officials to stop using the federal guidelines for certifying DBEs. But while this second suit was pending, Colorado altered its rules for certifying a DBE, in response to the district court's second decision in *Adarand v. Pena*, doing away with the presumption of disadvantage for particular groups. Instead, any applicant could simply certify itself as a disadvantaged group "based upon the effects of racial, ethnic, or gender discrimination."

A few days after Colorado implemented these new rules, the district court held a hearing on Adarand's suit against the state officials. The district court noted that in the other trial, it had just ruled that Adarand had been discriminated against by the federal government. Therefore, Adarand could declare itself a DBE—so the district court denied its request to order state officials to stop using the federal guidelines. A few days later, Adarand did indeed declare itself a disadvantaged business. As a result the appeals court ruled that its earlier case was now moot. (*Moot* means that a case no longer has any meaning and should be dismissed.) Adarand appealed this ruling of moot to the U.S. Supreme Court.

The Supreme Court heard this appeal in 2000, as *Adarand Constructors, Inc. v. Slater.* They disagreed that the case was moot and sent it back to the appeals court for a ruling. In September 2000, the appeals court overturned the district court's earlier ruling and said that even under strict scrutiny, the federal program was constitutional. In part, the Court was responding to changes made in the program under the leadership of President Bill Clinton, who in 1995 had responded to the first *Adarand* by saying that the proper approach to affirmative action should be "mend it, don't end it." Consequently, the Department of Transportation had revised its definition of DBE, adding women and veterans to the list of disadvantaged groups. Thus the program that the 10th Court of Appeals was ruling on in December 2000 was no longer the same program that the Supreme Court had considered in 1995.

Adarand appealed the new ruling to the Supreme Court yet again. The Court heard the case on October 31, 2001, and the Court's decision was much anticipated by observers on all sides of the issue, most of whom expected a definitive national ruling on the question of affirmative action. Given the conservative nature of the Court, it was generally believed that the final *Adarand* case would deal a death blow to federally funded programs that used race-based criteria—and, by implication, to minority business programs of all types around the country.

However, on November 28, the Court dismissed the case in a unanimous unsigned ruling. The justices said that the focus of the case appeared to have shifted to involve issues that the lower court had never reviewed. The justices also doubted whether the Adarand company still had legal standing to challenge minority business programs. By 2001, the state of Colorado no longer had such programs. Although some other states did have them, Adarand did not operate in those states and so could not be disadvantaged by them. Another race-based Department of Transportation program challenged by Adarand was no longer in use.

Affirmative action supporters regarded the Court's decision as a victory because it left in place an appeals court ruling in their favor. As of early 2002 observers continued to await a more definitive Court ruling on affirmative action.

APPEALS COURT CASES

PODBERESKY V. KIRWAN
38 F. 3D 147 (1994)

Background

The University of Maryland, College Park, had an all-expenses-paid minority scholarship program, the Benjamin Banneker Scholarships, that was open only to African Americans. Daniel J. Podberesky, a Costa Rican man with strong grades and good test scores, sued the university in 1989, naming, among others, the university president, William E. Kirwan, claiming that he was being discriminated against on the basis of race. The case rose to the Fourth District Court of Appeals.

Legal Issues

The main question in *Podberesky* was the issue of past discrimination. Could a scholarship program be restricted to African Americans on the grounds that they had been discriminated against in the past?

Also at issue in *Podberesky* was the concept of "strict scrutiny" as set forth by the Supreme Court in *City of Richmond v. Croson* (1989). In that case, the Supreme Court had found that any race-preferential law by state or local government must be subject to the most rigorous scrutiny to ensure that the equal protection clause of the Fourteenth Amendment was not being violated. In *Croson*, the Court had said that racial classification could be used only when:

1) The classification was needed to remedy continuing effects of discrimination in a specific area;

2) The classification was restricted to areas in which minorities faced discrimination and was used only as long as needed to compensate for past discrimination;
3) Race-neutral policies would not serve to remedy the existing discrimination.

The original district court had ruled in favor of the university. Appeals switched the decision twice, until it finally reached the Fourth District Court of Appeals, which has jurisdiction over Maryland, North Carolina, South Carolina, Virginia, and West Virginia. When the Supreme Court refused to hear a further appeal in 1995, the decision of the Appeals Court became final.

Decision

Using the precedent set in *Croson*, the appeals court found for the plaintiff, on the grounds that the university had not sufficiently proven the need to limit the Banneker scholarships by race. Once again, the burden of proof was on those who wished to show discrimination; simple results were not enough. Even if a college had been predominantly white for most of its existence, that did not necessarily mean that the school had practiced discrimination. As the court explained:

> *When we begin by assuming that every predominantly white college or university discriminated in the past, we are no longer talking about the kind of discrimination for which a race-conscious remedy may be prescribed. Instead, we are confronting societal discrimination, which cannot be used as a basis for supporting a race-conscious remedy.*

Impact

Podbereksy was the first major lawsuit in which the *Croson* precedents were applied to a college or university. The case was another example of the increasing difficulty of proving discrimination since *Croson* and *Ward's Cove*. No longer could affirmative action programs be justified merely by showing that a school or a workplace was all or nearly all white. Now a program had to be justified by proving that specific, current discrimination was actively being practiced—a claim that is often impossible to prove.

Thus, *Podberesky* led many college administrators to be concerned about their use of race-based scholarship programs, as legislatures around the country began to challenge the notion of race as a criterion for assisting students. Instead, financial need, geographic location, and family history (such as whether the student was the first in his or her family to attend college) were proposed as alternate bases for special aid.

Affirmative Action

SARAH P. WESSMAN V. ROBERT GITTENS
98-1657 (1998)

Background

Public schools in Boston have had a long history of racial segregation. In 1974, a federal court ordered a permanent injunction requiring Boston public schools to desegregate, mandating that each school have at least 35 percent minority enrollment.

The school known as Boston Latin is one of the most prestigious high schools in Massachusetts. Only 90 places are available in the ninth-grade class, and all applicants to this public school must take a written entry exam. Half the students admitted are chosen based on this exam and their junior high grades. The other half are chosen on these factors plus ethnic representation, with places allotted for African-American, Latino, Asian, and Native American students, according to their representation in the applicant pool.

Sarah Wessman, a white student, was denied admission to Boston Latin, although her test score and grade point average (GPA) were higher than those of some minority students who were admitted. Wessman sued the school, and her case reached the First Circuit Court of Appeals. (Robert Gittens, head of the Boston school committee, was also named in the suit.)

Legal Issues

As in federal Supreme Court cases concerning affirmative action, the Court of Appeals was concerned with whether the Boston Latin admissions procedure was narrowly tailored to accomplish a particular task. A narrowly tailored program might be constitutional; a program that used race-based criteria too broadly might violate the civil rights of white applicants under the equal protection clause of the Fourteenth Amendment.

The Boston School Committee (Boston's board of education) argued that its policy did not give preference to any one racial group; rather, the policy was based on the racial composition of the city and so could change over time. The school committee also argued that the 1974 permanent injunction constituted a "strong basis in evidence" that segregation had occurred in Boston and that affirmative action was needed to remedy it.

Decision

On November 19, 1998, the appeals court ruled that the Boston Latin program was not sufficiently narrowly tailored, and that Wessman's rights had been violated. Citing *Hopwood v. Texas* (see below) and other cases, the court took up the issue of diversity, going to great pains not to rule it out as a possible factor in admissions decisions. The court pointed out that the Supreme Court had not yet ruled definitively on diversity; therefore, "we assume . . . but we do not decide, that *Bakke* remains good law and that some iterations [assertions] of 'diversity' might be sufficiently compelling, in specific circumstances, to justify race-conscious actions."

However, the court continued, the Boston School Committee had not proven the educational value of diversity in this instance. It had only offered "generalities" and "abstractions" about the link between diversity and good learning.

As to the 1974 permanent injunction, the court ruled that it was a "negative" injunction that did not require "affirmative action." It prohibited discrimination; it could not be used to justify taking particular proactive steps.

Impact

Before the *Wessman* decision, most federal cases dealing with affirmative action in educational admissions had dealt with higher education. This was one of the first cases to deal with a high school. As magnet schools and other special public schools become more desirable to parents seeking quality education for their children, *Wessman* may herald an era in which lawsuits become more common among high school, junior high, and even elementary school students. Indeed, in Seattle, Washington, in 1999, a group of parents responded to the passage of I-200, an initiative designed to end affirmative action in the state, by suing the Seattle public school system, charging that the system was unconstitutional in using race to determine the allocation of contested places at the most desirable public elementary schools.

If suits like *Wessman* continue, and if they are successful, public schools will face some difficult choices. Since the 1970s, public education has been marked by a concern for integration, for ensuring that the best programs and the most desirable schools be equally available to all races and ethnicities. Historically, however, white students and some Asian-American students have done better than other groups on standardized tests. Whether this is due to inherent bias in the tests, to minority students being segregated into poor schools, or to white and Asian students' tendency to come from homes with more income and education, the fact remains that rewards allocated on the basis of test scores alone will tend to flow disproportionately to white and Asian students—reinforcing the conditions that led to educational disparity in the first place. *Wessman* shows that balancing the rights of individual students, respecting merit, and maintaining equality of opportunity will pose an enormous challenge for public education in the coming decade.

Affirmative Action

SMITH V. UNIVERSITY OF WASHINGTON LAW SCHOOL 233 F. 3D 1188 (2000)

Background

In 1994, a white woman, Katuria Smith, was denied admission to the University of Washington law school. She attended another law school and obtained her degree there. But in 1997, with the help of the Center for Individual Rights (CIR), a conservative public-interest law firm, she brought suit against the school that had rejected her, claiming that less-qualified minority students had been admitted and that she had been discriminated against because of her race. She was joined by Angela Rock, a white woman denied admission in 1995 who also got her law degree from another school, and Michael Pyle, a white man who had been denied admission in 1996 but who was accepted when he reapplied in 1999, by which time the race-based criteria in question had been eliminated.

The CIR sought to create a class-action suit on behalf of all "Caucasians and others" who had been denied admission because of the university's affirmative action policy. Smith's case went to district court, but meanwhile, on November 3, 1998, the people of Washington voted to pass I-200. In response, the university ended its affirmative action program and moved to dismiss the case on the grounds that I-200 had made it moot. Smith and her colleagues argued that the principle of affirmative action was still an important one, and they wanted the case to continue.

The district court agreed, but only in part. On February 10, 1999, it dismissed the plaintiffs' request for an injunction against the law school; on February 12, 1999, it ruled on the merits of the case, but found for the law school. Even though the institution no longer practiced affirmative action due to state law, the court held, there were no federal or constitutional reasons why the university's particular brand of affirmative action should not be practiced.

Legal Issues

In its decisions, the district court drew on the 1978 *Bakke* case, particularly the opinion written by Justice Lewis Powell, citing two principles:

1) Educational diversity could be a compelling governmental interest that meets the requirement of "strict scrutiny" for race-conscious measures under the Fourteenth Amendment. True, as Powell had said, using race in decision making was a grave matter that could not be done lightly; there had to be a "compelling interest" for the government to take such a potentially discriminatory step, and the courts

had to examine the government action rigorously—using "strict scrutiny." But the pursuit of "educational diversity" might indeed offer a compelling government interest and might hold up under the "strict scrutiny" test.

2) Race could be used as a factor in educational admissions decisions, even when not for strictly remedial purposes. In other words, even if a university had not specifically discriminated against a group in the past, it might still consider race as a factor in deciding whom to admit in the future.

The plaintiffs and the CIR the appealed the case to the Ninth Circuit Court of Appeals.

Decision

On December 4, 2000, the appeals court ruled that the question of enjoining the law school from future use of race in admissions decisions was indeed moot, as I-200 had invalidated the school's affirmative action program. However, the court ruled, the district court had been correct: The law school's admissions policies had not violated any constitutional principle, and had they not been outlawed on a state level, they would have been allowed to continue.

"There can be no doubt that the district court's decision faithfully followed Justice Powell's decision in *Regents of the University of California v. Bakke*," wrote Justice Ferdinand Fernandez, representing the panel of judges on the Ninth Circuit. But the *Bakke* case itself was confusing. While Powell's remarks on the constitutional permissibility of educational diversity had often been quoted in affirmative action law, Powell had not actually written the majority decision for the court. The Supreme Court had been unusually divided in *Bakke*, and it was difficult to know how to use that case as precedent.

Moreover, the Supreme Court had handed down many other affirmative action cases since then, notably *Croson* and *Adarand*. These were the cases that the Fifth Circuit Court of Appeals had cited in its *Hopwood v. Texas* ruling, to find that race-based criteria in pursuit of educational diversity were indeed unconstitutional.

But the Ninth Circuit Court of Appeals did not agree with the Fifth Circuit. It went through elaborate legal reasoning to explain first, why Powell's decision was the correct precedent to take from *Bakke*, and second, why *Bakke*, and not more recent cases, was the correct precedent for the current case. True, *Croson* and *Adarand* seemed to overrule *Bakke*—but those cases did not concern admissions decisions in higher education; *Bakke* did. The

Supreme Court had once explicitly said that if an earlier case seemed more relevant as a precedent than a later case, lower courts should use the earlier case, leaving it to the high court to eventually clarify the relevant law. "We, therefore, leave it to the Supreme Court to declare that the *Bakke* rationale regarding university admissions policies has become moribund, if it has. We will not," wrote Fernandez. In this case, then, the principle behind the University of Washington's affirmative action policies was upheld—even if the policies themselves were no longer in effect.

Impact

Although the plaintiffs and the CIR appealed *Smith* to the Supreme Court, the high court refused to hear the case, as it refused to hear a later appeal to *Hopwood*. Clearly, the Court will have to rule on affirmative action in higher education at some point—indeed, both *Gratz v. Bollinger* and *Grutter v. Bollinger*, concerning affirmative action at the University of Michigan, are likely to reach the high court during its 2001–02 season (see *Gratz* and *Grutter*, below). Meanwhile, the 1978 *Bakke* ruling stands as one precedent, while the rulings in *Adarand* and *Croson* stand as possible alternatives. The fact that federal courts could come to such varied conclusions—supporting affirmative action for the University of Washington law school in *Smith*; opposing it for the University of Michigan law school and the University of Texas law school in *Grutter* and *Hopwood*; supporting it for the University of Michigan undergraduate college in *Gratz*—demonstrates the need for a clear ruling.

At the same time, the impact of *Smith* includes the effect of I-200, the statewide initiative that outlawed affirmative action in state university admissions and made most of the *Smith* case moot. Opponents of affirmative action have been working in two areas: bringing class-action lawsuits such as the ones sponsored by CIR in Michigan and Washington and trying to get initiatives on the ballot, such as the ones sponsored by Ward Connerly in California, Washington, and Florida. It remains to be seen how activists working to end affirmative action will interpret the *Smith* decision, and what impact that will have on political activity around the nation.

Gratz v. Bollinger
122 F. Supp.2d 811 (2000)

Background

The Center for Individual Rights (CIR), a conservative public-interest law firm based in Washington, D.C., was looking for a case that might help change national affirmative action policy. The CIR decided that the

The Law of Affirmative Action

University of Michigan would make a good target for a landmark case, since the school was well known for its commitment to affirmative action. Moreover, its size made it likely to employ time-saving admissions measures, such as giving applicants bonus points on the basis of race, that could more easily be attacked in court. The CIR called upon four Republican state legislators, who used their in-state contacts to round up a number of white applicants turned down by the university. From these, the CIR chose two for a test case: Jennifer Gratz and Patrick Hamacher. Gratz had been rejected from the university's prestigious Ann Arbor campus, although she was accepted into the less prestigious Dearborn campus. When Hamacher was turned down by the University of Michigan, he enrolled at Michigan State University, also a less prestigious school. Their suit named, among others, university president Lee Bollinger.

The University of Michigan rated all applicants on a 150-point scale, with underrepresented minorities—African Americans, Latinos, and American Indians—given a 20-point bonus. The school also awarded 20 points to students from poor families; 20 points to recruited athletes; 10 points to Michigan residents; four points to children of alumni; and three points to those with special personal achievements. As a result, some 15 percent of the university's freshman class in 2000 was comprised of black, Latino, and Native American students. However, black enrollment at the university as a whole was only about 8.9 percent in a state that was about 14 percent black.

With the pro bono assistance of the CIR, Gratz and Hamacher brought suit against the university, claiming that its race-based admissions policy had violated their rights to equal protection under the Fourteenth Amendment. Later, the Citizens for Affirmative Action's Preservation, a group of students that included both minorities and white people, men and women, petitioned to be allowed to intervene in the case, arguing that they, too, had a stake in the maintenance of affirmative action at the university.

At the same time, Barbara Grutter was suing the University of Michigan law school, also with the help of CIR, also on the grounds that as a white woman she had been discriminated against. (See *Grutter v. Bollinger*, below.) The University of Michigan vowed to put on a thorough defense in both cases, bringing in scores of witnesses to defend the educational and economic benefits of affirmative action and campus diversity.

A striking feature of *Gratz* (and *Grutter*) was the participation of many Fortune 500 companies. Twenty of these corporations filed an amicus brief in support of the university, arguing that affirmative action was essential to good education. The companies included Microsoft, General Mills, Intel, Lucent Technologies, Eli Lilly, Kellogg, Texaco, Kodak, Dow Chemical, and Procter & Gamble. General Motors filed its own amicus brief in support of the university as well.

Affirmative Action

Legal Issues

Once again, as in the *Bakke* case of 1978, the question turned on the role of diversity in a student body and the rights of universities to use affirmative action as a means of overcoming the effects of past discrimination. Did the Fourteenth Amendment's guarantee of equal protection under the law mean that qualified white students could not be turned down by a public educational institution while apparently less-qualified minority students were accepted? Or did a university have some latitude in determining who was qualified, going beyond a consideration of test scores and grades alone? Was a university justified in making special efforts to include students from different racial backgrounds, if it also sought to include low-income students, top athletes, children of alumni, and students with special personal achievements? How did the Fourteenth Amendment apply to the rights of minority students in Michigan, who were currently underrepresented at their state university?

Decision

On December 13, 2000, Federal District Court Judge Patrick Duggan ruled in favor of the university, holding that it could indeed use race as a factor in its admissions policies. The CIR appealed to a higher court in February 2001.

Impact

Observers expect that the *Gratz* decision will be appealed to the Supreme Court by one side or the other, though it remains to be seen if the Court will be willing to hear the case. The impact of *Gratz* was muted, however, by the contradictory decision in *Grutter* on March 27, 2001, in which the district court judge found the law school's affirmative action policy to be unconstitutional. *Grutter*, too, is being appealed to a higher court and is expected to travel to the Supreme Court, although its future there is likewise uncertain.

Both *Gratz* and *Grutter* are part of a nationwide flurry of affirmative action cases concerning college admissions, including *Hopwood* and *Podberesky*. The Supreme Court's ultimate ruling on this case could determine national policy on affirmative action in higher education. If the Court uses *Gratz* to rule definitively against affirmative action, that could have an enormous impact, as statistics in California and Georgia have shown that ending affirmative action programs tends to drastically reduce the number of minority students, either in the system as a whole or on its most prestigious campuses. On the other hand, when the University of Florida system replaced that state's affirmative action program with Governor Jeb Bush's One Florida program, it instituted several recruitment plans as well, and the percentage of minority students in public colleges and universities rose to unprecedented levels. The impact of *Gratz*, then, remains to be seen as the national debate on affirmative action in education continues to unfold.

GRUTTER V. BOLLINGER
137 F. SUPP.ZD 821 (2001)

Background

Much of the background in *Gratz v. Bollinger* also applies in *Grutter v. Bollinger*, a suit brought by Barbara Grutter, a white applicant to the university's law school. Grutter was somewhat older than most first-year law students, and she was a woman; perhaps ironically, she, too, might have been considered a student in need of special consideration a decade or two ago. She was rejected by the law school, however, and with the help of the Committee for Individual Rights (CIR), brought suit against the University of Michigan. As in *Gratz*, the university mounted an ambitious defense of affirmative action's educational and economic benefits, with the support of an intervening group of students and the amicus briefs of several major corporations.

Legal Issues

The legal issues in *Grutter* were the same as those in *Gratz:* Did the university have the right to weigh race as one factor in admissions, or was that a violation of Barbara Grutter's rights to equal protection under the Fourteenth Amendment?

Decision

On March 27, 2001, Federal District Judge Bernard Friedman ruled against the University of Michigan, holding that Grutter had been unfairly rejected by the law school. The case was promptly appealed to a higher court.

Impact

The decision in *Grutter* might have led the University of Michigan law school to change its affirmative action policies, at least temporarily, but on April 6, 2001, a federal appeals panel ruled that the law school could continue with its current practice, pending its appeal. Like *Gratz*, *Grutter* is expected to travel to the Supreme Court, where it, too, may play a part in defining national affirmative action policy in higher education.

Affirmative Action

HOPWOOD V. TEXAS
861 F. SUPP. 551 (2001)

Background

In 1977, even as the *Bakke* case was making its way through the lower courts, a federal court ordered the U.S. Justice Department's Office of Civil Rights (OCR) to investigate claims that higher education in Texas was still segregated. Texas public higher education had traditionally been white-only; indeed, the 1950 Supreme Court case *Sweatt v. Painter* concerned the state's attempts to defend the segregated law school at the University of Texas (for more on *Sweatt v. Painter*, see chapter 1). A quarter-century later, the OCR found that Texas had failed to eliminate the effects of this history of segregation, and demanded that the state come up with a new plan to encourage minority enrollment at every one of the state's colleges and universities. Negotiation and litigation involving the OCR continued for more than 20 years, with the OCR continuing to maintain that Texas has not yet fully integrated public higher education.

In response to the OCR, the University of Texas Law School created an affirmative action program in 1983. Details of the plan changed in various ways over the years, but the policy proved strikingly successful in attracting students of color. Minority law students at Texas graduated at higher rates than at most of the nation's other law schools, and most of those graduates went on to successful law careers. By the mid-1990s, the University of Texas law school had trained more African-American and Mexican-American lawyers than any other historically white law school.

However, minorities were still significantly underrepresented at the University of Texas Law School based on their share of the state population. In 1994, for example, the year of the *Hopwood* trial, some 11 percent of the state was African American, whereas only 3 to 9 percent of the law school was black; without affirmative action, that figure would have been 1 to 4 percent. In the same year, some 31 percent of the state was Mexican American (Chicano), while 8 to 14 percent of the law school was Chicano, a figure that would have been 5 to 8 percent without affirmative action. Put another way, 58 percent of the state's population was neither black nor Chicano, that 58 percent had 80 to 87 percent of the law school places with affirmative action, and would have had 89 to 94 percent of all slots without the policy. (These figures come from the opinion of the district court handed down after the first *Hopwood* trial.)

In 1992, Cheryl Hopwood and some other rejected white applicants sued the law school, claiming that they would have been admitted had the affirmative action program not been in place. They had high grades and test scores, but the law school claimed that they had had weak majors at weak undergraduate institutions; even without affirmative action, the law school argued, Hopwood and her fellow plaintiffs would not have been accepted. The law school pointed out that most of its applicants were clustered within a very narrow range of grades and test scores. Within that range, it was no longer meaningful to make selections based on the minor differences between GPAs and scores; other factors—including but not limited to race—became more significant.

Nevertheless, Hopwood and her fellow plaintiffs wanted a judgment that the law school's admissions policy was unconstitutional, an injunction against further use of that policy, and money damages for the costs they had incurred through being denied admission.

Legal Issues

The legal issues in *Hopwood* are familiar to anyone even slightly acquainted with affirmative action law. The plaintiffs alleged a violation of their Fourteenth Amendment rights to equal protection under the law, regardless of race, the law school claimed that it was pursuing the "compelling state interest" of achieving desegregation, that it sought to remedy past discrimination in public education, and that it wanted to ensure diversity in the classroom.

The plaintiffs argued that if some minority applicants had won admission partly on the basis of their race, then some white applicants had been denied admission partly on the basis of their race. The law school acknowledged this as a mathematical fact, but it argued that its policies could withstand the "strict scrutiny" that had been called for in similar cases because the need for the policy was so compelling and because, given the large number of applicants and the small number of places, the "racial cost" of the program was spread out thinly among a large number of white applicants; the effect of the policy on any individual white person was thus relatively small.

One of the reasons that the *Bakke* decision had ruled against the University of California, Davis, medical school was because there had been two separate admissions committees, general and special (for minorities and economically disadvantaged whites). In 1992, the University of Texas law school also had two separate committees, which later received a great deal of publicity; during the actual trials, however, this fact was generally considered unimportant by both sides, and by the appeals court. In the law school's view, looking at all the minority applications together made it easier to identify the strongest candidates in the group and to determine how much weight racial preference should be given. The plaintiffs, however, objected to the whole notion of racial preference, whether it was administered by two committees or one; they wanted race to be irrelevant in the law school's choices.

Initially, U.S. District Judge Sam Sparks ruled that the law school could consider race in admissions so long as the goal was to maintain diversity (since the *Bakke* decision had suggested that was "constitutionally permissible"), and/or to remedy past discrimination (since that had been found acceptable in numerous other affirmative action decisions).

Decision

The *Hopwood* case was long and complicated. The initial decision by the Fifth U.S. Circuit Court of Appeals, handed down in 1996, was to overrule the district court, finding any consideration of race, even as one factor among many, to be unconstitutional. In June 1996, the U.S. Supreme Court declined to review the decision, putting an end to affirmative action in all admissions decisions at Texas public colleges.

The case was sent back to the district court for further findings of fact, however, and in March 1998 Judge Sparks found that even if the University of Texas had used a color-blind admissions system, it still would not have accepted Cheryl Hopwood and her coplaintiffs. The plaintiffs had been requesting more than $5 million compensatory damages, based on emotional distress and on a lifetime of lost earnings from not having graduated from the law school. When the judge found against the plaintiffs, he awarded them each one dollar for having been subjected to a discriminatory system. In order to avoid another trial if the decision were overturned on appeal, the judge also gave his opinion as to how much money the plaintiffs would have been entitled to if they had been acceptable students: $40,000 to one student to reimburse him for the additional tuition that he had paid at the Southern Methodist University law school, and $6,000 to Cheryl Hopwood for emotional distress. These figures were, of course, only theoretical, but the plaintiffs had also requested more than $1.5 million in court costs—and the judge did award them about $775,000. He also issued a formal order implementing the appeals court decision. All of his decisions were appealed, and, in December 2000, all of them were upheld by the Fifth Circuit Court of Appeals. In April 2001, Texas once again asked the U.S. Supreme Court to review the decision, and in June 2001, the Court declined. The *Hopwood* case had finally ended.

Impact

The abolition of affirmative action has done very little to increase the chances of any given white student to attend the University of Texas law school. With or without the program, the average applicant had less than a

25 percent chance of admission, for every year there are at least 4,000 applicants for about 500 places. Affirmative action affected only 2 to 3 percent of the white students who applied.

On the other hand, minority enrollment at the University of Texas law school has been deeply affected by *Hopwood*. In 1996, the first year without affirmative action, black enrollment dropped more than 90 percent in the first-year class, from 38 to four, while Mexican-American enrollment fell nearly 60 percent, from 64 to 26. This decrease is even more dramatic than it first appears when one considers that first-year students are divided into four sections, and that upper-level students are divided into dozens of possible courses. Without affirmative action, many classes have no students of color at all, depriving white students of that perspective; many other classes have only one or two minority students, which creates a vastly different experience for both minorities and whites than if there are four or five minority students.

Eventually the numbers began to creep up again, very slowly, though they are still well below their affirmative action levels:

Year	African American	Mexican American
1995 (the last year with affirmative action)	7.4 percent	12.5 percent
1996 (partial affirmative action)	1.7 percent	8.6 percent
1997 (no affirmative action)	0.9 percent	5.6 percent
1998	1.7 percent	6.4 percent
1999	1.4 percent	6.6 percent
2000	3.8 percent	7.1 percent

In 2000, the state's minority population was approximately 42 percent, whereas the law school's minority population was about 11 percent.

Part of the reason that minority enrollment rose at all was because the law school has other ways of recruiting minorities. The school encourages students, faculty, and alumni volunteers to recruit qualified minority applicants and to encourage admitted students to attend. Alumni and other volunteers help pay for application fees, and they have raised more than $1.2 million in private funds for minority scholarships. The school also works with undergraduates at the University of Texas's El Paso, San Antonio, Pan American, and Brownsville campuses, providing free or reduced-cost summer preparatory classes and helping the schools develop their prelaw curriculum. Finally, the law school has tried to develop a mentoring program for all newly admitted students, so that current students and alumni can make the law school more hospitable and can help with academic difficulties. In 2000, 18 African Americans joined the law school's first-year class, compared to only nine the year before; the number of Mexican Americans rose from 32 to 34.

The *Hopwood* case has also had a ripple effect on affirmative action in hiring and recruitment of professors. For example, in 1999, the University of Texas, Austin, ended a $300,000-a-year program intended to recruit minority professors, for fear that it violated the court ruling to end the use of racial preferences in admissions.

JOHNSON V. BOARD OF REGENTS OF UNIVERSITY OF GEORGIA
WL 967756 O.A. 11 (GA.) (2001)

Background

In the mid-1990s, University of Georgia officials had developed an admissions system designed to create a racially diverse student body. The University of Georgia had only begun admitting black students in 1961, and had accepted no black students at all during its first 160 years. At this time, therefore, it was sensitive to the need for diversity. Despite the university's efforts, however, its main campus at Athens had never been more than 6 percent black, even though almost one-third of Georgia's state population is African American.

The University of Georgia system was based on the Total Student Index (TSI), under which students who were not automatically admitted to the school on the basis of grades and test scores were assigned numerical scores based on about a dozen factors. Race was one of the factors; so were such issues as whether the student would be the first in his or her family to attend college. Race, however, carried the most weight. Only about 10 percent of all University of Georgia students were admitted based on their TSI scores; the other 90 percent were admitted based on grades and test scores. The school justified the TSI system by citing Justice Lewis Powell's 1978 *Bakke* decision, which held that attaining a diverse student body was a constitutionally permissible goal and that "ethnic diversity" could be one of the factors a school considered in admissions decisions. The TSI system also awarded bonus points for being male, in an effort to boost gender balance on the campus.

In 1999, three white women who were not admitted to the university (one of whom was named Johnson) brought a suit claiming that they would have been accepted had they been men or from a minority group. U.S. District Judge B. Avant Edenfield ruled that the university's use of race in admissions was an instance of "naked racial balancing," and was not a compelling state interest that deserved constitutional protection. The judge ordered the women to be admitted for the fall 2000 semester and had the University of Georgia compensate them for the extra money they had paid to attend other colleges. The university put its admissions systems on hold while the case was appealed—purely on the grounds of race—to a three-judge panel at the 11th Circuit Court of Appeals.

Legal Issues

At issue was the question of whether the "educational diversity" referred to in the *Bakke* case was synonymous with "racial diversity." Another key question was whether every student had to be considered solely as an individual, or whether such categories as race might be taken into consideration.

Decision

On August 27, 2001, the appeals panel ruled unanimously that the university's admissions policy was unconstitutional, for the university had failed to prove that having more nonwhite students on campus would actually lead to a more diverse student body. "Racial diversity alone is not necessarily the hallmark of a diverse student body," the judges found, "and race is not necessarily the only, or best, criterion for determining the contribution that an applicant might make to [a] broad mix of experience and perspectives." In the opinion written by Judge Stanley Marcus, the court gave the example of a white student from rural Appalachia, who might contribute more to on-campus diversity than a black student from suburban Atlanta. Although the court stopped short of saying that race could never be considered as a factor in encouraging diversity, it criticized the university for assuming that every nonwhite student would make the school more diverse.

Therefore, the court found, if race was to be taken into account, it had to be on a purely individual basis, student by student. If the university wanted "to ensure diversity through its admissions decisions, and wants race to be part of that calculus," the judges wrote, "then it must be prepared to shoulder the burden of fully and fairly analyzing applicants as individuals and not merely as members of groups when deciding their likely contribution to student body diversity."

Impact

The impact of the *Johnson* case was felt immediately. The University of Georgia saw a 20 percent drop in fall enrollment of new African-American freshmen and a 40 percent drop in applications from black high school seniors. Campus observers predicted that the numbers would continue to fall if steps were not taken to counteract the trend. Within a few days of the ruling, the University of Florida announced that it too would discontinue more than 50 minority scholarships, fearing similar lawsuits. Further changes are expected in the state university systems of Alabama, Florida, and Georgia, the states within the 11th Circuit.

Certainly, the *Johnson* decision sends a strong message nationwide that considering race in admissions decisions may be unconstitutional. Schools that do not have the resources to consider each student individually, as the court suggested, may simply eliminate race as a category and rely entirely on test scores and high school grades, a move almost certain to reduce the number of minorities attending college.

The week after the ruling, African-American leaders announced their own response to the decision. They argued that if the university could no longer use race-based criteria for admissions, it should also be required to stop favoring legacies, the children of alumni. University president Michael F. Adams, meanwhile, has expressed pride in his defense of affirmative action; in late 2001 he had not yet given any indication of what the school's eventual response might be.

Meanwhile, several university-admissions decisions are being appealed to the Supreme Court for the 2001–02 season, and legal observers expect the Court to eventually clarify its stance on this issue. The Supreme Court has not ruled on affirmative action in university admissions since the 1978 *Bakke* case, leaving the door open for people on all sides of the issue to cite various decisions, particularly that of Justice Lewis Powell. The impact of the *Johnson* case might thus also be felt in the growing pressure on the Supreme Court to further define national affirmative action policy.

STATE SUPREME COURT CASES

MCDONALD V. HOGNESS
598 P. 2D 707, 717 (WASH.) (1979)

Background

McDonald, a white male, was denied admission to the University of Washington medical school, despite the fact that he had higher grades and test scores than some minority students who were admitted. McDonald brought suit, naming the school's dean, John P. Hogness, among others, claiming that his Fourteenth Amendment rights to equal protection under the law had been violated.

The Law of Affirmative Action

Legal Issues

In 1978, a year before the *McDonald* decision, the U.S. Supreme Court had found in favor of Allan Bakke, a white male denied admission to the University of California, Davis (UC Davis) medical school. Yet a decision written by Justice Lewis Powell had held that educational diversity was a reasonable goal for a state university, and that some admissions policies—even if not UC Davis's—could meet that goal by considering race in a constitutional way.

The University of Washington cited *Bakke*, claiming that educational diversity was a key part of its admissions process. The university also claimed that McDonald had been incorrect to charge racial discrimination on the basis of grades and test scores. These objective criteria were only the initial part of the screening process, but other factors were also important: The minority students accepted in McDonald's place had in fact excelled in ways that McDonald did not. Therefore, there had been no discrimination.

McDonald, on the other hand, argued that his Fourteenth Amendment right to equal protection under the law regardless of race had been violated: as a white man, he said, he had been discriminated against.

Decision

The Washington State Supreme Court found for the university. It, too, cited Justice Powell's *Bakke* decision holding that achieving a diverse student body was a "compelling interest" warranting the use of "race-based" criteria. The Washington high court ruled that race could indeed be a factor in admissions when it was designed to serve a compelling state interest and when it did not insulate an applicant from competition with remaining applicants. The admissions procedure considered in *Bakke* had insulated white and minority applicants from competing with each other; not so in *McDonald*, where a single admissions committee had looked at all applicants—and had found McDonald wanting on a number of grounds, including his inability to contribute to the diversity of the student body.

Impact

The *McDonald* decision showed that even after *Bakke*, courts could support race-based admissions criteria in affirmative action programs that were better designed than the one at UC Davis. Not until the mid-1990s would the public-policy tide turn against affirmative action in state colleges and universities. Meanwhile, *McDonald* was part of a growing body of law that upheld affirmative action programs in public higher education.

Affirmative Action

INITIATIVES AND REFERENDUMS
Proposition 209

In 1995, University of California regent Ward Connerly, a conservative African-American businessman, led a successful fight to abolish affirmative action policies at the University of California. Connerly was also leading a campaign to get Proposition 209 on the California ballot. Proposition 209 held that the state could not discriminate against or grant preferential treatment to any individual or group on the basis of race, sex, color, ethnicity, or national origin in public employment, public education, or public contracting. Nor could race be used as a factor in admissions decisions in the public university systems in California. If a majority of California voters supported Proposition 209, affirmative action in the state of California would effectively be rendered illegal.

Opponents of Proposition 209 claimed that its anti–affirmative action stance was a violation of the U.S. Civil Rights Act of 1964 and other federal civil rights legislation, as well as an effort to bypass the federal legal procedure that involved the Supreme Court. In opponents' view, national policy as written by Congress and interpreted by the Supreme Court could not be circumvented by a state initiative. Supporters of Proposition 209 argued that in fact, the measure's language was in keeping with the Constitution and with federal legislation, and that California voters had the right to express their opinion on this issue at the polls.

On November 3, 1996, California voters passed Proposition 209, spurring challenges to the measure by a number of legal groups. The challenges led all the way to the Supreme Court which, on November 3, 1997, rejected the challenge without comment. The Court let stand a lower court decision which said that the anti–affirmative action measure did not violate anyone's constitutional rights.

The success of Proposition 209 led to another successful statewide anti–affirmative action campaign, also led by Connerly, Washington State's I-200. Connerly went on to campaign for a similar measure in Florida, and plans to continue, state by state, throughout the nation.

Meanwhile, in California, challenges to the measure continued as various state and city organizations struggled to retain some part of their affirmative action policies, with varying degrees of success. Minority enrollment at the state's public universities plummeted, then slowly recovered, but observers noted that minority enrollment has never reached pre-1997 levels at the Berkeley and Los Angeles campuses of the University of California, the system's top schools. In 2000, the University of California Board of Regents restored affirmative action in its university system; it is still unclear how that decision will fit into the anti–affirmative action context created by Proposition 209.

Initiative 200

After his success in getting California voters to pass Proposition 209, conservative African-American businessman Ward Connerly started a similar campaign in Washington State, where he sought to place Initiative 200 (I-200) on the November 1998 ballot. A heated debate ensued, in which Microsoft head Bill Gates and other local business leaders donated heavily to the No!200 campaign; the *Seattle Times* ran its own series of newspaper ads to defeat the measure. Nevertheless, on November 3, 1998, 58 percent of Washington state voters cast a "yes" vote for I-200, and the measure was passed.

The impact of I-200 was felt both immediately and over the long term. Before I-200 had passed, a lawsuit had been pending against the University of Washington's law school, with the university accused of bias due to the race-based preferences it used in admissions. In February 1999, a federal judge found that I-200 had made much of the suit moot, since the university could no longer make affirmative action a part of its admissions policy. At the same time, university officials found that the number of African-American applicants had fallen 41 percent since the previous year. In 1999, university officials considered retaining some form of race- and gender-based scholarships to restore minority admissions to their previous levels, and in October 2000, the university president announced a $65.6 million scholarship program with that goal.

I-200 also had an impact on local public education. In July 1999, parents went to federal court requesting that the Seattle School District be prohibited from discriminating on the basis of race. The parents were reacting to a program that allowed them to choose their children's schools, but in which race was used as a "tiebreaker" to decide school assignments in cases when there were conflicts. The parents claimed that the school district's policy violated I-200, among other laws.

In 1998, a number of organizations said that they would not hold their conventions in Washington State if I-200 was passed. In August 2000, new figures revealed that Seattle tourism had indeed fallen as a result of I-200.

CHAPTER 3

―――――――

CHRONOLOGY

This chronology represents an overview of the main events in the history of affirmative action, from the beginning of U.S. history through early 2002. Naturally, in such a dynamic field, the situation continues to change, particularly as the Supreme Court and the lower courts consider new issues and hand down new rulings, and as legislators and voters across the country create new affirmative action policies. However, precisely because the political and legal situations can change so quickly, a chronological listing of major events is extremely useful, as a way of marking the trends and landmarks in the U.S. treatment of race and gender.

1776

- *July 4:* Declaration of Independence is signed, proclaiming that "all men are created equal."

1787

- U.S. Constitution, including the Bill of Rights (the first 10 amendments), is adopted. Although there is no mention of equality, the Fifth Amendment guarantees due process of law, a right that will be invoked later by supporters of affirmative action.

1848

- Women gather at Seneca Falls, New York, to discuss their political situation and formulate demands, including the right to vote.

1857

- The Supreme Court hands down a landmark decision in *Dred Scott v. Sanford*, ruling that African Americans, as "subordinate and inferior beings," cannot constitutionally be citizens of the United States, whether they were slaves or free.

1863

- *January 1:* President Abraham Lincoln signs the Emancipation Proclamation, which frees the slaves in the Confederate states.

1865

- *December 6:* The Thirteenth Amendment to the Constitution is ratified, permanently abolishing slavery throughout the United States. States of the former Confederacy begin to pass Black Codes, reaffirming the separate legal status of African Americans. Many Union states likewise have laws on the books affirming the distinct legal status of people of color.

1866

- The so-called Radical Republicans in Congress object to the South's unwillingness to grant African Americans legal and social equality. They also object to President Andrew Johnson's veto of the Civil Rights Act of 1866. For the first time in history, Congress overrides a presidential veto and impeaches and tries a president.

1867

- The Radical Republicans engage in affirmative steps to enforce the policies of Reconstruction, including massive voter registration drives throughout the South, focusing on freed slaves and Radical Republicans of all races. The Freedman's Bureau provides emergency assistance to displaced Southerners of all races and oversees special tribunals to settle racial disputes. Contingents of the Union army are stationed in the South to enforce these reforms. In the 10 states of the former Confederacy, more black people than white people are registered to vote, and legislatures are controlled by African Americans and Radical Republicans.
- *April:* The Ku Klux Klan, a group organized to preserve white supremacy, meets for the first time at Maxwell House in Nashville, Tennessee.

1868

- *July 9:* The Fourteenth Amendment is ratified. The amendment applies the Bill of Rights to the actions of state and local governments; confers citizenship on all persons born in the United States; and requires the states to provide all persons with equal protection of the laws and due process of law before taking away life, liberty, or property.

1870

■ The Fifteenth Amendment is ratified, guaranteeing voting rights to all citizens, including freed slaves.

1874

■ The Ku Klux Klan, Confederate army veterans, and white leagues have organized to preserve white supremacy in the South. The 1874 state and local elections throughout the South are marked by mob violence and intimidation.

1875

■ Congress passes the Civil Rights Act of 1875, the last piece of Reconstruction legislation. The act bars discrimination by nongovernmental entities.

1876

■ *November:* Republican Rutherford B. Hayes and Democrat Samuel Tilden run against each other in an indecisive presidential election. The electoral college is split, and Congress must decide the outcome.

1877

■ In the Compromise of 1877, Democrats agree to concede the election to Hayes if he will withdraw federal troops from the South, putting an end to Reconstruction.

1883

■ The Supreme Court strikes down the Civil Rights Act of 1875, opening the door to a host of local and state Jim Crow laws excluding African Americans from virtually all sectors of public life, establishing segregated schools, theaters, restaurants, transportation, and employment.

1886

■ In *Yick Wo v. Hopkins* the Supreme Court rules that even if a law makes no mention of race, it is unconstitutional if it can be applied "with an evil eye and an unequal hand." The case concerned a San Francisco ordinance requiring laundry owners to get permission from the Board of Supervisors to operate. The case reveals that 200 Chinese were denied permission but 80 non-Chinese were granted permission.

1896

■ The Supreme Court decides *Plessy v. Ferguson*, ruling that separate but equal accommodations for African Americans do not violate the Constitution. Jim Crow law is thus ruled constitutional so long as the separate black facilities are deemed equal to white facilities.

1900

■ Eighteen northern and western states have laws against racial discrimination, even as Jim Crow laws, poll taxes, and literacy tests continue to be customary in the South.

1905

■ W. E. B. DuBois begins the Niagara Movement of African-American intellectuals, calling for equal rights and expanded suffrage.

1909

■ The Niagara Movement and white reformers join forces to create the National Association for the Advancement of Colored People (NAACP), one of the major civil rights organizations in the United States.

1917

■ The Supreme Court rules in *Buchanan v. Warley*, holding that a system of residential segregation enforced by the city of Louisville, Kentucky, violates the Fourteenth Amendment.

1936

■ The exclusion of African Americans from the University of Maryland is challenged in *Pearson v. Murray*.

1938

■ In *Missouri ex rel. Gaines v. Canada*, the Supreme Court invalidates a Missouri plan that denies African-American law students admission to the state university law school but pays their tuition at law schools outside the state.

Affirmative Action

1941

- Union leader and socialist A. Philip Randolph organizes thousands of black workers into the Negro March on Washington Movement, in which Randolph threatens a massive march on Washington, D.C. To prevent the march, President Franklin D. Roosevelt agrees to sign Executive Order 8802, barring segregation by government defense contractors.

1948

- In *Sipuel v. Board of Regents*, the Supreme Court requires the University of Oklahoma law school to enroll an African-American law student, since the state has no separate law school for African Americans.

1950

- In *McLaurin v. Oklahoma State Regents*, the Supreme Court finds unconstitutional the practice of physically segregating African-American students from the rest of the class during lectures at the state university.
- In *Sweatt v. Painter*, the Supreme Court rules that a separate law school established by the state of Texas to keep African Americans from attending the University of Texas is not sufficiently equal to justify the separate facility.

1953

- President Harry Truman's Committee on Governmental Contract Compliance urges the Bureau of Employment Security to "act positively and affirmatively" to implement nondiscrimination in a number of its functions.

1954

- Under Chief Justice Earl Warren, the Supreme Court overturns *Plessy v. Ferguson* with its ruling in *Brown v. Board of Education*, when it holds that "Separate educational facilities are inherently unequal." The Court orders the desegregation of public schools "with all deliberate speed." Arguing the case before the Court was NAACP legal director Thurgood Marshall. The Warren Court will go on to apply this principle to many other public facilities, including libraries, parks, beaches, and hospitals.

1961

- *March 6:* President John F. Kennedy's Executive Order 10925 makes the first reference to "affirmative action," when Kennedy's order creates the

Equal Employment Opportunity Commission (EEOC) and mandates that contractors working on federally financed projects must "take affirmative action" to ensure that hiring and employment are conducted without regard to race, creed, color, or national origin.

1963

- The U.S. District Court in Alabama rules that the University of Alabama's dean of admissions must adhere to a 1955 court order requiring the university to admit African-American students.
- *August 28:* In response to 250,000 people marching on Washington, D.C., for racial justice, President Kennedy urges Congress to go beyond simply barring discrimination and to pass a comprehensive civil rights statue that would expand educational and employment opportunities, including special apprenticeship and training programs, for people of color.

1964

- *July 2:* President Lyndon B. Johnson signs the Civil Rights Act of 1964, which prohibits discrimination based on race, color, religion, or national origin. The act includes Title II, prohibiting discrimination in privately owned facilities open to the public; Title VI, outlawing racial discrimination by any institution—public or private—that receives federal funds; and Title VII, banning discrimination by both private and public employers.

1965

- Congress passes the Voting Rights Act, giving the U.S. Department of Justice broad authority to eliminate discrimination that concerns the right to vote.
- *June 4:* President Johnson gives a commencement speech at Howard University, a traditionally black institution, in which he in effect lays out the philosophy behind affirmative action, saying, "We seek . . . not just equality as a right and a theory, but equality as a fact and as a result."
- Executive Orders 11246 and 11375 make the Department of Labor responsible for affirmative action, requiring government contractors and subcontractors at various levels (based on the amount of government funds they receive and/or the number of employees they hire) to "take affirmative action" to ensure that employees are hired and then treated during employment "without regard to their race, color, religion, sex, or national origin." Contractors must submit affirmative action plans analyzing the demographics of their current workforces and explaining what they plan to do to create greater equality.

1967

- *October 13:* Executive Order 11246, which established affirmative action, is amended to include discrimination on the basis of gender.

1968

- Civil rights leader Martin Luther King, Jr., is assassinated.
- Congress passes the Civil Rights Act of 1968, the nation's first open housing law.

1969

- President Richard M. Nixon initiates the Philadelphia Plan, the most far-reaching plan so far to guarantee fair hiring practices in construction jobs. Embodied in Labor Department Order No. 4, the plan requires several companies and educational institutions to initiate affirmative action plans to employ and promote people of color.

1971

- The Philadelphia Plan is expanded to include women.
- The U.S. Commission on Civil Rights reports that federal equal employment opportunity programs and agencies are failing at their task.
- The Eighth Circuit Court of Appeals rules that hiring preferences are constitutional if they can be shown to be necessary to overcome the effects of a given employer's past discrimination.

1972

- Inspired by the Civil Rights Commission report, Congress passes the Equal Employment Opportunity Act of 1972, extending the EEOC's jurisdiction to include all employers of more than 15 employees; unions with at least 15 members; and all government agencies. The act gives greater emphasis to systemic discrimination, making it easier to bring class-action suits.
- Title IX of the Education Amendments of 1972 is passed, banning gender-based discrimination by public and private institutions receiving public funds.

1973

- The Rehabilitation Act of 1973 requires that qualified people with disabilities be included in affirmative action requirements for contractors receiving federal funds.

Chronology

1974

- The Vietnam Era Veterans' Readjustment Act of 1974 requires that qualified individuals with disabilities be included in affirmative action requirements for federal contractors.
- The Supreme Court hands down *DeFunis v. Odegaard*, the first case to consider the constitutionality of affirmative action in college admissions, concerning the challenge to the affirmative action program at the University of Washington law school by a white applicant who argued that he would have been accepted had the program not been in place. The trial court had ruled DeFunis must be admitted to law school; Washington State's Supreme Court upheld the program; the Supreme Court rules that the case is moot, since DeFunis is in his final quarter of law school by the time the case reaches the high court.

1975

- The Supreme Court rules in *Albemarle Paper Co. v. Moody* that federal antidiscrimination initiatives have two purposes: to "bar [similar] discrimination in the future" and to "eliminate the discriminatory effects of the past."

1976

- The U.S. District Court for the District of Columbia rules that Georgetown University Law Center's race-based scholarship program is reverse discrimination that cannot be justified by a claim of affirmative action.

1978

- ***June 28:*** The Supreme Court rules in *Bakke v. Regents of the University of California* that while race is a legitimate factor in school admissions, it is unconstitutional to apply inflexible quotas such as those used at the medical school of University of California, Davis (UC Davis). The Court was responding to the challenge of white applicant Allan Bakke, who had twice been refused admission to the medical school, while the school had accepted applicants of color with significantly lower test scores, under a program that had reserved 16 of 100 places for minority and economically disadvantaged applicants and created a separate admissions program for them. The decision addresses only a few of the many questions that have arisen about affirmative action.

- In *United Steelworkers v. Weber*, the Court upholds a voluntary affirmative action plan agreed to by a private company and its union, even in the absence of governmental findings of past racism.
- The U.S. Department of Health, Education and Welfare (HEW) issues its interpretation of Title VI in light of the *Bakke* decision. HEW finds that no changes are needed in the regulations designed to implement the statute.
- In *McDonald v. Hogness*, Washington State's Supreme Court upholds the state university medical school's affirmative action program, despite the *Bakke* ruling. The Washington court points out that unlike the affirmative action plan at the UC Davis medical school, the Washington State plan does not call for separate consideration of minority applicants.
- In *Weber v. Kaiser Aluminum Co.*, the Supreme Court endorses a voluntary affirmative action plan of a private employer under the Civil Rights Act Title VII, if three conditions are met: there is "manifest racial imbalance" in the major job category of the program; the jobs had been "traditionally segregated"; and the plan did not "unnecessarily trammel" white employees' interests.

1980

- Ronald Reagan is elected president, with opposition to affirmative action as one of the major planks of his campaign. Citing the decision in *Weber*, Reagan asserts that white people are suffering from reverse discrimination.
- In *Fullilove v. Klutznick*, the Supreme Court upholds the minority business enterprise provision of the Public Works Employment Act of 1977, a remedial program created by Congress to eliminate traditional barriers in public contracting. The Court finds that the "narrowed focus and limited extent" of the affirmative action program in question does not violate the rights of nonminority contractors, because there was no "allocation of federal funds according to inflexible percentages solely based on race or ethnicity."

1981

- President Ronald Reagan takes office and begins to appoint opponents of affirmative action to key positions within his administration. He names Clarence Thomas and Clarence Pendleton, Jr., to the EEOC and appoints Antonin Scalia and Anthony Kennedy to the Supreme Court. During his two terms in office, Reagan cuts the funding of the EEOC and other agencies designed to monitor affirmative action; supports repeal of the Voting Rights Act (although this is never accomplished); and frequently criticizes affirmative action as a program of "racial quotas" and "reverse discrimination."

- In *DeRonde v. Regents of the University of California*, the California Supreme Court upholds the validity of an affirmative action plan at the UC Davis law school.
- The Supreme Court's ruling in *Valentine v. Smith* upholds an affirmative action program that is part of a court-ordered plan to desegregate the faculty of the Arkansas state college and university system.
- The Supreme Court finds in *Mississippi University for Women v. Hogan* that a man cannot be denied admission into a woman-only nursing program at a public university solely on the basis of his gender, as the restriction serves no important governmental interest.

1983

- The state of Texas commits to practicing affirmative action in its professional school admissions program and to setting goals for minority enrollment, in response to a desegregation order from the Office of Civil Rights, a division of the U.S. Department of Justice.

1984

- The 11th Circuit Court of Appeals upholds race-conscious hiring goals for faculty in *Palmer v. District Board of Trustees of St. Petersburg* [Florida] *Junior College*.

1986

- *May 19:* In *Wygant v. Jackson Board of Education*, the Supreme Court upholds a challenge to a school board's policy of protecting minority employees by laying off nonminority teachers first, in violation of seniority. The Supreme Court holds that the injury suffered by nonminorities cannot be justified by the benefits to minorities: "Denial of a future employment opportunity is not as intrusive as loss of an existing job."
- In *Local 93, International Association of Firefighters v. City of Cleveland* and *Local 28 of the Sheet Metal Workers' International Association v. EEOC*, the Supreme Court upholds court-ordered (as opposed to voluntary) race-conscious hiring and promotion policies, after intentional discrimination has been proved.

1987

- In *Johnson v. Transportation Agency, Santa Clara County*, the Supreme Court upholds an affirmative action plan against an allegation by a white male employee that a less qualified woman was promoted ahead of him, in violation of Title VII of the Civil Rights Act.

■ **February 25:** In *United States v. Paradise*, the Supreme Court upholds a court-ordered plan to remedy persistent race discrimination by promoting one African American for each white person promoted in the state of Alabama's Department of Public Safety until 25 percent of the department's upper ranks are African Americans. The case had begun with a July 1970 federal court finding that the department had systematically discriminated against African Americans in hiring. Twelve years and several lawsuits later, the department still had not promoted any African Americans above entry level, nor had it implemented a fair hiring system. In response, a federal court had ordered the plan that the Supreme Court upholds in *Paradise*.

1988

■ President George H. W. Bush is elected, in a campaign that is less explicitly opposed to affirmative action than that of President Ronald Reagan. Advocates of affirmative action, however, point out that Bush was Reagan's vice president, and so had been implicitly supportive of Reagan's positions.

1989

■ **January 23:** In *City of Richmond v. Croson*, the Supreme Court rules that a set-aside program for minority subcontractors violates the Fourteenth Amendment's equal protection clause. The city of Richmond, Virginia, had set aside 30 percent of city construction funds for African American–owned firms, a program that the Supreme Court found unjustifiably restrictive in the absence of proof that racial discrimination was "widespread throughout [the construction] industry."
■ In *Ward's Cove v. Antonio*, the Supreme Court reinterprets the Civil Rights Act of 1964, reversing the past 18 years of legal precedent by moving the burden of proof in "discriminatory impact" cases from the employer to the victim of discrimination.
■ In *Patterson v. McLean Credit Union*, the Supreme Court holds that the Civil Rights Act of 1866 does not prohibit racial harassment on the job.

1990

■ **October:** President Bush vetoes the Civil Rights Act of 1990, which he characterizes as a "quota bill."

1991

■ Clarence Thomas is approved as a Supreme Court justice, despite the sexual harassment claims made by his former employee, Anita Hill.

- Bush supports the Civil Rights Act of 1991, a moderate version of the legislation he had vetoed the previous year.
- U.S. Secretary of Education Lamar Alexander proposes Title VI policy guidelines that would require race neutrality in scholarships awarded by colleges and universities unless there is a judicial, agency, or legislative finding that past discrimination continues to have present effects. Although these guidelines are not adopted, they are a significant step forward in the shifting of the burden of proof from the employer or institution accused of discrimination to the person claiming discrimination.

1992

- Bill Clinton is elected president. His ties to civil rights leaders raise the hopes of supporters of affirmative action.
- The U.S. Department of Education and the University of California, Berkeley (UC Berkeley) agree that the university will no longer separate applicants into different pools on the basis of race.
- Cheryl Hopwood and other students sue the University of Texas, claiming that they were denied admission to the law school because of the school's admission policy, which gave unconstitutional preference to black and Latino students. *Hopwood v. Texas* will become a major case in affirmative action law.

1993

- President Clinton takes office, appointing four African Americans, three women, and two Latinos to his cabinet, the greatest percentage of women and minorities in history. His other executive appointments likewise include more women and minorities, further raising the hopes of the civil rights community. That community quickly becomes disillusioned, however, when under pressure from conservatives, Clinton withdraws his appointment of Philadelphia law professor Lani Guinier to head the Justice Department's Civil Rights Division. Guinier's support for affirmative action has led conservatives to call her "the quota queen."
- The Office of Civil Rights and the U.S. Department of Education rule that the state of Connecticut's decision to exclude Native Americans and Asian Americans from a program designed to recruit and retain minority students violates Title VI.

1994

- The Fourth District Court of Appeals, with jurisdiction over Maryland, North Carolina, South Carolina, Virginia, and West Virginia, makes the final ruling in *Podbereksy v. Kirwan*, a case that involves the Benjamin Banneker Scholarships for African Americans within the Maryland public university system. The appeals court finds that the scholarships' racial preferences are unconstitutional, since the university has not proved the need to limit them by race. When the Supreme Court refuses to hear the case in 1995, this decision becomes final.

- *February 23:* U.S. Secretary of Education Richard Riley issues a statement, published as 59 Fed. Reg. 8756–8764, that colleges and universities can award scholarships to remedy past discrimination and to promote diversity on college campuses.

- *November:* Republicans win control of both houses of Congress, enabling them to claim a mandate for the conservative Contract with America, a program of proposed legislation. A key portion of the contract is the abolishment of affirmative action.

- *November:* California voters pass Proposition 187, which bans illegal immigrants and their children from receiving public education or social services and which requires a variety of public employees to report children and families suspected of being illegal immigrants.

1995

- *February 5:* The new Senate majority leader and potential Republican presidential candidate, Bob Dole, a longtime supporter of affirmative action, expresses his support for a proposed 1996 California ballot initiative that would abolish state-sponsored affirmative action. Later, Republican presidential hopeful Senator Phil Gramm says that his opposition to race and gender preferences will be central to his campaign.

- Under pressure from a conservative Congress, President Clinton announces an "urgent review" of federal affirmative action by a new task force.

- *March:* The federal Glass Ceiling Commission, established during the Bush administration and headed by then-Secretary of Labor Elizabeth Dole, issues *Good for Business: Making Use of the Nation's Human Capital*, a fact-finding report on affirmative action. The report says that "progress has been disappointingly slow" in including minorities and women in senior corporate management.

- *June 12:* The Supreme Court hands down *Adarand Constructors, Inc. v. Pena*, a decision that restricts—but fails to strike down—affirmative action in the granting of federal highway contracts. The Court again calls for "strict scrutiny" in determining whether discrimination exists before putting a federal affirmative action program in place. It defines strict scrutiny as finding a "compelling government interest" to be met by the program, which must be "narrowly tailored" to fit a particular situation. In dissenting opinions, Justices Clarence Thomas and Antonin Scalia call for a complete ban on affirmative action.

- *July 19:* President Clinton announces the results of his own five-month review of affirmative action in a speech at the National Archives, where he claims that *Adarand* "actually reaffirmed the need for affirmative action and reaffirmed the continuing existence of systematic discrimination in the United States." A White House memo issued the same day calls for the elimination of any program that "(a) creates a quota; (b) creates preferences for unqualified individuals; (c) creates reverse discrimination; or (d) continues even after its equal opportunity purposes have been achieved."

- *July 20:* The Regents of the University of California vote to phase out affirmative action in admissions, hiring, and contracting. This decision deals a huge blow to affirmative action, setting a precedent for public university systems across the nation. California governor Pete Wilson, who had supported affirmative action while mayor of San Diego, U.S. senator, and governor, now ends affirmative action in the University of California system, despite massive protest.

1996

- Attorneys general in Georgia, Texas, and Colorado recommend that universities and colleges stop using race as a criterion when deciding upon admissions and scholarships. The University of Houston ignores that advice.

- In *United States v. Virginia*, the Supreme Court rules that the Virginia Military Institute cannot exclude women from admission to that institution's "unique educational opportunities."

- A lawsuit against Texas A & M University by a white student seeking access to a summer program sponsored by the National Science Foundation is settled when the institution agrees to stop excluding white people from the program.

- A lawsuit against Ohio State University is settled when that institution agrees not to consider race in awarding painting contracts. Previously, the university had wanted to assign 100 percent of its painting contracts to minority contractors.

- *March 18:* In *Hopwood v. University of Texas Law School*, the U.S. Fifth Circuit Court of Appeals finds that the University of Texas "may not use race as a factor in law school admissions." The appeals court argues that Justice Lewis Powell's decision in *Bakke* did not represent the majority decision of the Supreme Court. (Powell had written that programs designed to increase diversity were indeed constitutional.) The Supreme Court later declined to consider *Hopwood*, leaving its opinion—that "educational diversity is not recognized as a compelling state interest"—as the ruling precedent in the Fifth Circuit: Texas, Mississippi, and Louisiana.

- *June:* The U.S. Supreme Court declines to review the *Hopwood* decision. All affirmative action ends in admissions to public universities in Texas.
- *November 3:* California voters pass Proposition 209, a state ban on all forms of affirmative action. The action has the strong support of Governor Pete Wilson, despite Wilson's previous support of affirmative action throughout his career. The next day, the American Civil Liberties Union (ACLU) and a coalition of civil rights groups file suit to block enforcement of the law. U.S. District Judge Thelton Henderson issues a preliminary injunction against the legislation, ruling that the ACLU is substantially likely to prevail.

1997

- *January 6:* Chief U.S. District Judge Thelton Henderson denies a motion by California governor Pete Wilson to allow a state court to review Proposition 209 before Henderson decides whether the measure is unconstitutional. Proposition 209 is the initiative that bans affirmative action in California.
- *February 18:* The U.S. Supreme Court denies Philadelphia's plea to preserve a city law setting aside one-fourth of its public works spending for African American–owned or women-owned businesses. Officials cited figures showing that less than 1 percent of the 8,050 construction firms in the metropolitan area are owned by African Americans, and claimed that this figure was evidence of discrimination. A lower court concluded that, on the contrary, the low number of minority entrepreneurs was the reason that so few of them were awarded contracts.
- *March 19:* The Colorado Senate Judiciary Committee abandons a bill by Colorado Republicans to enact legislation similar to California's Proposition 209. The Colorado bill, which would have banned affirmative action by the state, dies in committee despite the Colorado attorney general's assertion that recent Supreme Court decisions make the law a necessity.
- *April 9:* Three Ninth Circuit Court justices rule that Proposition 209, an initiative abolishing affirmative action in California, is indeed constitutional.
- *April 10:* The Clinton administration vows to continue its challenge of Proposition 209.
- *May:* In response to *Hopwood*, the Texas legislature requires all public colleges and universities to allow admission to anyone in the top 10

percent of his or her graduating classes in any public or private high school in the state.

- *May 18:* In a commencement speech, UC Berkeley chancellor Chang-lin Tien criticizes the university system's dismantling of affirmative action. He says that he has encountered evidence of demoralization among inner-city high school students: "Why should I work hard anymore? I'm not welcome. I'm a second-class citizen."
- *June:* Professors of California State University, Northridge, release the results of a 30-year demographic study of the median incomes of minority and majority ethnic groups, finding that African-American and Chicano incomes have dropped relative to those of white people. They also discover than some 90 percent of all southern California lawyers are white.
- *June 14:* At a speech in San Diego, President Clinton launches a year-long initiative on race called One America, forming an advisory board headed by historian John Hope Franklin. Republicans respond soon after when Senator Mitch McConnell and Representative Charles Canady introduce bills entitled Civil Rights Act of 1997, aimed at eliminating affirmative action. These bills are never passed.
- *June 18:* House Speaker Newt Gingrich calls for the elimination of quotas, preferences, and set-asides in government contracts, hiring, and university admissions.
- *July 11:* The U.S. Department of Education announces its intent to investigate whether the University of California's dismantling of affirmative action has led to violations of federal civil rights law.
- *August 21:* The U.S. Ninth Circuit Court of Appeals upholds Proposition 209.
- *August 28:* Proposition 209 goes into effect, and affirmative action in California is now banned. Thousands join a protest march in San Francisco.
- *August:* The prestigious Boalt Law School of UC Berkeley announces that none of the 15 African-American students admitted this year have decided to enroll. A student who had deferred admission from the previous year becomes the only African American in an entering class of 270 students.
- *September:* After *Hopwood*, no African-American student accepts offers of admission to the University of Texas law school.
- *October:* An alumnus sues UC Berkeley, charging that the school has purposely circumvented Proposition 209.
- *October 14:* The Center for Individual Rights, which initiated the *Hopwood* lawsuits at the University of Texas, files a lawsuit at the University of Michigan on behalf of two white students denied admission the previous year, claiming that the school's policies discriminate against "qualified" white people in favor of "unqualified" students of color.

- *October 20:* Reverend Jesse Jackson begins a bus tour through California to rally opposition to Proposition 209.
- *October 27:* Reverend Jesse Jackson's tour culminates in a Save the Dream march and rally at the state capital in Sacramento, calling on Democrats to resist efforts to end affirmative action and to overturn Proposition 209 (which had ended affirmative action) and Proposition 187 (which curtailed the rights of illegal immigrants).
- *November 3:* The U.S. Supreme Court declines to hear a challenge to Proposition 209. Because it is not an actual decision by the Supreme Court, a national precedent has not been set, but anti–affirmative action drives continue in Congress as well as in Texas, Michigan, and Washington State.
- *November 4:* Houston voters approve a measure that keeps the city's affirmative action policies in force, by a vote of 55 percent to 45 percent.

1998

- *January:* Opponents of affirmative action in Washington State file a petition that will put Initiative 200 (I-200) on the ballot in November. Like California's Proposition 209, I-200 would ban affirmative action at state agencies, including public colleges and universities.
- *February 10:* The Washington state legislature does not pass I-200, a measure that seeks to end affirmative action statewide, so the measure will go to the voters in November.
- *March:* U.S. District Judge Sparks finds that none of the plaintiffs in the *Hopwood* case would have been admitted to the University of Texas law school, even had race played no part in the university's decisions. Sparks also enters a formal order implementing the 1996 Court of Appeals decision, prohibiting all future consideration of race in Texas public higher education. The plaintiffs appeal the first part of the decision; the university appeals the second.
- *March 26:* Some 41 students of all races, including both women and men, file a motion to intervene in *Grutter v. Bollinger.* They are joined by three Michigan pro–affirmative action coalitions. *Grutter* is the suit sponsored by the Center for Individual Rights on behalf of two white students claiming discrimination for having been denied admission to the University of Michigan's law school.
- *April:* University of California affiliates announce sharp declines in minority enrollment in the wake of Proposition 209, the initiative that ended affirmative action in California. At UC Berkeley, the number of African Americans in the freshman class has dropped by 66 percent since 1997, and there are 53 percent fewer Latinos. At UCLA, the numbers fell

by 43 percent and 33 percent. Meanwhile, UC Santa Cruz accepts 7.4 percent more Latinos, while UC Riverside accepts 42 percent more African Americans. UC Riverside and UC Santa Cruz are both considered less prestigious than UC Berkeley or UCLA, and the new figures raise fears of a two-tier system.

- *May 1:* The Oakland Education Association and a number of student groups, professors, and civil rights groups sponsor a rally to call for the immediate admission of the 800 minority students with 4.0 GPAs who were denied admission to UC Berkeley because of the repeal of affirmative action.

- *June 1:* Members of minority journalism groups representing African Americans, Latinos, Asian Americans, and Native Americans, debate whether to hold their Unity '99 convention in Seattle, because of concerns that Washington voters will pass I-200, a measure that would end affirmative action statewide.

- *June 16:* A Republican and African American, Mary Radcliffe, joins the otherwise all-white leadership of the I-200 campaign to become the movement's spokeswoman. I-200 is a Washington State ballot initiative that would abolish affirmative action statewide.

- *July 12:* A *Seattle Times* poll among Washington voters reveals that most believe that minorities and women still face discrimination; however, most do not believe that affirmative action is the appropriate remedy.

- *August 28:* Microsoft donates $25,000 to the No!200 campaign, designed to defeat the ballot measure known as I-200, which would end affirmative action in Washington State.

- *September 9:* A study conducted by two former presidents of Ivy League universities, Derek Bok of Harvard, a political scientist, and William Bowen of Princeton, an economist, concludes that affirmative action policies over the past 20 years were central in the creation of the African-American middle class and helped show white students the value of integration. Published in book form as *The Shape of the River: Long-Term Consequences of Considering Race in College and University Admissions*, the study surveyed more than 60,000 white and African-American students from the classes of 1976 and 1989. The study also disputes the "fit" hypothesis, which claims that affirmative action brought minority students to colleges for which they were unfit.

- *September 16:* Despite Proposition 209, which bans affirmative action statewide, a panel of San Francisco supervisors vote to extend the city's program of race and gender preferences in contracting until 2003 and to expand it to include companies owned by Arab Americans and American Indians. Unless the entire Board of Supervisors passes the measure, affirmative action in contracting will expire on October 31.

- *September 17:* In the face of an upcoming ballot measure designed to end affirmative action in Washington State, a poll shows that most Washington State business leaders believe that U.S. society is growing apart but that college courses about diversity can help pull it together. The business leaders predict that their own workforces will grow more diverse in 20 years, so that people will need to learn to work together.

- *September 22:* The San Francisco Board of Supervisors votes unanimously to extend and expand the minority-preference program in city contracting. The program will now extend until 2003 and will include Arab Americans and Native Americans as well as women, African Americans, Latinos, Asian Americans, and Pacific Islanders.

- *October 13:* In one of the first applications of the *Hopwood* decision, which banned the use of race-based criteria in University of Texas admissions, the Fifth Circuit U.S. Court of Appeals revives a lawsuit charging that the university's Austin branch discriminated against white applicants.

- *October 21:* Students and professors at some 25 colleges and universities across the country hold pro–affirmative action teach-ins, rallies, and walkouts, but the events attract only small crowds.

- *October 23:* A white male college student brings federal suit against the Oklahoma State Regents for Higher Education, challenging a scholarship program that sets different test-score requirements for members of different racial groups and for men and women.

- *November 3:* Washington State voters vote for I-200. The measure wins 58 percent of the vote.

- *November 9:* Nine white firefighters in Chicago lose a Supreme Court appeal; the firefighters had claimed that they were unconstitutionally passed over for promotion in favor of African Americans and Latinos.

- *December 1:* The Miami-Dade County Commission votes to ban discrimination against lesbians and gay men in employment, housing, and public accommodations.

- *December 2:* A California judge turns down Governor Pete Wilson's request to invalidate a law that critics say gives employment preferences to women and some minorities.

- *December 3:* I-200 goes into effect in Washington, making it the second state to abolish affirmative action.

- *December 9:* A report issued by Pew Health Professions Commission urges medical schools to take steps to admit more minority applicants, despite recent setbacks for affirmative action.

- *December 11:* A cartoon about affirmative action at the University of Rhode Island leads to protests and a cutoff of the paper's funding, exposing racial tensions at the school.

- *December 13:* A report from the Association of American Medical Colleges reveals that after two decades of steady growth, the number of women applying to U.S. medical schools has reached a plateau.
- *December 14:* The Federal Communications Commission (FCC) announces that it will not urge the Supreme Court to revise the FCC's affirmative action rules, which encourage radio and television stations to hire more women and minorities.
- *December 15:* The National Science Foundation announces $13.7 million in grants to be awarded to some 200 women in science and engineering through its Professional Opportunities for Women in Research and Education. The individual grants begin at $13,000 and range up to $150,000.
- *December 21:* The 95,000-member Screen Actors Guild issues a report revealing severe underrepresentation of women, Latinos, Asian Pacific Americans, Native Americans, the disabled, and seniors on prime-time and daytime television.

1999

- *January 4:* The University of Texas, Austin, terminates a $300,000-per-year program intended to recruit minority professors; the university fears being in violation of a court ruling against using racial preferences in admissions.
- *January 11:* A federal judge finds unconstitutional an admissions program used during 1990–95 by the University of Georgia to grant preferences to African-American applicants.
- *January 20:* Statistics released today reveal that African-American and Latino enrollment at UC Berkeley has dropped more than 10 percent for next year's incoming freshman class, although the number of minority students applying to the system as a whole has increased.
- *January 22:* A federal judge finds the University of North Texas guilty of discrimination because it paid an African-American professor less than his white colleagues. University officials plan to appeal the order.
- *February 2:* Eight minority students and three minority groups file a class-action suit against UC Berkeley, charging that the university is violating a federal antibias law in its admissions decisions by placing too much emphasis on standardized test scores and completion of advanced placement courses.
- *February 3:* Boston school officials decide not to ask the U.S. Supreme Court to rule on *Wessman v. Gittens*, a race-based school admissions program found unconstitutional by a federal appeals court. School officials are afraid that the Supreme Court will also rule against the admissions program, thus setting a national precedent against affirmative action.

- *February 4:* Stanford University is investigated by the U.S. Department of Labor to find whether the school has violated federal affirmative action law by not having a plan to hire and promote female faculty.

- *February 5:* A federal judge dismisses two gender-discrimination lawsuits brought by four women athletes at the University of Minnesota, Duluth, finding that the women had no legal standing to sue the school.

- *February 10:* A federal judge narrows the scope of the lawsuit against the University of Washington's law school. The university had been accused of bias in the race-based preferences it used in admissions. The judge finds that I-200, an initiative banning affirmative action statewide, has made much of the suit moot. However, the case still has national import, for the judge will consider whether the now-abandoned admissions policy did in fact discriminate against the three white applicants who brought the suit.

- *February 15:* Federal judge Thomas S. Zilly says that the 1978 *Bakke* decision is still valid and will be used to decide the lawsuit against race-based criteria in the admissions policy of the University of Washington law school. The *Bakke* decision, while ruling against the admissions policy at UC Davis, also affirmed the constitutionality of some race-based criteria in order to achieve racial diversity.

- *February 19:* The University of Massachusetts, Amherst, announces that socioeconomic status and extracurricular activities will count more in admissions and financial aid decisions, while race will count less. College officials predict that minority enrollment at the school will consequently drop from 19 percent of the student population to somewhere between 13 and 16 percent.

- *March 9:* The Supreme Court refuses to hear two affirmative action cases, though the Court indicates that it is still looking for a good test case to rule on the issue. Meanwhile, however, the Court declines to rule on the suit of a white University of Nevada professor claiming discrimination, and an effort by Miami-Dade County, Florida, seeking to reinstate a program for affirmative action in city contracting.

- *March 14:* Ward Connerly reveals that Florida will be the next state in which he tries to get an anti–affirmative action measure on the ballot. Connerly has already gotten such measures on the ballot in California and Washington State, and the measures passed in both states.

- *March 15:* Officials at the University of Washington law school announce that the number of African-American applicants is down 41 percent since last year, in the wake of I-200, the voter initiative that banned affirmative action statewide.

- *March 18:* University of Washington officials announce that they may retain race- and gender-based scholarships, although applicants for such awards would have to pass a screening process based on neutral factors.

This represents a turnaround for university officials, who had initially thought that the passage of I-200, banning affirmative action statewide, would require ending the scholarship program.

- *March 19:* The University of California Board of Regents agrees that the top 4 percent of graduates from each high school in the state should be automatically allowed entrance into the university.
- *March 23:* A joint study by two University of California research centers finds significant decreases in minority applicants, admissions, and enrollments in the state's medical schools.
- *April 1:* A lecturer who claims that being white put him out of the running for a tenure-track post at San Francisco State University wins a jury award of $2.75 million.
- *April 2:* The University of California releases enrollment figures showing that the number of minority applicants for the coming fall's freshman class is approximately equal to the figure for 1997, the last year affirmative action was in place. However, one of the system's top schools, UC Berkeley, has far fewer minority students.
- *April 6:* Officials of historically black colleges speak out at their annual meeting against the abolition of affirmative action and the curtailment of remedial classes, claiming that these policies are restricting the access of African Americans to higher education.
- *June 16:* The U.S. Department of Education plans to award more than $21 million in grants to improve teaching in schools whose students have limited proficiency in English.
- *June 22:* Congressional hearings are held on the U.S. Department of Education's controversial draft guidelines on the use of standardized tests in admissions policies. Civil rights groups have urged college leaders to support the guidelines.
- *June 25:* Ward Connerly seeks the support of Texas governor George W. Bush and Florida governor Jeb Bush for his planned ballot measure to end affirmative action in Florida.
- *June 30:* Oklahoma eliminates race-based preferences for female and minority students in a state scholarship program.
- *July 12:* A federal judge dismisses a lawsuit that challenges the University of Georgia's use of race-based criteria to admit minority students. However, the judge also criticizes university officials for supporting the policy, which he says is probably unconstitutional.
- *July 15:* Florida's Board of Regents votes to spend up to $2.5 million on scholarships and other programs to recruit minority students rather than creating two new public law schools. Many African-American and Latino lawmakers criticize the decision, arguing that Florida needs new schools to train an increased number of minority lawyers.

- *July 20:* President Clinton meets with 150 leaders in the legal profession and asks the nation's law schools to increase their racial and ethnic diversity.
- *July 21:* The Alliance for Equity in Higher Education is formed through the union of three higher-education associations that join to lobby for colleges serving minority students.
- *July 28:* California governor Gray Davis vetoes a bill that would have permitted outreach programs for women and minorities, despite the anti–affirmative action ban put in place by Proposition 209. Meanwhile, a branch of the American Civil Liberties Union (ACLU) sues California for not making advanced placement courses equally available to African-American, Latino, and low-income students, putting minority and low-income students at a disadvantage for college admissions.
- *July 28:* A federal judge rules against the University of Wisconsin's affirmative action plan, holding that the school did not justify its use of race in a decision involving a faculty hire.
- *July 28:* The National Research Council releases a report holding that colleges should not rely too heavily on standardized tests in their admissions decisions.
- *July 31:* Ward Connerly has gathered 43,000 signatures on petitions to get his anti–affirmative action measure on the ballot in Florida.
- *August 5:* A poll of 1,820 law students at Harvard and the University of Michigan finds that most students—most of whom are white—report that their learning was enhanced by having classmates of a different race.
- *August 18:* The University of Georgia plans to cease giving automatic preferences to male applicants, following a lawsuit in which a woman claims discrimination on the grounds of being white and female.
- *September 17:* Bill and Melinda Gates donate $1 billion to fund scholarships for minority college students, calling for "a new generation of leaders," and responding to such anti–affirmative action plans as Washington State's I-200.
- *October 4:* The NAACP president announces that if the Supreme Court were a private company, it would be found guilty of discrimination; the leader calls for greater diversity in the hiring of law clerks at the high court.
- *October 6:* The Supreme Court hears arguments on who should be considered a native Hawaiian in response to a suit from a white man whose ancestors settled in Hawaii five generations ago; the man wants to be allowed to vote on distribution of a fund set aside for descendants of aboriginal peoples and claims discrimination. The fund was intended to acknowledge the unjust seizure of the land of native Hawaiians some 100 years ago.

- *November 4:* A survey finds that more women and minorities are earning Ph.D.'s than ever before, despite the shortage of women and minorities in such key fields as business and engineering.
- *November 4:* A poll by two Florida newspapers, the *Miami Herald* and the *St. Petersburg Times,* finds that Florida voters favor a ban on affirmative action by two to one.
- *November 10:* Florida governor Jeb Bush signs an order to abolish racial preferences in many areas of contracting and university admissions, but he does not favor Ward Connerly's efforts to completely abolish affirmative action in the state. Bush's own plan is called One Florida.
- *November 16:* Florida's Board of Regents endorses Governor Jeb Bush's plan to end affirmative action in admissions to the state's public universities and colleges, despite protests from students and civil rights leaders.
- *November 17:* Florida state senator Daryl Jones, who had supported Governor Jeb Bush's voluntary racial-diversity plan, does an abrupt reversal and criticizes the governor, in the face of threats that Jones might be removed as chair of the legislature's Black Caucus.
- *November 22:* African-American lawmakers in Florida organize a petition campaign to oppose Governor Jeb Bush's One Florida campaign, which would abolish many aspects of affirmative action in the state.
- *November 24:* Florida's attorney general asks the state Supreme Court to stop Ward Connerly's effort to end affirmative action in Florida.
- *December 16:* In response to a ruling by Suffolk Superior Court judge John Zifaras, the Boston Police Department ends its 19-year practice of giving preference to minority officers in promotions, even if some white officers may have higher civil service test scores. Police Commissioner Paul Evans announces the promotion of 31 white officers who had not been promoted three years ago so that the department could meet affirmative action standards. However, Evans says, he will use race as a tiebreaker between candidates with equal scores.

2000

- *January 18:* In Florida, two African-American lawmakers stage a sit-in in Lieutenant Governor Frank Brogan's office, saying that they will not leave until Governor Jeb Bush rescinds his plan to eliminate affirmative action in that state.
- *February 17:* The Florida Board of Regents votes unanimously to support Governor Jeb Bush's One Florida plan, which would abolish many aspects of affirmative action in the state.
- *February 22:* The Florida legislature approves the education portion of Governor Jeb Bush's One Florida initiative.

- *February 25:* The U.S. Department of Education criticizes Florida's decision to abolish affirmative action.
- *March 7:* Thousands join a protest at the Florida state capital in Tallahassee in response to Governor Jeb Bush's executive order abolishing race and gender preferences in university admissions and state contracting.
- *March 9:* The President's Advisory Commission on Educational Excellence for Hispanic Americans announces that colleges and universities must try harder to recruit and enroll Latinos. The commission estimates that if Latinos attended college at the same rate as Anglos, their earnings would grow by some $118 billion, providing an additional $41 billion to the nation in taxes.
- *March 20:* The Supreme Court lets stand a decision concerning the Montgomery County, Maryland, school system's policy of denying transfers to some students to maintain racial balance in its schools.
- *March 20:* The American Council on Education conference features a panel in which university officials discuss the innovative policies that have been put in place to substitute for newly banned affirmative action policies. Some of the replacement policies include new types of recruitment and expanded scholarship programs.
- *April 4:* The University of California announces that the number of minority students entering the next year's freshman class has exceeded the number in 1997, the last year that affirmative action policies were in place. However, the most competitive campuses have fewer minority students, while the second-place campuses have more, leading to fears of a two-tier system.
- *April 11:* The U.S. Commission on Civil Rights releases a report strongly criticizing the newly prevalent practice of state universities replacing affirmative action policies with programs that permit entrance to everyone in the top percentage of a high school graduating class. These plans are "no substitute for strong race-conscious affirmative action in higher education," according to the commission. However, the commission says, at least Texas's 10-percent policy guarantees admission to the state's best school, whereas similar policies in California and Florida promise only admission to *some* public institution. The news comes as Pennsylvania officials are considering a top-15-percent policy for their state.
- *July 18:* Parents go to federal court to ask that the Seattle School District be prohibited from discriminating on the basis of race. The parents are reacting to a program that allows them to choose their children's schools, but that uses race as a tiebreaker to decide school assignments in cases where there is a conflict. Parents Involved in Community Schools claims that the policy violates I-200, the federal Civil Rights Act of 1964, and the U.S. Constitution.

Chronology

- *August 16:* The University of Georgia plans to appeal a recent federal court decision striking down the school's use of affirmative action.
- *August 27:* Seattle tourism is down as a result of I-200, the 1998 ballot measure that ended affirmative action in Washington.
- *October 16:* A state law with the goal of diversifying Texas colleges, signed by Texas governor George W. Bush in 1997, is running into trouble with the Federal Educational Rights and Privacy Act. Though in theory, the top 10 percent of every high school's graduating class is guaranteed admission to Texas state schools, the privacy acts forbids release of the statistical information that colleges need to identify the 10 percent.
- *October 17:* A *New York Times* editorial announces a landmark study published in the *Journal of Economic Literature*, in which economists Harry Holzer of Georgetown University and David Neumark of Michigan State University review more than 200 scientific studies of affirmative action. They discover that affirmative action offers concrete benefits for the economy as a whole, as well as for women and minorities.
- *October 17:* A number of Fortune 500 companies declare their support for the University of Michigan's efforts to preserve affirmative action in the face of a hostile lawsuit. Supportive companies include Microsoft, Lucent, Texaco, and Johnson & Johnson.
- *October 21:* The president of the University of Washington announces a $65.6 million scholarship program that seeks to restore the number of incoming minority students to levels that match those before I-200 went into effect; I-200 was the 1998 ballot measure that abolished affirmative action in Washington State.
- *November–December:* In a lengthy and contested electoral process, George W. Bush is finally declared president of the United States. While his Democratic opponent, Al Gore, supports affirmative action, Bush has long been an opponent of the policy, as demonstrated by actions he took as governor of Texas.
- *December:* The Fifth U.S. Circuit Court of Appeals upholds Judge Sparks's decision in *Hopwood* that the plaintiffs in the case would not have been admitted to the University of Texas law school, even if race had played no part in the school's decision. It also reaffirms its earlier decision that race should play no part in any admissions decisions made in Texas public higher education.
- *December 7:* The Pathways to College Network plans to identify and replicate programs that are successful at preparing minority and low-income students for college. The new group is formed by a coalition of foundations, colleges, and government agencies.
- *December 13:* In *Gratz v. Bollinger,* a federal judge rules that using race as a factor in admissions to the University of Michigan is indeed constitu-

tional, given that preference is also granted to the children of alumni, scholarship athletes, and other groups; thus, reasons the judge, the program serves "a compelling interest" by allowing students to benefit from a diverse student body.

- *December 18:* The U.S. Education Department's Office for Civil Rights releases a guidebook on the use of standardized tests, a form of evaluation that supporters of affirmative action have claimed discriminates against minorities and low-income students. A draft of the guidelines had been released in April 1999 to great controversy; these toned-down guidelines are received with little fanfare.

2001

- *January 10:* Linda Chavez, President Bush's nominee for U.S. Labor Secretary, questions whether U.S. women still need affirmative action.
- *January 22:* The Reverend Jesse Jackson calls on President Bush to improve public school funding and support affirmative action programs.
- *January 31:* Minority applications to the University of California system are on the rise, which some attribute to the changing ethnic makeup of state high schools, while others point to the lack of necessity for affirmative action.
- *February 1:* Protests calling for the reinstatement of affirmative action continue at UC Berkeley.
- *February 3:* Attorney General John Ashcroft is confirmed. Ashcroft has been a longtime opponent of affirmative action, although he stressed inclusiveness and racial sensitivity in his confirmation hearing.
- *February 8:* Harvard University professors and students react angrily to the statement of a Harvard professor that grade inflation at Harvard was linked to the increased admission of African Americans in the 1970s.
- *February 8:* In the wake of a ban on affirmative action in California, the percentage of female faculty hired in the University of California system has dropped dramatically. In 1995–96, women constituted 35.8 percent of university hires, but in 1999–2000, only 25.1 percent of faculty hires were women.
- *February 17:* University of California president Richard C. Atkinson recommends dropping the main Scholastic Aptitude Test (SAT) as an admission requirement, calling the test an unfair way to measure student abilities.
- *February 28:* A federal judge rules that the University of Michigan law school does not need to use affirmative action to remedy past discrimination. The judge was ruling on the intervention by students who supported affirmative action and who joined the case in opposition to the original

plaintiffs, white applicants who claimed that the school had discriminated against them on the basis of race.

- *March 2:* UC Berkeley students who assist in minority recruitment to their school threaten to actually discourage students from enrolling if the ban against affirmative action on campus is not repealed; students say they are tired of trying to diversify the campus without the university's support.

- *March 9:* Thousands rally at UC Berkeley in support of affirmative action. While police put the crowd at slightly more than 1,000, organizers estimate 6,000 people were at Berkeley as part of a statewide protest.

- *March 14:* A crowd of students takes over a hall at UCLA to demand restoration of affirmative action on University of California campuses. The University of California Board of Regents abolished affirmative action on campus in 1995, and a statewide ballot measure ended the policy statewide the following year.

- *March 26:* The Supreme Court agrees to hear a challenge to the U.S. Department of Transportation's revised highway construction program, whose guidelines are designed to favor minority-owned and other disadvantaged businesses.

- *March 27:* In a case similar to *Gratz v. Bollinger,* the University of Michigan case in which a judge allowed undergraduate admissions officials to use affirmative action, another judge draws the opposite conclusion when ruling on admissions to state law schools in *Grutter v. Bollinger,* invalidating the school's affirmative action policy and ruling that "intellectual diversity bears no obvious or necessary relationship to racial diversity."

- *March 30:* Nearly 1,000 students gather at the University of Michigan to protest the ruling against use of affirmative action in admissions policy to the law school. Reverend Jesse Jackson urges the crowd to fight for a reversal of Judge Bernard Friedman's decision.

- *April 4:* The percentage of minority students admitted to the University of California has nearly reached affirmative action levels; some 18.6 percent of incoming freshmen are African American, Latino, Chicano, or American Indian. In 1997, the last year affirmative action was in place in the university system, the minority percentage was 18.8 percent.

- *April 6:* A federal appeals panel rules that the University of Michigan's law school can continue using affirmative action in its admissions, pending the appeal of the lower court ruling of the previous week.

- *April 14:* Ward Connerly has begun an initiative in California to put a new measure on the ballot, one that would prohibit the state from collecting racial data on individuals. Without race-based statistics, it would be impossible to measure minority participation in education and employment. If Connerly is successful, the initiative will be on the ballot in March 2002.

Affirmative Action

- *April 17:* Patrick Barrett is suing the state of Hawaii in federal court on the grounds of discrimination; he claims that the policy of Hawaii's Office of Hawaiian Affairs (OHA), which offers privileges to ethnic Hawaiians, is a violation of his own right to equal protection under the Fourteenth Amendment.
- *April 17:* Texas Attorney General John Cornyn asks the U.S. Supreme Court to review *Hopwood,* a case in which federal courts ruled against the use of affirmative action in the admissions decisions of Texas state universities.
- *May 16:* After weeks of political maneuvers, the University of California Board of Regents votes to overturn its 1995 ban on affirmative action.
- *May 29:* The U.S. Supreme Court lets stand a lower court ruling that allows race-based admissions criteria for the purpose of creating diversity on campus. The lower court had ruled on a case involving admission to the University of Washington's law school, using the *Bakke* decision of 1978, in which the Supreme Court had allowed race-based admissions criteria if diversity was the goal.
- *June 25:* The Supreme Court refuses to hear the *Hopwood* case, concerning the use of affirmative action in admissions to the University of Texas. Since lower courts had ruled against the use of affirmative action, Texas will continue its five-year-old policy of avoiding race-based criteria in its admissions. A national precedent has not yet been set, however.
- *June 26:* Gerald A. Reynolds, an opponent of affirmative action, receives President Bush's nomination to head the civil rights office of the Department of Education, the division responsible for protecting the civil rights of women, minorities, and the disabled from kindergarten through graduate school.
- *June:* The District of Columbia Circuit Court of Appeals declines to review a lower court ruling that strikes down equal opportunity rules of the Federal Communications Commission (FCC), urging the hiring of women and minorities at FCC-licensed stations.
- *July 19:* The University of California's Board of Regents approves a dual admissions program that is expected to dramatically increase the university system's number of disadvantaged and minority students.
- *July 23:* The University of California, San Diego (UC San Diego) is warned by the university's attorneys that a privately funded scholarship program intended to attract minority students may be illegal.
- *July 25:* The American Bar Association asks Texas Southern University's law school to raise admissions standards, even though this may prevent many African-American and Latino law students from having access to a legal education.
- *August 10:* The Bush administration urges the Supreme Court to uphold a federal affirmative action policy, despite the administration's general op-

position to affirmative action. However, the administration is also committed to supporting federal law.

- *August 12:* African-American enrollment in the incoming class at the University of Florida is expected to be down from 12 percent last year to about 6 or 7 percent this year, as a result of the state's cutback on affirmative action.

- *August 14:* More than three-quarters of all roles in film go to white actors, according to the Screen Actors Guild 2000 Employment Statistics Report.

- *August 15:* Robert Farmer, age 40 and white, had sued the University of Maryland School of Medicine, claiming that he was rejected by the school because of his race. His case is dismissed by a federal judge, who declines to address the constitutional issues raised by Farmer's case.

- *August 27:* A three-judge panel of the Atlanta-based 11th Circuit Court of Appeals throws out the University of Georgia's affirmative action program in *Johnson v. Board of Regents of University of Georgia.*

- *September 4:* A state appeals court strikes down California's major affirmative action laws on the grounds that they violate Proposition 209, the statewide anti–affirmative action initiative.

- *September 4:* African-American leaders in Georgia announce that if the University of Georgia cannot use race-based criteria for admissions, as found in the recent *Johnson* ruling, the school should also be required to stop favoring legacies, the children of alumni.

- *September 6:* The Bush administration considers a change in the rules for government contracting that would move work from the public to the private sector while facilitating access of women- and minority-owned businesses to government contracts.

- *September 10:* An internal audit at the University of California finds that potentially illegal scholarships for minorities at UC San Diego may cost the system $1 million, even though the privately funded program is now canceled.

- *September 26:* The Houston City Council puts a referendum on the November 6 ballot to ban same-sex partner benefits; the measure would explicitly ban Houston from providing medical and other benefits to the same-sex partners of city employees. While the city does not currently offer such benefits, it had considered doing so.

- *October 1:* Houston city attorneys recommend that their city approve an out-of-court settlement of a reverse discrimination suit that would eliminate race as a factor in the selection of police officers and firefighters.

- *October:* The Nellie Mae Education Foundation releases a report stressing that colleges and universities in the New England area do not "lower the bar" or use quotas to admit minority students.

- *November:* The University of Georgia announces that it will not seek a Supreme Court review of the federal appeals court decision that struck down its use of race in undergraduate admissions decisions.
- *November 15:* The University of California Board of Regents adopts a new admissions policy that takes into account personal hardships that a student has to overcome in a response to the school's elimination of affirmative action. The new policy, known as comprehensive review, is said by supporters to be a race-neutral program, while opponents say it is a covert way of reintroducing race into the admissions process.
- *November 27:* The University of Texas announces that it will no longer appeal the *Hopwood* case. When the Supreme Court refused to hear the case in June, the university had the option of appealing another portion of the Circuit Court's decision, but it decides instead to simply end the case.
- *November 29:* A lawsuit by minority and female contractors against Contra Costa County, California, was dismissed by a federal judge on the grounds that there was no evidence of intentional discrimination. Contra Costa was the first California county to repeal its affirmation action program after the 1996 passage of Proposition 209. In 1998, women and minorities filed a suit claiming that the county had known for years that its contracting system had favored white men, but had done nothing about it. The ruling found that even if the county's system had a discriminatory effect, there was no evidence that discrimination was its intent.
- *December:* The controversy continues over the role of affirmative action and the department of Afro-American studies at Harvard University. The conflict began when Harvard president Lawrence H. Summers allegedly declined to make a strong statement supporting affirmative action when he met with members of the department in summer 2001. Summers also reportedly criticized Professor Cornel West for recording a rap CD, leading a political committee supporting Reverend Al Sharpton's bid for U.S. president, and writing popular rather than academic books. In December, West abruptly takes a leave of absence, while Summers insists that he intended no offense.
- *December 7:* A federal appeals court hears arguments on the constitutionality of using race as one factor in the University of Michigan's admissions decisions for its undergraduate programs and law school.

2002

- *January:* The John J. Heldrich Center for Workforce Development at Rutgers University releases a report revealing that black Americans and white Americans have strikingly divergent views of economic opportunity and advancement on the job. According to the report, entitled "A Workplace Divided," many whites believe they can advance as far as their education, skills, and talent will permit, while minorities attest that they are not equally rewarded for their skill and education. The report also finds that minorities also tend to describe their employers as supporting diversity in theory but not actually implementing it.

- *January 3:* Harvard president Lawrence Summers expresses his commitment to diversity at Harvard and to the strength of the Afro-American studies department.
- *January 4:* Harvard professor Cornel West meets with Summers, apparently ending the dispute that began the previous summer, when Summers had reportedly rebuked West for unprofessional behavior and had allegedly failed to express strong support for affirmative action.
- *January 27:* Harvard professor K. Anthony Appiah announces his move to Princeton University, which observers see as a response to the recent controversy over affirmative action at Harvard.
- *January 30:* Harvard hires Professor Michael C. Dawson, director of the University of Chicago's Center for the Study of Race, Politics, and Culture, to become a professor of government and African-American studies, beginning in July 2002. Meanwhile, Harvard professors Cornel West and Henry Louis Gates, Jr., chairman of the Afro-American studies department, are considering positions at Princeton University.
- *February 1:* In the wake of a 2001 decision by the University of California system to move away from using standardized tests in admissions decisions, U.S. college officials meet in Washington to preview a new generation of college entrance exams, including a test that is supposed to measure creativity and help colleges boost minority enrollment without specifically resorting to affirmative action.
- *March:* Controversy continues at the University of Oregon over the recommendations of a consultant on how the university can establish a truly diverse student body. Currently, minorities make up 11 percent of the university's 625 tenure-track faculty, up only 0.2 percent from five years ago, while 12.7 percent of the student body are minorities, up less than 1 percent over the past five years. However, only 13 percent of Oregon residents are minorities. The university reaffirms its commitment to increasing minority hiring and enrollment, as critics accuse it of being lukewarm on the issue.
- *March 2:* Texas's two leading Democratic contenders for governor—who are both Latino—debate in both English and Spanish as the state's primary campaign heats up. According to the National Association of Latino Elected and Appointed Officials, this is the first time that candidates for the governor of a state respond to questions and debate in Spanish.

Affirmative Action

- *March 6:* A group of demonstrators in Florida continues its annual protest against Governor Jeb Bush's efforts to end affirmative action in that state.
- *March 29:* President George W. Bush appoints a strong critic of affirmative action to head the civil rights division of the U.S. Education Department. Gerald A. Reynolds, named assistant secretary of education for civil rights, wrote a 1997 article in the conservative *Washington Times*, criticizing the "civil rights industry" and calling affirmative action "a corrupt system of preferences, set-asides, and quotas." Reynolds's nomination is opposed by more than two dozen groups, including the American Association of People with Disabilities, the National Organization for Women (NOW), the National Association for the Advancement of Colored People (NAACP), and the Leadership Conference on Civil Rights, an umbrella group representing dozens of civil rights organizations. Bush had originally named Reynolds in June 2001, but the nomination had not yet been confirmed by the Senate. The March action is a "recess appointment," made while Congress is in recess and allowing the president to appoint candidates who will serve through the next session of Congress—the end of 2003.
- *April:* The University of California announces that it has admitted a greater proportion of minorities in its 2002 fall freshman class than in 1997, the last year affirmative action was in force in that state. The number of Latino students rises to record levels for the second straight year, while the number of African-American students rises to some extent. However, the percentage of Latinos and African Americans remains virtually unchanged at Berkeley, the state's most prestigious campus, though minority attendance is up at UCLA.
- *April:* Despite his earlier insistence that he was prepared to remain at Harvard, Professor Cornel West leaves Harvard for Princeton, raising further questions about the future of affirmative action and African-American studies at Harvard.

CHAPTER 4

BIOGRAPHICAL LISTING

Allan Bakke, the plaintiff in the Supreme Court case *Bakke v. Regents of the University of California* (1978). Bakke had twice been refused admission to the medical school at the University of California, Davis (UC Davis), while the school had accepted applicants of color with significantly lower test scores, under a program that had reserved 16 of 100 places for minority and economically disadvantaged applicants and created a separate admissions program for them. Although Bakke had been refused admission to 10 other medical schools, he claimed that he would have been admitted to UC Davis had it not been for the affirmative action program, and he charged that as a white man, he was being denied his Fourteenth Amendment rights of equal protection under the law without regard to race or color. The Court ruled 5-4 that while race might be a consideration in some college admissions decisions, the UC Davis program had considered race in an unconstitutional way. Justice Lewis Powell wrote a famous concurring decision in which he cited "educational diversity" as a constitutionally permissible goal of affirmative action. Bakke's case is generally considered the beginning of the anti–affirmative action backlash, although Powell's decision and the notion of educational diversity have also been cited numerous times in defense of affirmative action.

Linda Brown, child of the plaintiff in the Supreme Court case *Brown v. Board of Education* (1954). Brown was an elementary school student living in Topeka, Kansas. Because schools in Topeka were rigidly segregated, Brown had to ride the bus five miles to the school for black people each day, although there was a white school only four blocks from her home. The Supreme Court ruling in *Brown* required schools throughout the country to end segregation, ending the previous legal notion of separate but equal schools and public accommodations.

George H. W. Bush, U.S. president from 1988 to 1992. Bush was known for continuing the anti–affirmative action policies of his predecessor,

President Ronald Reagan, although his 1988 presidential campaign was less explicitly opposed to affirmative action than Reagan's campaigns had been. Bush vetoed the Civil Rights Act of 1990, which he characterized as a "quota bill," although he supported the Civil Rights Act of 1991, a more moderate version of the same legislation. He nominated Clarence Thomas to the Supreme Court; Thomas was a staunch opponent of affirmative action and under Reagan had served as chair for the Equal Employment Opportunity Commission (EEOC), where he took part in Reagan's efforts to dismantle affirmative action "from within." Bush's secretary of education, Lamar Alexander, once proposed Title VI policy guidelines that would have required race neutrality in scholarships awarded by colleges and universities unless there was a judicial, agency, or legislative finding that past discrimination continues to have present effects. Although these guidelines were not adopted, they were a significant step forward in the shifting of the burden of proof from the employer or institution accused of discrimination to the person claiming discrimination.

George W. Bush, U.S. president starting in 2000– . An opponent of affirmative action, George W. Bush is nevertheless known for having more people of color and women in his cabinet than any previous president. Commentary in the months following Bush's swearing-in focused on the president's mixed messages regarding affirmative action, which he seemed neither to support nor to oppose outright. However, Bush did nominate staunch opponents of affirmative action to two key positions: Attorney General John Ashcroft and Health and Human Services Secretary Tommy Thompson, as well as making a "recess appointment"—bypassing the congressional confirmation process—of the the anti–affirmative action Gerald A. Reynolds to civil rights chief at the U.S. Department of Education.

Jeb Bush, governor of Florida, son of former president George H. W. Bush and brother to President George W. Bush. Bush initiated the One Florida program, intended to end affirmative action in that state. However, he opposed the efforts of Ward Connerly to put an anti–affirmative action initiative on a statewide ballot, as Connerly had done in California and Washington State; Bush considered Connerly's efforts "divisive."

Charles Canady, the Republican member of Congress who introduced the Civil Rights Bill of 1997 to the House of Representatives. The bill—which was never passed—was intended to eliminate affirmative action.

Linda Chavez, prominent conservative columnist and president of the Center for Equal Opportunity, an anti–affirmative action group; author of *Out of the Barrio: Toward a New Politics of Hispanic Assimilation.* In January 2001, she was nominated by President George W. Bush to lead the

Department of Labor, but she withdrew her name a week later after news organizations and Democrats challenged her relationship with an illegal immigrant. Chavez, a conservative immigration specialist, served with the Civil Rights Commission under the administration of former president Ronald Reagan and was Bush's immigration adviser during his presidential campaign.

Bill Clinton, U.S. president from 1992 to 2000. Clinton was considered to have a mixed record on affirmative action; while he often took pro–affirmative action positions, he was under a great deal of pressure from conservatives who bitterly opposed the policy. Soon after he took office, Clinton withdrew his appointment of Philadelphia law professor Lani Guinier to head the Justice Department's Civil Rights Division, largely because Guinier's support for affirmative action has led conservatives to call her "the quota queen." In 1994, as Republicans in Congress sought to end affirmative action under the Contract with America, Clinton's secretary of education, Richard Riley, declared that colleges and universities could award scholarships to remedy past discrimination and to promote diversity on college campuses. In 1995, Clinton announced an "urgent review" of federal affirmative action by a new task force and five months later called for the elimination of any program that "(a) creates a quota; (b) creates preferences for unqualified individuals; (c) creates reverse discrimination; or (d) continues even after its equal opportunity purposes have been achieved." On the same day, however, he made a speech asserting the need for continued affirmative action, and he helped rework federal regulations in response to *Adarand v. Pena*, saying "mend it, don't end it," was the proper response to affirmative action. In 1997, the Clinton administration announced its intention to challenge California's Proposition 209, a referendum that sought to abolish affirmative action statewide. Later that year, Clinton launched a year-long initiative on race called One America, forming an advisory board headed by historian John Hope Franklin.

Ward Connerly, conservative African-American businessman who led the initiative for Proposition 209, the 1995 ballot measure to end affirmative action in California. The initiative was successful, and affirmative action was banned in the state in 1996. Connerly went on to lead a similarly successful anti–affirmative action campaign in Washington State with Initiative 200, which abolished affirmative action in Washington in 1998. He then went to Florida, where he clashed with anti–affirmative action Governor Jeb Bush, who considered him divisive; Connerly was unable to get his measure on the ballot there. He is currently president of the American Civil Rights Initiative, an outgrowth of his California Civil Rights Initiative.

Newt Gingrich, congressman from Georgia and the Speaker of the House in 1994. He led a group of conservative members of Congress in a program of proposed legislation known as the Contract with America; one of the cornerstones of that program was the abolishment of affirmative action. During the mid-1990s, Gingrich was enormously influential, both within Congress and as an intellectual who helped to shape debate in conservative circles, and for a time, he was considered a strong contender for a possible Republican nomination for president. In 1995, however, he retained his post as Speaker by only three votes; although he won the position again in 1997, challenges from within his own party and criticism for ethics violations led him to step down in 1998. Soon after that he resigned from Congress.

Lani Guinier, a law professor at Harvard and the coauthor, with Columbia professor Susan Sturm, of *Who's Qualified?*, a defense of affirmative action. Guinier won renown in 1993 when she was appointed by newly elected president Bill Clinton to head the Justice Department's Civil Rights Division; her nomination was later withdrawn when Guinier's support for affirmative action led conservatives to call her "the quota queen."

Anita Hill, a conservative law professor at the University of Oklahoma who had worked for Clarence Thomas when he headed the the Equal Employment Opportunity Commission (EEOC) under President Ronald Reagan. During Thomas's confirmation hearings for his appointment to the Supreme Court, Hill came forward, charging Thomas with sexual harassment. As part of the Reagan Revolution, Thomas had been responsible for dismantling from within many of the affirmative action policies associated with the EEOC. He was bitterly opposed by many civil rights leaders, while women's groups opposed him because of his strong opposition to abortion rights. Hill's charges provoked an enormous controversy, but eventually, the Senate voted 52-48 to confirm Thomas, and the relatively conservative Hill went on to become a spokeswoman for civil rights and feminist causes.

Cheryl Hopwood, a white student who brought a suit against the University of Texas law school when she was denied admission in 1992. Hopwood charged that the law school's consideration of race in its admissions decision discriminated against her as a white person. Her case, *Hopwood v. Texas*, was successful at the Fifth Circuit Court of Appeals in that it led to the abolishment of affirmative action in the Texas university system; however, subsequent trials found that Hopwood would not have been admitted to the law school even without the affirmative action policy, and she was awarded none of the financial damages she had sought, although she did receive a considerable sum for legal fees. The Supreme Court refused to hear the case in 2001.

Reverend Jesse Jackson, civil rights leader who has been an outspoken supporter of affirmative action. In 1998, when the state of Washington was considering I-200, an initiative to end affirmative action, Jackson called on supporters of the policy to rally in defense of affirmative action. (The anti–affirmative action measure eventually passed.) When affirmative action was under attack at the University of Michigan in the *Gratz v. Bollinger* and *Grutter v. Bollinger* cases, Jackson took part in rallies and protests to defend the policy, most recently in 2001. He has also led actions in California in response to protests against both state and university decisions to end affirmative action.

Lyndon B. Johnson, U.S. president from 1964 to 1968. Johnson eloquently defended the principles of affirmative action in a 1965 commencement address at Howard University and established affirmative action in Executive Order 11246, which called upon the Department of Labor's Office of Federal Contract Compliance Programs (OFCCP) to require government contractors to "take affirmative action" to ensure that workers were employed and treated "without regard to their race, color, religion, or national origin," later amended to include sex as well. Johnson also presided over the passage of the Civil Rights Act of 1964, which outlawed employment discrimination, and the Voting Rights Act of 1965, which was passed in response to a long history of law, custom, and violence that had denied African Americans their right to vote, particularly in the South.

John F. Kennedy, U.S. president from 1960 to 1963, and the first president to use the phrase "affirmative action." Kennedy issued Executive Order 10925 in 1961, creating the Equal Employment Opportunity Commission (EEOC), the agency responsible for overseeing equal employment opportunity; the order also called upon contractors working with federal funds to take affirmative action to ensure that workers did not face discrimination based on "race, creed, color, or national origin."

Martin Luther King, Jr., perhaps the most prominent civil rights leader of the 1950s and 1960s, leader of numerous protests and boycotts that helped spur Presidents John F. Kennedy and Lyndon Johnson to institute affirmative action in the mid-1960s.

Thurgood Marshall, a Supreme Court justice nominated by President Lyndon Johnson. Marshall was one of the staunchest supporters of affirmative action on the Court, as well as the Court's first African-American justice. Marshall was also the legal director of the National Association for the Advancement of Colored People (NAACP) in the mid-1950s, in which capacity he brought to the Supreme Court the landmark case of *Brown v. Board of Education* (1954), which led to the abolition of the "separate but equal" principle and to the integration of public education.

Richard M. Nixon, U.S. president from 1968 to 1974. Although Nixon was a Republican and a conservative, he was for a time a supporter of affirmative action. In 1970, he instituted the Philadelphia Plan, a pilot program in the Philadelphia construction industry administered by Assistant Secretary of Labor Arthur Fletcher, one of the few African Americans in Nixon's administration. The Philadelphia Plan was an attempt to integrate the traditionally all-white construction industry by requiring unions and contractors to hire minority workers; in 1971 the plan was amended to require the hiring of women workers as well. Observers saw the plan as part of a Nixon strategy to attract black voters into the Republican Party—an attempt that was never successful. Toward the end of his term, he supported a constitutional amendment (never passed) that would have prohibited busing schoolchildren to achieve desegregation.

Ronald Reagan, U.S. president from 1980 to 1988. A conservative Republican, Reagan instituted the so-called Reagan Revolution, whose goals included the abolition of affirmative action. While affirmative action remained official government policy, Reagan's strategy was to frustrate the implementation of the policy by staffing the various federal agencies and departments responsible for its oversight with conservatives such as Clarence Thomas, who would dismantle it "from within." Reagan also helped set a national tone that was critical of affirmative action while advocating individual effort and personal responsibility. Under his administration, several black conservatives came to prominence, including economist Thomas Sowell, another opponent of affirmative action.

Justice Clarence Thomas, a conservative Supreme Court justice who is one of the Court's staunchest opponents of affirmative action. Thomas had served as head of the Equal Employment Opportunity Commission (EEOC) under President Ronald Reagan, where he was part of the Reagan Revolution with the job of helping to dismantle affirmative action "from within." He came to prominence during Senate confirmation hearings for his nomination to the Supreme Court when he was charged with sexual harassment by former employee Anita Hill; Thomas later called the hearings "a high-tech lynching for uppity blacks." Eventually, the Senate voted 52–48 to confirm him, and Thomas took his place on the Court, where he is known for his strong opposition to affirmative action as well as abortion rights.

Pete Wilson, governor of California from 1991 to 1999, a U.S. senator from 1983 to 1991, and the mayor of San Diego from 1971 to 1983.

While governor of California, Wilson played a key role in the support of Proposition 209, the 1995 ballot initiative that ended affirmative action in California. He faced criticism from civil rights groups for his advocacy of Proposition 187, a 1987 ballot measure that banned illegal immigrants from receiving state-funded social, educational, or public health services; similar criticism followed his support for Proposition 209.

CHAPTER 5

GLOSSARY

ableism   A term coined by the disability rights movement to denote bias against people with disabilities.

affirmative action   The principle that institutions should take positive action to overcome discrimination and ensure broad representation within their ranks. Affirmative action in employment might involve active efforts to recruit employees from among underrepresented minorities and/or women; to expand the presence of minorities and/or women in largely white and/or male departments; and to increase the numbers of minorities and/or women in management. Affirmative action in education might entail efforts to increase enrollment by minorities and/or women.

ageism   Discrimination or bias against people on the basis of age.

amicus curiae   Latin for "friend of the court." A legal term referring to briefs filed by people who are interested in a case but not actually a party to it. For example, if a case involves civil liberties, the American Civil Liberties Union may file an amicus brief to enter its opinion into the court record.

applicant pool   The people who have applied to work, from whom employees are chosen.

backlash   The reaction against something. Historians often speak of the backlash against affirmative action, in which white people and/or men began to express their resentment at what they perceived to be the special treatment of women and minorities.

Bakke case   A landmark Supreme Court affirmative action case in 1978, which found that Allan Bakke, a white man, had been discriminated against on the basis of race when he was not accepted to the medical school at the University of California, Davis.

Civil Rights Act of 1964   The most prominent piece of civil rights legislation since Reconstruction, banning discrimination based on "race, color, religion, or national origin" in public establishments that had a connection to interstate commerce or were supported by the state. The

148

Glossary

Civil Rights Act was later amended to include discrimination based on sex, as well. The various parts of the civil rights act are called titles.

civil rights movement The movement that began in the 1950s in which African Americans and their allies demanded an end to segregation and the beginning of fully equal opportunity for people of color.

class action suit A suit brought by a group, or class, of people, all claiming to be injured by the same problem. For example, a group of employees might claim that they all suffered from discrimination by the same employer.

compelling interest (compelling governmental interest) A legal term referring to reasons that the state might take action, especially action restricting something that is otherwise considered a legal right. For example, if the state has a compelling interest to end discrimination, it may enact legislation to achieve that end. Part of the Supreme Court's job is to determine cases in which the state needs a compelling interest to act, and then to determine whether it in fact has such a compelling interest.

complainant The person, group, or institution bringing a lawsuit or making a complaint.

concur Agree. A Supreme Court justice will frequently write a concurring opinion when he or she agrees with the main decision but has something more to say.

consent decree A kind of contract between the parties in a suit, in which a defendant voluntarily agrees to correct the situation that the plaintiff claims is illegal. However, no fault is found and no punishment or sentencing is involved.

constitutional Acceptable under the U.S. Constitution. The Supreme Court's job is to decide which laws are constitutional.

defendant The person against whom a suit is being brought or a charge is being made.

disability rights A concept coined in the 1980s referring to the need to respect the rights of people with disabilities. The term is a reference to the civil rights movement, which concerned the rights of people of color.

discrimination Action or policy that is unfair to a particular group, keeping them from enjoying the same opportunities as other people.

dissent Disagree. Supreme Court justices frequently write dissenting opinions, in which they express their disagreement with the Court's ruling.

due process clause The clause of the Fifth Amendment guaranteeing every citizen due process of law.

due process of law The principle that the law will work the same way in every case, for every citizen; a right guaranteed by the Fifth and Fourteenth Amendments of the Constitution.

educational diversity   A principle mentioned by Justice Lewis Powell in the 1978 *Bakke v. University of California Board of Regents* case and frequently cited thereafter in affirmative action cases; the ideal of a student body formed of many diverse types of people as an educational goal.

enjoin   Prohibit. When a court enjoins an action, the court order is an *injunction.*

Equal Employment Opportunity Commission (EEOC)   A regulatory agency created in a 1972 amendment to the 1964 Civil Rights Act, charged with protecting the equal rights of U.S. citizens in employment, as defined by the 1964 and 1972 laws.

equal protection   The principle that every citizen deserves the same protection of the law; a right guaranteed by the equal protection clause of the Fourteenth Amendment.

Equal Rights Amendment   A proposed constitutional amendment that would have guaranteed women equal rights under the Constitution, for which there was a campaign in the 1970s; however, the amendment failed to win the necessary support and was never ratified by a sufficient number of states.

executive order   An order by the executive branch of U.S. government; that is, the president. Although federal laws can be passed only by Congress, an executive order has the force of law unless overruled by Congress.

Executive Order 10925   Issued on March 6, 1961, by President John F. Kennedy, establishing the President's Committee on Equal Employment Opportunity. It required that every federal contract include a nondiscrimination pledge and that the contractor would "take affirmative action, to ensure that applicants are employed, and that employees are treated during employment, without regard to their race, creed, color, or national origin"; the first time the U.S. government called for affirmative action.

Executive Order 11246   Issued by President Lyndon B. Johnson on September 24, 1965. This executive order called for government contractors to have a written plan of remedy for past discrimination in hiring and stated that contractors would not discriminate against any employee because of race, color, religion, or national origin; later amended to include sex as well.

Fifth Amendment   An amendment to the Constitution guaranteeing, among other things, that every citizen shall have access to due process of law; the due process clause is often cited in affirmative action cases.

Fourteenth Amendment   An amendment to the Constitution, passed soon after the Civil War in response to continuing discrimination against the newly freed slaves. It holds that the states should make no laws depriving any citizen of the equal protection of the law, without regard to race, color, creed, or previous condition of servitude. The Fourteenth Amendment's equal protection clause is frequently invoked in affirmative action cases.

free market   The principle that the economy—including the allocation of resources, the setting of prices, the behavior of corporations, and the awarding of jobs and promotions—should be allowed to work freely and without interference. Opponents of affirmative action claim that it interferes with the free market by forcing employers to hire or promote people who in a free market would be passed over.

glass ceiling   Term coined to express the perception that women could rise only to a certain level in an institution, after which they hit a glass ceiling—an unofficial invisible barrier that nevertheless was impassable.

Hopwood   A reference to *Hopwood v. Texas*, the 1996 case brought by Cheryl Hopwood, a white student who charged that the race-based admissions criteria at the University of Texas law school had discriminated against her. Hopwood won her case on appeal, ending affirmative action at the University of Texas.

intermediate scrutiny   Less rigorous examination used to determine whether a law or program is constitutional; by contrast to "strict scrutiny," the most rigorous form of examination. See also **strict scrutiny.**

initiative   A citizen-initiated effort to get a measure on the ballot. Citizens can then vote directly on whether the initiative should become law, rather than depending on the state legislature. Several anti–affirmative action initiatives were placed on the ballot in various states in the 1990s.

Initiative 200 (I-200)   The 1998 initiative in Washington State abolishing affirmative action statewide.

injunction   Legal requirement or prohibition that a citizen may seek from a court. An applicant to a law school who believes that he or she has been unfairly excluded from the program might seek an injunction ordering his or her immediate acceptance, for example. See also **enjoin.**

institutionalized racism   A concept coined by supporters of the civil rights movement to indicate the kinds of discrimination that were practiced via the policy of institutions rather than because of individual decisions. For example, if a college degree is required to work at a particular job, and if few African Americans in the area have college degrees, the policy may be considered an example of institutionalized racism, especially if it can be shown that the knowledge represented by the degree has no actual relationship to the job.

integration   A term meaning intermixing or made part of the whole; often used to refer to the process of bringing people of color and white people together in schools, jobs, and public accommodations. The opposite of *segregation.*

Jim Crow   Colloquial term referring to a set of laws and practices in the South that officially and unofficially segregated African Americans and other people of color, preventing African Americans from voting and giving white people more credibility in legal proceedings.

level playing field   A term used to express fairness or equal opportunity, suggesting that everyone must start out at the same point so that only individual merit will determine success.

majority opinion   The ruling of five or more Supreme Court justices.

minorities   A term used to refer to people of color; considered acceptable in the 1970s, it came under attack in the 1980s, when people of color pointed out that in fact, white people were in the minority worldwide and in some parts of the United States.

minority opinion   The losing opinion in a Supreme Court case; held by fewer members than either a majority or a plurality opinion.

One Florida   A program established by Florida governor Jeb Bush in 1999 to replace affirmative action.

open admissions   A policy adopted by some public educational institutions whereby anyone with a high school diploma (and, in some cases, a minimum grade point average) is accepted; an effort to make higher education more widely available and to avoid discriminatory decisions about who should attend college.

plaintiff   The person, group, or institution "complaining," or bringing a lawsuit.

precedent   Past case or cases used to make a decision in a current lawsuit. The U.S. legal system is supposed to operate according to precedent, with new cases following the principles established in the old ones.

prima facie   Latin for "first face"; a legal term that means "on its face," or "based on how it looks." For example, if an employer has a workforce of 100 that includes no African Americans, and yet the surrounding labor force is 50 percent African American and many African Americans live in the surrounding area, that might be considered a prima facie case of discrimination: the numbers alone make the case, without having to show that the employer intended to discriminate or took active steps to discriminate. Prima facie cases of discrimination were very important in the early days of affirmative action law; later, courts were more likely to want proof of employer intent.

Proposition 209   The 1996 initiative ending affirmative action in California, the result of a campaign led by conservative black businessman Ward Connerly.

quota   A fixed proportion or amount; used to refer to the principle that there should be a fixed number of a certain type of student or employee. For example, a quota might be used to say that only three places in a school will be given to Jews, or it might be used to say that at least 10 percent of an entering class should be female. Quotas have been seen as a discriminatory measure but also as a way of ensuring diversity.

referendum A measure voted on by the citizens of a city or state; if the referendum passes, it becomes law.

regents Literally, "rulers"; trustees or board members; the regents of a university system make the final policy decisions for that system.

remedial Correcting; a remedial action is used to counteract an existing problem. Legal language often contrasts remedial actions with policies designed to achieve general goals; thus a legal decision that required an employer to rehire someone who had been fired unjustly would be remedial, whereas a decision requiring an employer to hire people from a minority group might not be remedial, particularly if it could not be shown that the employer in question had ever been guilty of discrimination against that group.

reverse discrimination A term coined in response to affirmative action efforts, claiming that people who had once suffered from discrimination, like African Americans and women, were now discriminating against others.

reverse racism A term coined in response to affirmative action efforts, claiming that the victims of historic racism were now practicing their own racism against white people.

segregation Literally, separation; refers to the primarily southern system of law and custom that kept African Americans and other people of color separate from white people in employment, schools, and public accommodations.

seniority length of service in a job A seniority system at work awards raises, promotions, and other benefits on the basis of seniority rather than according to the personal preference of the employer. Because of historic patterns of segregation, white people often have more seniority or seniority in better positions than people of color; challenges to seniority are sometimes part of affirmative action plans.

separate but equal The principle established in the 1896 Supreme Court decision *Plessy v. Ferguson*, asserting that African Americans could be segregated into separate schools and public accommodations as long as those separate institutions were equal to those of white people. The concept represented an effort to continue segregation despite the equal protection clause of the Fourteenth Amendment, which asserts that every citizen has an equal right to due process of law, regardless of race, color, or creed.

sexism Discrimination on the basis of sex; generally used to mean discrimination against women, but occasionally used to mean discrimination against men.

state The legal term referring both to the government of an individual state and to government in general.

strict scrutiny Rigorous examination; a term used to indicate that a policy must be strictly examined to see whether it is necessary, as opposed to intermediate scrutiny or other less rigorous types of scrutiny. Strict scrutiny is generally called for in the case of programs that a judge believes may violate individual rights: strict scrutiny is needed to see whether such violations are indeed necessary for a larger purpose. Strict scrutiny is often used to determine compelling interest.

structural inequality Akin to *institutionalized racism*, the term refers to a kind of inequality that results from the structure of a situation rather than a specific intent. For example, if a greater proportion of African Americans than white people cannot afford college tuition and are educated in inferior schools, that creates structural inequality between the two groups with regard to college admissions.

suit Lawsuit.

title Portion of a law.

Title VI The provision of the 1964 Civil Rights Act that declares that "no person in the United States shall on the ground of race, color, or national origin, be excluded from participation in, be denied the benefits of, or be subjected to discrimination under any program or activity receiving federal financial assistance."

Title VII The portion of the Civil Rights Act of 1964 that prohibits employment discrimination on the basis of race, creed, color, or national origin (and, as amended, by sex) by any employer engaged in interstate commerce.

Title IX A portion of the Education Amendments of 1972, prohibiting discrimination on the basis of sex by any educational institution receiving federal funds; instrumental in helping to establish and expand school sports programs for girls, among other things.

Voting Rights Act Legislation passed by the U.S. Congress in 1965 in response to the march of Martin Luther King, Jr., from Selma to Montgomery, Alabama, in March 1965, to dramatize the problem of African-American voting in the South. The Voting Rights Act implemented a number of measures designed to facilitate black voting. It authorized the U.S. attorney general to send federal examiners to register African-American voters under certain circumstances and suspended literacy tests in states in which less than 50 percent of the voting-age population was registered or had voted in the 1964 election. (Literacy tests, or tests of the ability to read and write, had been used to disqualify black citizens from voting.) The Voting Rights Act was readopted and strengthened in 1970, 1975, and 1982.

PART II

GUIDE TO FURTHER
RESEARCH

CHAPTER 6

HOW TO RESEARCH
AFFIRMATIVE ACTION

One of the biggest challenges faced by the researcher of affirmative action is keeping up with the rapidly changing legal and political landscape. Because affirmative action has been so profoundly defined by the court decisions that set the boundaries for the policy, the entire national picture of the issue can be changed by a single court decision. It can be difficult to determine when a case has reached the end of the road and when it is slated to continue on to a higher court; moreover, since higher courts may refuse to hear a case even on appeal or remand a case back to a lower court for a new trial, it can be hard even to figure out what a case's status might be.

Another problematic—if interesting—aspect of researching affirmative action is the extent to which the Supreme Court has left the legal field undefined, particularly with regard to educational policy. As of mid-2002, the only Supreme Court case on affirmative action in education is the 1978 *Bakke* case; the *Bakke* case is notoriously open to interpretation, as there was a majority vote but no majority decision. (See chapter 2.) Thus district courts and appeals courts around the country cite *Bakke* to opposite effects, while some courts also hold that other, more recent affirmative action cases should serve as precedents, even though they deal with issues other than education. This tangle of precedent and varying interpretation can make it difficult for a beginning researcher to follow the thread of a legal argument. Moreover, court decisions themselves can be difficult to read and interpret; and since so much of affirmative action research depends on an understanding of the legal issues, the serious researcher really cannot avoid reading at least some excerpts from court decisions.

Finally, affirmative action is a highly controversial field with intensely polarized opinions, so much so that the beginning researcher, reading various commentators, might be hard-pressed to understand how they can all be talking about the same issue. This is as true for Supreme Court opinions as it is for op-ed articles: Some observers write as though racism were a thing of the past or were primarily a problem for white people; others write as though it were a burning issue that requires concerted, immediate action; still others acknowledge the existence of racism but feel strongly that affirmative action makes the problem worse, not better. Being aware of the various perspectives on an opinion is always important when doing research, but it is particularly important when researching affirmative action, so that the researcher can form his or her own judgment about the validity of the observer's viewpoint.

How, then, can researchers proceed? Here are some general suggestions, followed by more specific advice about where to find material.

TIPS FOR RESEARCHING AFFIRMATIVE ACTION

- **Define the Topic as Specifically as Possible.** When researching affirmative action, it is common to find either too much material on a topic or far too little. One court case might merit several hits on a search engine; another might turn up only as a passing reference in the discussion of another case. Certain news events are covered in every major newspaper in the country; others find their way only into the pages of a local newspaper—yet they may prove important months later, if a local issue turns into a landmark case. Knowing exactly what question is to be answered is key for sorting through the excess material and for knowing how and where to persist when material is in short supply.

- **Keep a Historical Context in Mind, and Remember the Diversity of Opinion.** Try to be able to describe all the major opinions about a particular issue or event in such a way that people on every side would recognize and accept that version of their opinion. When both sides cite the Fourteenth Amendment as evidence for the correctness of their position, for example, it is important to understand how each side views the problem of racial equality and the role of the U.S. government in protecting it. When people who bitterly disagree both declare that racism and discrimination are evils that must be overcome, it is important to understand the different means by which each side proposes to do that. It is equally important to measure all opinions against one's own view of the history and current reality of the United States.

- **Be Aware of the Legal History and Terminology.** A helpful place to start is the discussion in chapters 1 and 2 of "compelling interest" and "strict scrutiny," and of the legacy of the *Bakke* case. A review of the court cases presented in chapter 2 will also yield some useful background information. Since each court case builds on a history of precedent, it helps to understand previous cases in order to grasp the significance of the ones that come later. It also helps to read the decisions and to decide personally if the court is really following precedent or if it is simply claiming to follow a previous case while actually breaking new ground. Remember that it is rare and extremely difficult for any court opinion to acknowledge that it is departing from a previous ruling. Yet when two appeals courts, for example, cite the same case as their precedent for two opposing opinions, clearly at least one court is reading the previous case according to its own lights.

- **Read the Dissenting Opinions.** Sometimes the dissenting opinions can be as important as the deciding opinions in helping to understand the contours of the debate. In addition, Supreme Court justices who wrote dissenting opinions on one case may write the majority opinions on another, so an understanding of how they reason and what matters concern them will help clarify the issues while reading through the cases.

- **Use the Syllabus.** Every Supreme Court case is published with a syllabus, a one-, two-, or sometimes three-page single-spaced summary of the major issues in the case, the key points in the majority opinion, and the final count of how each justice voted. While it is often important to read the actual opinions on both sides, reading the syllabus will at least make available the main points in a case so that its significance can be seen in the larger context. The syllabus will also cite previous cases, allowing readers to follow the legal reasoning from case to case, even if they read only the syllabus.

- **Know the Source.** When reading commentary or news articles, be aware of the vastly different points of view on this issue—and assess the material accordingly. Recall that few people are objective on this issue, so it helps to know where the writer is coming from before beginning.

GETTING STARTED: HOW TO FIND HELPFUL SOURCES

NEWSPAPERS AND MAGAZINES

One excellent way to research affirmative action is simply to key the words "affirmative action" into a database, deciding in advance how far back in time the search will go. In preparing this book, ProQuest, a database formerly used by the New York Public Library, was very helpful, but many others are available. Most databases will provide both an abstract and the full article; however, the *New York Times* provides only abstracts free of charge for anything published before December 1999. Other periodicals have followed the *Times's* example and have begun instituting a fee for examining or printing a full article.

Another useful approach to researching affirmative action is to choose a periodical that expresses a particular point of view, so as to find out how various pro– or anti–affirmative action sources are analyzing a particular event. It may also be useful to read particular writers as a way of tracking the general political climate. Here are some suggestions:

> *Useful Pro–affirmative action Periodicals:* Ms., The Nation, National NOW News, The Village Voice
> *Useful Anti–affirmative action Periodicals:* Commentary, National Review, Wall Street Journal
> *Useful Pro–affirmative action Commentators:* Derrick Bell, Katha Pollitt, Adolph Reed, Patricia Williams, Cornel West
> *Useful Anti–affirmative action Commentators:* Mona Charen, Ann Coulter, Charles Krauthammer, John McWhorter, Charles Murray, George F. Will

THE INTERNET

The Internet can be an invaluable resource for the researcher on affirmative action: to locate a court case, get background on a key figure, find out the latest news on a particular topic, or to track the history of a court case.

The search engine Google (http://www.google.com) is an amazingly effective way of answering particular questions or locating specific information on affirmative action. Searches conducted in the course of writing this book turned up information as diverse as a thumbnail biography of California governor Pete Wilson, a website featuring more than 60 conservative commentators (http://www.townhall.com), a pro–affirmative action website featuring a plethora of news reports and essays (http://www.aadap.org), and a brief history of women in the United States. Moreover, every Supreme Court case involving affirmative action is available on the Web, as are summaries of national legislation and regulations on affirmative action. Researchers looking to read a wide range of opinions on a topic, or to quickly find the pro– or anti–affirmative action position on a particular development, can easily meet their needs on the Internet. Indeed, because of the fast-changing nature of the topics, the Internet is a useful place to find the information that has not yet been published in book form. Just be careful: often information on the Net is not marked with a date, and researchers can easily find themselves using out-of-date information without realizing it.

Researchers looking for specific court cases and legislation can turn to one of the many free sources for legal information on the Web. Unfortunately, electronic law libraries—including Westlaw and Lexis-Nexis—are all fee-based, either via subscription or on a per-use basis. They are the only really reliable way to get comprehensive online access to court cases before 1990, other than Supreme Court cases, which are readily available through Findlaw (http://findlaw.com) and the Legal Information Institute (http://lii.cornell.edu). Findlaw also offers a comprehensive directory of various Internet legal resources, including a state-by-state guide, while the Legal Information Institute offers pages that focus on educational policy, employment policy, and discrimination law. Be aware that many states do not offer online texts of court cases; many others go back only a few years or, at most, to 1990.

CHAPTER 7

ANNOTATED BIBLIOGRAPHY

The following bibliography contains four major sections: books, general-interest articles, law review articles, and websites.

The books section is by no means a comprehensive listing of all the books on this ever-changing subject, but it is a selection of important volumes discussing the key issues and representing the major viewpoints about the topic. It includes at least one book by most of the major commentators on the issue and covers theoretical and political analyses, journalistic reports, and personal experiences.

The general-interest articles were drawn primarily from daily newspapers around the United States, as well as from some newsweeklies, such as *Time* and *Newsweek*. Some journals of opinion, such as *The Nation* and *National Review*, are also represented, as are a few scholarly publications. Again, a wide range of opinions can be found in the editorials and journals of opinion included here, and an effort was made to provide at least one article from each well-known commentator on the issue.

The law review articles are a useful resource for a field that is largely defined by court rulings and legal principles. Although these articles are only a small sampling of the legal writing available on this issue, they do provide a useful overview for the beginning researcher, and a handy summary for the experienced legal scholar.

There are relatively few websites dealing with affirmative action, and many of those that are available are specialized and technical, oriented to personnel departments, government agencies, and small businesses applying for special programs. While new material is always coming online, the beginning researcher can rest assured that the website listing includes the vast majority of sources for the general researcher and a good many specialized sources as well.

BOOKS

Bacchi, Carol Lee. *The Politics of Affirmative Action: "Women," Equality and Category Politics.* London: Sage, 1996. The author, a professor of politics at the University of Adelaide, explores the contradiction between affirmative action, which focuses on women as a distinct category, and on the distaste that many feminists have for seeing women as a separate class of people. Drawing on material from the United States, Canada, Norway, Sweden, the Netherlands, and her own Australia, Bacchi explores the political uses of creating separate categories for various types of people.

Ball, Howard. *The* Bakke *Case: Race, Education, and Affirmative Action.* Lawrence: University of Kansas Press, 2000. Part of the Landmark Law Cases and American Society series, this book analyzes the *Bakke* case and the many issues that arose from it. When Allan Bakke's claim of reverse discrimination was heard by the Supreme Court in 1978, it proved to be a turning point in the history of affirmative action, opening the door to numerous other such suits and beginning a process that includes numerous recent state initiatives intended to abolish affirmative action. Ball, a veteran of the civil rights movement, looks at both the *Bakke* case and its contemporary legacy.

Beckwith, Francis J., and Todd E. Jones, eds. *Affirmative Action: Social Justice or Reverse Discrimination?* Contemporary Issues Series. Amherst, N.Y.: Prometheus Books, 1997. Francis J. Beckwith opposes most forms of affirmative action, while Todd Jones defends affirmative action; the two editors have created this volume to represent both sides of the debate about affirmative action regarding race and gender. Contributors include well-known radicals, liberals, and conservatives on all sides of the issue, including Ronald Dworkin, Stanley Fish, Louis Pojman, Michael Levin, Cornel West, Shelby Steele, Ward Connerly (who led the anti–affirmative action movement in California and Florida), and President Lyndon Johnson (who initiated the concept in the 1960s).

Bell, Derrick. *And We Are Not Saved: The Elusive Quest for Racial Justice.* New York: Basic Books, 1987. Bell, an African-American law professor, is skeptical about any efforts to overcome racism in America, while also arguing that standardized tests and similar "objective" measurements in fact seriously discriminate against black Americans.

Bergmann, Barbara. *In Defense of Affirmative Action.* New York: Basic Books, 1996. The author argues that women need affirmative action, as do people of color, to improve their standing in the labor market; she claims that black men and women earn substantially less than their white counterparts even when education, experience, and geographical factors are corrected for.

Bolick, Clint. *The Affirmative Action Fraud: Can We Restore the American Civil Rights Vision?* Washington, D.C.: Cato Institute, 1996. This volume, published by the conservative Cato Institute, argues that affirmative action represents a divergence from the original color-blind vision of the early civil rights movement. Bolick explores the ways that, in his view, the United States got "off track" and suggests ways of restoring the original vision.

Bowen, William G., and Derek Bok. *The Shape of the River: Long-Term Consequences of Considering Race in College and University Admissions.* Princeton, N.J.: Princeton University Press, 1998. The results of a 20-year study drawing on academic records and survey responses concerning some 45,000 students affected by affirmative action, following the lives of students who entered college in 1976 and 1989. The authors conclude that affirmative action provided the backbone of the black middle class and gave white students valuable experiences of diversity.

Cahn, Steven M., ed. *The Affirmative Action Debate.* New York: Routledge, 1995. This collection of philosophic essays spans two decades of writing on the topic, with contributors from all sides of the issue, including Steven M. Cahn, James W. Nickel, J. L. Cowan, Paul W. Taylor, Michael D. Bayles, William A. Nunn III, Alan H. Goldman, Paul Woodruff, Robert A. Shiver, Judith Jarvis Thomson, Robert Simon, George Sher, Robert Amdur, Robert K. Fullinwider, Bernard A. Boxhill, Lisa H. Newton, Anita L. Allen, Celia Wolf-Devine, Sidney Hook, Richard Wasserstrom, Thomas E. Hill Jr., and John Kekes.

Caplan, Lincoln. *Up against the Law: Affirmative Action and the Supreme Court* New York: Twentieth Century Fund Press, 1997. An analysis by a respected legal writer on the ways that the Supreme Court has shaped U.S. affirmative action policy.

Carter, Stephen L. *Reflections of an Affirmative Action Baby.* New York: Basic Books, 1992. The author, an African-American graduate of Yale Law School, acknowledges that he was accepted into Yale in 1977 "because I am black—so what?" He argues that all decisions should be based on merit, and that affirmative action—or, in his view, "racial preference"— further isolates African Americans by keeping them from competition with the top people in their field. He further objects to the "taint"—the sense that black professionals have succeeded because of race rather than merit; and to the idea that a dark skin implies taking part in a single "correct" black ideology.

Chavez, Lydia. *The Color Bind: The Campaign to End Affirmative Action.* Berkeley: University of California Press, 1998. An account of the 1995 initiative to end affirmative action in California, Proposition 209, written by a professor at the University of California, Berkeley, who supports affirmative action. The *New York Times* praised Chavez's account as a "fair and well-written book."

Cohen, Carl. *Naked Racial Preference: The Case against Affirmative Action.* Lanham, Md.: Madison Books, 1995. Cohen, a philosopher, argues that race-based preferences are morally indefensible in admissions requirements at law and medical schools and in hiring. He also claims that they actually harm both the institutions and the people that they were intended to help. Cohen looks at landmark court cases on affirmative action as well as at their consequences.

Crosby, Faye, and Cheryl Vandeveer, eds. *Sex, Race, and Merit: Debating Affirmative Action in Education and Employment.* Ann Arbor: University of Michigan Press, 2000. A collection of articles that focus on both race and gender in the affirmative action debates.

Curry, George E., and Cornel West, eds. *The Affirmative Action Debate.* Cambridge, Mass.: Perseus Press, 1996 (updated in 1998). A collection of essays from a range of political viewpoints, including such opponents of affirmative action as Linda Chavez and William Bradford Reynolds and such supporters as Cornel West and Manning Marable; it includes a copy of Lyndon B. Johnson's 1965 Harvard commencement speech, in which he described his rationale for affirmative action.

Decter, Midge. *An Old Wife's Tale.* New York: HarperCollins, 2001. The autobiography of one of the United States's most prominent female opponents of feminism and affirmative action for women. Decter argues that feminism is antiwomanhood and antimotherhood, and that women are desperate to return to traditional values.

Delgado, Richard. *The Coming Race War?: And Other Apocalyptic Tales of America after Affirmative Action and Welfare.* New York: New York University Press, 1996. University of Colorado law professor Richard Delgado argues that U.S. law is inherently racist in that it guarantees that a white elite will maintain power at the expense of oppressed people of color. Delgado presents his arguments as a series of dialogues between an unnamed professor and a younger colleague of mixed race. Delgado argues, among other things, that only judges of color can protect the rights of people of color; that court decisions striking down laws against hate speech are incorrect; and that affirmative action should be maintained. He also presents the apocalyptic vision of conservatives who want to end welfare in order to provoke a rebellion by minorities that would lead to the creation of U.S. apartheid.

Drake, W. Avon, and Robert D. Holsworth. *Affirmative Action and the Stalled Quest for Black Progress.* Urbana: University of Illinois Press, 1996.

The authors explore the reasons why African-American progress seems to have "stalled." They examine the early history of affirmative action, in which progress seemed assured, contrasting it with the setbacks that occurred in the wake of the 1978 *Bakke* decision.

Eastland, Terry. *Ending Affirmative Action: The Case for Colorblind Justice.* New York: Basic Books, 1996. Eastland looks at the goal of equal opportunity and the actual results of affirmative action. He argues that affirmative action should be abolished but stresses that the programs to replace it must be carefully crafted.

Edley, Christopher, Jr. *Not All Black and White: Affirmative Action and American Values.* New York: Farrar, Straus and Giroux, 1998. Edley was the leader for President Clinton's review of affirmative action. In this volume, he draws on material from law, the social sciences, and public policy to make his case for the idea that affirmative action has not yet outlived its usefulness.

Eisenberg, Susan. *We'll Call You If We Need You: Experiences of Women Working Construction.* Ithaca, N.Y.: Cornell University Press, 1999. Eisenberg, a master electrician, interviewed 30 women in the building trades to explore the experience of the gender that holds only 2 percent of the 4 million U.S. construction jobs. Eisenberg argues that improving conditions for women on job sites would also make things better for men.

Fair, Bryan K. *Notes of a Racial Caste Baby: Color Blindness and the End of Affirmative Action.* New York: New York University Press, 1999. The author, a law professor and administrator at the University of Alabama, Tuscaloosa, offers numerous perspectives on affirmative action: the personal narrative of his own childhood poverty and the role of affirmative action in helping him and most of his siblings achieve a better life; an analysis of racial privilege and power in the United States; and a legal history of affirmative action.

Feinberg, Walter. *On Higher Ground: Education and the Case for Affirmative Action.* New York: Teachers College Press, 1997. A defense of affirmative action on moral grounds. Feinberg argues that affirmative action has three "morally defensible" goals: to correct "systematic ruptures" in the principle of equal opportunity; to advance the standing of groups that have suffered from discrimination based on race or gender; and to address a historical debt.

Grapes, Bryan J., ed. *Affirmative Action.* Farmington Hills, Mich.: Gale Group, 2000. A collection of articles on affirmative action, presenting a wide spectrum of views, oriented to grades nine through 12.

Guinier, Lani, and Susan Sturm. *Who's Qualified?* (New Democracy Forum). Boston: Beacon Press, 2001. Lani Guinier is a law professor at Harvard, and Sturm teaches law at Columbia. Guinier also came to national prominence when she was appointed by President Clinton to head the Justice Department's Civil Rights Division; her nomination was later withdrawn when Guinier's support for affirmative action led some conservatives to call her "the quota queen." In this volume, Guinier and Strum argue that affirmative action is usually instituted in places where a false meritocracy is already being practiced, so that in fact, even before affirmative action, merit was not the only basis for admissions, hiring, or promotion. Thus, affirmative action is incorrectly perceived as opposing "justice" to "merit," whereas in fact we need new ways of evaluating merit. The book includes commentary on their argument from a dozen scholars, most of whom also support affirmative action.

Halstead, Ted, and Michael Lind. *The Radical Center: The Future of American Politics.* New York: Doubleday, 2001. An ambitious book that one reviewer called "part historical tract, part policy agenda, and part visionary manifesto," *The Radical Center* opposes affirmative action while calling for "a new social contract" that would enable all workers to feel secure while capitalists are still enabled to get rich. They propose replacing the category of race with the notion of class and argue for improving social services for people of all races.

Henry, William. *In Defense of Elitism.* New York: Anchor, 1994. The author argues that supporters of affirmative action for women and people of color want to "change the ground rules" by allowing people to "have their cake and eat it too"; women, for example, want the right both to have children and to work, without considering who will care for the child while women are working, or without considering that an employed mother has "divided loyalties," so that she deserves to be compensated at a lower rate than a single-minded nonparent.

Hill, Anita Faye, and Emma Coleman Jordan, eds. *Race, Gender, and Power in America: The Legacy of the Hill-Thomas Hearings.* New York: Oxford University Press, 1995. A collection of articles about the ways that race and gender affect the distribution of power in the United States in the wake of the confirmation hearings on Clarence Thomas's nomination to the Supreme Court, at which Anita Hill testified that Thomas had sexually harassed her.

Ibarra, Robert A. *Beyond Affirmative Action: Reframing the Context of Higher Education.* Madison: University of Wisconsin Press, 2000. Ibarra puts affirmative action in the context of U.S. higher education, which he claims focuses in harmful ways on individual achievement rather than teamwork, on discrete pieces of knowledge rather than the big picture, and on in-house scholarship rather than communicating with the world at large. He argues that reframing our notions of higher education will make colleges and universities more attractive to women, minorities, and even some "majority males," both as students and as ranking professors.

Jordan, June. *Affirmative Acts: Political Essays.* New York: Doubleday, 1998. Activist, poet, and professor June Jordan is also a political essayist. In this collection she takes on the underlying racism that she claims continues to persist beneath a facade of apparent multiculturalism. She argues that the "calculated racialization of poverty, inequality, immigration, and education," makes it appear that these problems are "race problems" rather than issues that affect us all—and indeed, they do affect people of color in disproportionate numbers. Her perspective is evident in essay titles such as "We Are All Refugees," "My Mess and Ours," and "Notes on a Model of Resistance."

Kahlenberg, Richard D. *The Remedy: Class, Race, and Affirmative Action.* New York: HarperCollins, 1997. The author, a former law professor at George Washington University and a current Center for National Policy Fellow, argues that the original purpose of affirmative action has changed, from "racial preferences as a temporary bridge to color-blindness" to "racial preferences as a permanent way of life." Kahlenberg analyzes what he sees the successes and failures of affirmative action and calls for a new affirmative action based not on race, but on economic need.

Lindsay, Beverly, and Manuel J. Justiz, eds. *The Quest for Equity in Higher Education: Toward New Paradigms in an Evolving Affirmative Action Era.* Frontiers in Education Series. Albany: State University of New York Press, 2001. A look at affirmative action from the point of view of public debates, voter referendums, and legislative efforts. The contributors argue that the quest for equity that affirmative action represents will actually help students by providing them with information and critical skills and preparing them for the world of work.

Lowe, Eugene Y., Jr., ed. *Promise and Dilemma: Perspectives on Racial Diversity and Higher Education.* Princeton, N.J.: Princeton University Press, 1999. A collection of articles on affirmative action in higher education, offering a broad spectrum of views.

McWhirter, Darien A. *The End of Affirmative Action: Where Do We Go From Here?* New York: Carol Publishing Group, 1996. McWhirter is an Austin, Texas, attorney who describes himself as a "disillusioned liberal." He was inspired to write the book by the 1995 California initiative, Proposition 209, which ended affirmative action in that state; now McWhirter asks where the quest for equal opportunity should go next. He analyzes the social and legal history of affirmative action, arguing that racial preferences foster resentment among white people and self-doubt among people of color. He suggests that selecting qualified applicants for schools and jobs at random might benefit minorities without creating the kinds of problems to which race-based programs have led.

McWhorter, John. *Losing the Race: Self Sabotage in Black America*. New York: Free Press, 2000. A controversial account of race relations by a 36-year-old linguistics professor at the University of California, Berkeley, and Bay Area actor, in which McWhorter argues that the problem for African Americans is neither lack of ability nor white racism but a dysfunctional black culture plagued by a sense of victimization, a drive toward separatism, and a commitment to anti-intellectualism. McWhorter's seminal moment came as a child in 1968, when a group of black children in his integrated Philadelphia neighborhood teased him for being smart.

Mosley, Albert G., and Nicholas Capaldi. *Affirmative Action: Social Justice or Unfair Preference?* Lanham, Md.: Rowman and Littlefield, 1996. A look at the liberal-conservative debate over affirmative action, as the two authors debate each other. The book includes a summary of relevant case law and a concise overview of the main issues.

Nordquist, Joan, ed. *Affirmative Action: A Bibliography*. Santa Cruz, Calif.: Reference and Research Services, 1996. Although many important events in the history of affirmative action took place after 1996, this is a comprehensive bibliography of materials on the topic up to that date.

Post, Robert, and Michael Rogin, eds. *Race and Representation: Affirmative Action*. Cambridge, Mass.: MIT Press, 1998. Collected as a response to the anti–affirmative action decisions in California and Texas of the late 1990s, these essays focus on the ways in which affirmative action has been presented in popular culture and the news media, inviting readers to view affirmative action within the broader context of U.S. race relations.

Reed, Adolph, Jr. *Without Justice for All: The New Liberalism and Our Retreat from Racial Equality*. Boulder, Colo.: Westview Press, 2001. A scathing analysis of the ways that liberals, too, have retreated from what the author considers a full commitment to racial justice, which in Reed's view includes a commitment to affirmative action.

Robinson, Jo Ann Oiman, ed. *Affirmative Action: A Documentary History*. Primary Documents in American History and Contemporary Issues. Westport, Conn.: Greenwood Press, 2001. The book provides 395 documents that trace the history of affirmative action; includes arguments both for and against the controversial concept. One of the few books to include information on race, gender, and disability.

Rubio, Philip F. *A History of Affirmative Action, 1619–2000*. Jackson: University Press of Mississippi, 2001. Rubio argues that to truly understand the current debates over affirmative action, U.S. racial history must be looked at, from colonial times through the present. In Rubio's view, a misunderstanding of affirmative action's history is the primary reason that white people have trouble seeing their own privilege, both current and historical. Rubio's own experience as a blue-collar worker, labor and community activist, and jazz musician informs his look at African-American, labor, and social history.

Skrentny, John David. *The Ironies of Affirmative Action: Politics, Culture, and Justice in America*. Morality and Society Series. Evanston, Ill.: University of Chicago Press, 1996. Skrentny is a sociologist at the University of Pennsylvania who claims to see a number of ironies of affirmative action: that it was opposed by early civil rights leaders, including Martin Luther King, Jr., as working against the goal of a color-blind society; that Republican president Richard Nixon instituted affirmative action as a cynical way of splitting the Democratic Party coalition of African Americans and unions; and that support for affirmative action was often motivated by fear that the Soviet Union would seize upon U.S. racism as a propaganda tool. Now that the cold war is over, he claims, affirmative action is suddenly far more vulnerable.

Sowell, Thomas. *Civil Rights: Rhetoric or Reality*. New York: William Morrow, 1985. Economist Thomas Sowell rose to prominence in the 1980s as one of the new black conservatives whose criticisms of affirmative action and the welfare state dovetailed with the Reagan revolution. Sowell's project is to contrast the rhetoric of the civil rights establishment with what he sees as the reality of U.S. society and U.S. law.

Spann, Girardeau A. *The Law of Affirmative Action: Twenty-Five Years of Supreme Court Decisions on Race and Remedies*. New York: New York University Press, 2000. A comprehensive look at the Supreme Court's involvement with affirmative action, beginning with the *DeFunis v. Odegaard* (1974) and the landmark *Bakke* decision (1978) and continuing through the 1998–99 term. Since Supreme Court decisions are so central to the status of affirmative action, this look at legal history illuminates the history of affirmative action.

Tomasson, Richard F., Faye J. Crosby, and Sharon D. Herzberger, *Affirmative Action: The Pros and Cons of Policy and Practice*. Lanham, Md.: Rowman and Littlefield, 2001. A comprehensive look at how affirmative action has worked in practice, updated from a 1996 edition.

West, Cornel. *Race Matters*. New York: Vintage, 1994. West, a prominent philosopher, argues that "the fundamental crisis in black America is twofold: too much poverty and too little self-love." While West supports affirmative action, he argues that it is "neither a major solution to poverty nor a sufficient means to equality."

Williams, Patricia. *The Alchemy of Race and Rights*. Cambridge, Mass.: Harvard University Press, 1991. The great-great-granddaughter of a slave and a white Southern lawyer considers the complicated and contradictory ways that race, gender, and class intersect in her own narrative as she becomes a lawyer. Williams was a law professor at University of Wisconsin when she wrote this book; she is currently a professor at Columbia University and a columnist for the progressive magazine the *Nation*.

Welch, Susan, and John Gruhl. *Affirmative Action and Minority Enrollments in Medical and Law Schools*. Ann Arbor: University of Michigan Press, 1998. When affirmative action plans were first adopted by universities, the focus was often on increasing the number of minority doctors and lawyers. This book analyzes how affirmative action policies have actually affected minority enrollments in law and medical schools.

Zelnick, Bob. *Backfire: A Reporter's Look at Affirmative Action*. Washington, D.C.: Regnery Publishers, 1996. Zelnick, an ABC reporter, offers this scathing look at affirmative action, which he criticizes as unfair, clumsy, misguided, and destructive to people of all races. Zelnick also considers the issues of racial self-segregation in campus housing, the practice of tracking in high school, and the existence of historically black colleges and universities.

ARTICLES

LAW REVIEW

Adams, Jr., Frank. "Why *Brown v. Board of Education* and Affirmative Action Can Save Historically Black Colleges and Universities." *Alabama Law Review*, 1966, vol. 47, p. 481. A look at the problem of "separate but equal" in affirmative action decisions as it relates to historically black institutions of higher education.

Albritton, Erin. "*Hopwood v. Texas:* Affirmative Action Encounters a Formidable and Fatal Match in the Fifth Circuit." *Tulane Law Review*, 1966, vol. 71, p. 303. A look at the impact of the *Hopwood* decision, in which a federal judge found race unconstitutional as a factor in admission to the University of Texas law school.

Aldave, Barbara Bader. "*Hopwood v. Texas:* A Victory for 'Equality' That Denies Reality—An Afterword." *St. Mary's Law Journal*, 1996, vol. 28, p. 147. A critical look at *Hopwood v. Texas*, in which white students denied entry to the University of Texas law school successfully charged reverse discrimination.

Alt, Robert D. "Toward Equal Protection: A Review of Affirmative Action," *Washburn Law Journal*, 1997, vol. 36, p. 179. An overview of affirmative action law and its relationship to the equal protection clause of the Fourteenth Amendment.

Anderson, Corinne E. "A Current Perspective: The Erosion of Affirmative Action in University Admissions." *Akron Law Review*, 1999, vol. 32. p. 181. The author explores the gradual erosion of affirmative action in university admissions in the wake of such anti–affirmative action decisions as *Hopwood v. Texas* and *Podbereksy v. Kirwan*.

Arriola, Elvia R. "Difference, Solidarity and Law: Building Latina/o Communities through LATCRIT Theory." *Chicano-Latino Law*, 1998, vol. 19, p. 1. The author looks at how critical theory and difference theory might involve gender and ethnicity in the building of community.

Badiani, Purvi. "Affirmative Action in Education: Should Race or Socioeconomic Status Be Determinative?" *Georgia Journal on Fighting Poverty*, 1997, vol. 5, p. 89. Many critics have argued that replacing race-based criteria with class-based factors would solve both the legal and the ethical problems of affirmative action while still acting affirmatively to bring about minority inclusion; the author explores those arguments.

Beyers, Melanie Ryan. "Affirmative Action in Post-secondary Education: When Race Matters." *Detroit College of Law Michigan State University Law Review*, 1997, p. 955. A look at the ways that race matters—and does not matter—in relationship to affirmative action.

Bloom, Lackland H., Jr., "*Hopwood, Bakke* and the Future of the Diversity Justification." *Texas Tech Law Review*, 1998, vol. 29, p. 1. The author looks at the landmark affirmative action case of *Bakke v. Regents of the University of California* (1978) and one of the most recent affirmative action cases, *Hopwood v. University of Texas*, in light of how each case justified—or failed to justify—affirmative action on the grounds of educational diversity.

Boger, John Charles. "Willful Colorblindness: The New Racial Piety and the Resegregation of Public Schools." *North Carolina Law Review*, 2000, vol. 78, p. 1719. One result of affirmative action cases that require colorblindness in admissions decisions is that schools at all levels are becoming increasingly segregated by race. The author explores the impact of anti–affirmative action cases and racial segregation.

Booher, Ross I. "Constitutional Law—Fourteenth Amendment Equal Protection Clause—Racial Preferences in College and University Admissions." *Tennessee Law Review*, 1997, vol. 64, p. 497. The cornerstone of anti–affirmative action cases has been the equal protection clause of the Fourteenth Amendment; the author explores the role of the Fourteenth Amendment in recent law.

Brooks, Jennifer C.. "The Demise of Affirmative Action and the Effect on Higher Education Admissions: A Chilling Effect or Much Ado about Nothing?" *Drake Law Review*, 2000, vol. 48, p. 567. Many observers have argued that the end of affirmative action has a chilling effect on the admission and hiring of minorities; the author argues that the effects of anti–affirmative action cases may well have been exaggerated.

Brown, Kevin. "*Hopwood:* Was This the African-American Nightmare or the African-American Dream?" *Texas Forum on Civil Liberties & Civil Rights,* 1996, vol. 2, p. 97. Some African Americans have argued that the end of affirmative action is a huge blow to minorities, but conservative African-American leaders such as Ward Connerly are deeply opposed to affirmative action. This article examines the controversy as it relates to the *Hopwood* case, which ended affirmative action at the University of Texas law school.

Brown-Nagin, Tomiko. "A Critique of Instrumental Rationality: Judicial Reasoning about the 'Cold Numbers' in *Hopwood v. Texas.*" *Law & Inequality Journal,* 1998, vol. 16, p. 359. A closer look at the *Hopwood* case, in which a white student charged reverse discrimination by the University of Texas law school.

Bybee, Keith J. "The Political Significance of Legal Ambiguity: The Case of Affirmative Action." *Law & Society Review,* 2000, vol. 34, p. 263. Affirmative action in educational admissions has been ruled by legal ambiguity since the 1978 *Bakke* decision; the author explores the political meanings of legal ambiguity.

Byrne, Jennifer R. "Toward a Colorblind Constitution: Justice O'Connor's Narrowing of Affirmative Action." *St. Louis Law Journal,* 1998, vol. 42, p. 619. Since her accession to the Supreme Court, Justice Sandra Day O'-Connor has been one of the most vigorous and articulate opponents of affirmative action on the bench; she has authored many landmark anti–affirmative action decisions that maintain the need for colorblindness in educational and employment decisions. The author explores O'-Connor's influence on this key field of law.

Byrnes, Erin E. "Therapeutic Jurisprudence: Unmasking White Privilege to Expose the Fallacy of White Innocence: Using a Theory of Moral Correlativity to Make the Case for Affirmative Action Programs in Education." *Arizona Law Review,* 1999, vol. 41, p. 535. The author argues that the presumption of "white innocence"—the argument that "innocent" white people are being made to suffer through affirmative action policies—is really a cover for white guilt.

Carcieri, Martin D. "A Progressive Reply to Professor Oppenheimer on Proposition 209." *Santa Clara Law Review,* 2000, vol. 40, p. 1105. The author criticizes Proposition 209, the colorblind statute that bans affirmative action in the state of California.

Carleton, Francis, and Jennifer Nutt Carleton. "An Ethic of Care Applied: A Critical Analysis of Affirmative Action Jurisprudence." *Temple Politics & Civil Rights Law Review,* 1998, vol. 8, p. 87. A review of affirmative action law in light of the apparently "uncaring" decisions that have characterized jurisprudence in recent years.

Chang, Lisa E. "Remedial Purpose and Affirmative Action: False Limits and Real Harms." *Yale Law & Policy Review*, 1997, vol. 16, p. 59. In affirmative action law, the notion of remedial purpose is key, as conservative jurists hold that only to remedy specific past discrimination can race-based criteria be justified—and sometimes not even then. The author explores this concept as it has played out in recent jurisprudence.

Chen, Jim. "Diversity and Damnation." *UCLA Law Review*, 1996, vol. 43, p. 1839. The notion of educational diversity has been a cornerstone of affirmative action law since Justice Lewis Powell mentioned the concept in his 1978 decision in *Bakke v. University of California Regents*. Jim Chen further explores the notion of diversity.

Colaluca, Thomas L., and Gina A. Kuhlman. "The Future of Affirmative Action: The Legal Imperative Nationally and the Ohio Experience." *Cleveland State Law Review*, 1998, vol. 46, p. 765. A look at Ohio's experience with affirmative action law in the context of national developments.

"Constitutional Law—Equal Protection—Affirmative Action—Fifth Circuit Holds That Educational Diversity Is No Longer a Compelling State Interest—*Hopwood v. Texas*." *Harvard Law Review*, 1997, vol. 110, p. 775. A report on the *Hopwood* case, in which the Fifth Circuit Court of Appeals seemed to overturn Justice Lewis Powell's *Bakke* decision by holding that educational diversity was no longer a compelling enough reason for the state to use race-based criteria in college admissions.

"Constructing Reality after *Hopwood*." *Texas Hispanic Journal of Law & Policy*, 1998, p. 45. A look at the effects of *Hopwood*, the 1996 case in which educational diversity was ruled an insufficient reason for a university to use race-based admissions criteria.

Cosner, Krista L. "Affirmative Action in Higher Education: Lessons and Directions from the Supreme Court." *Indiana Law Journal*, 1996, vol. 71, p. 1003. A review of the Supreme Court's affirmative action law and its implications for affirmative action in higher education; although the Supreme Court has not ruled directly on a higher education case since 1978, many observers believe its other affirmative action decisions hold significant for education as well.

Daniel, Philip T. K., and Kyle Edward Timken. "The Rumors of My Death Have Been Exaggerated: *Hopwood's* Error in 'Discarding' *Bakke*." *Journal of Law & Education*, 1999, vol. 28, p. 391. A controversial aspect of the *Hopwood* case was its apparent disregard of the precedent set by *Bakke*; whereas Justice Lewis Powell had written in *Bakke* that educational diversity was a constitutionally permissible goal that might justify race-based criteria in educational admissions, *Hopwood* indicated that race-based criteria were never acceptable. The authors criticize the *Hopwood* decision.

Dassance, Ellen R. "Affirmative Action Implications for Colleges and Universities beyond the Scholarship and Student Admissions Areas." *William & Mary Bill of Rights Journal*, 1997, vol. 5, p. 661. Most policy makers and legal observers have focused on the effects of affirmative action decisions in education on scholarships and admissions; this author looks beyond those areas at the further implications.

Dayton, John, and Anne P. Dupre. "Equal Protection of the Laws: Recent Judicial Decisions and Their Implications for Public Educational Institutions." *Education Law Report*, 1997, vol. 114, p. 1. An analysis of how recent affirmative action law has affected public colleges and universities.

Delgado, Richard, and Jean Stefancic. "California's Racial History and Constitutional Rationales for Race-Conscious Decision Making in Higher Education." *UCLA Law Review*, 2000, vol. 47, p. 1521. Delgado, the controversial and provocative author of several books about affirmative action and racism, coauthors this analysis of racism in California, the site of much affirmative action controversy in recent years.

Donahue, Robert J. "Racial Diversity as a Compelling Governmental Interest." *Indiana Law Review*, 1997, vol. 30, p. 523. Many recent affirmative actions have turned on the question of whether the state has a "compelling interest" to intervene using race-based criteria. The author argues that racial diversity is itself a compelling governmental interest.

D'Souza, Dinesh, and Christopher Edley. "Affirmative Action Debate: Should Race-Based Affirmative Action Be Abandoned as a National Policy?" *Albany Law Review*, 1996, vol. 60, p. 425. D'Souza, a noted opponent of affirmative action, and Edley, a supporter, debate the merits of affirmative action as a national policy.

Early, Shawna A. "Can Affirmative Action Survive in Education?" *North Carolina Central Law Journal*, 1996, vol. 22, p. 177. The author explores the future of affirmative action in education given the numerous setbacks such as *Hopwood*, the case that ended affirmative action at the University of Texas law school.

Essix, Shalond N. "*Hopwood v. Texas:* The Future of Remedial Justification for Past and Present Disabling Effects of Discrimination: Will the 5th Circuit's *Hopwood* Be a Barrier to Diversification?" *Southern University Law Review*, 1996, vol. 24, p. 121. The author explores the notion of remedial justification—the principle that affirmative action must be justified on the grounds of remedying a specific ill—and considers the effect of *Hopwood*, which banned race-based criteria in admissions decisions at the University of Texas law school.

Feeny, Kira M. "Race-Conscious Admissions Programs in Higher Education: It's Not a Black and White Issue." *Dayton Law Review,* 1999, vol. 25, p. 109. The author explores the complexities involved in race-conscious admissions to colleges and universities.

Forbath, William E., and Gerald Torres. "Merit and Diversity after *Hopwood.*" *Stanford Law & Policy Review,* 1999, vol. 10, p. 185. Many observers of affirmative action have presented the issue as one of merit versus diversity. The authors explore this notion in light of the *Hopwood* decision, which eliminated the goal of racial diversity as a legal rationale for using race-based admissions criteria.

Forde-Mazrui, Kim. "The Constitutional Implications of Race-Neutral Affirmative Action." *Georgetown Law Journal,* 2000, vol. 88, p. 2331. In the wake of many court decisions that have banned the explicit use of race in admissions decisions, college officials are exploring the possibility of "race-neutral" affirmative action—programs that would attract minority students without explicitly mentioning race. The author examines the constitutional questions involved.

Freedman, Shane H. "Affirmative Action: An Idea Whose Time Has Gone." *Seton Hall Law Review,* 1997, vol. 27, p. 1579. Affirmative action has been called obsolete by many observers who see it as unnecessary in this post–civil rights era. The author explains the reasons behind this view.

Friedl, John. "Making a Compelling Case for Diversity in College Admissions." *University of Pittsburgh Law Review,* 1999, vol. 61, p. 1. Diversity has been mentioned as the rationale for affirmative action in college admissions since the 1978 decision by Justice Lewis Powell in *Bakke v. Regents of the University of California.* The author explores the notion of diversity as it applies to affirmative action.

Garfield, Leslie Yalof. "*Hopwood v. Texas:* Strict in Theory or Fatal in Fact." *San Diego Law Review,* 1997, vol. 34, p. 497. A look at the notion of strict scrutiny as it applies to *Hopwood,* the case ending affirmative action at the University of Texas.

Gee, Harvey. "Changing Landscapes: The Need for Asian Americans to Be Included in the Affirmative Action Debate." *Gonzaga Law Review,* 1996–97, vol. 32, p. 621. Despite years of historic discrimination, Asian Americans have recently done well in educational and employment achievement, scoring high on standardized tests and receiving good grades in high school and undergraduate schools; as a result, they are often ignored in an affirmative action debate that pits "whites" against African Americans and Latinos. The author argues for Asian Americans to be included in the debate.

Goldsmith, Therese M. "*Hopwood v. Texas:* The Fifth Circuit Further Limits Affirmative Action Educational Opportunities." *Maryland Law Review,*

1997, vol. 56, p. 273. A look at the ways that *Hopwood*, which ended affirmative action at the University of Texas, will affect educational opportunities in the future.

Goring, Darlene C. "Private Problem, Public Solution: Affirmative Action in the 21st Century." *Akron Law Review*, 2000, vol. 33, p. 209. A look into the future of affirmative action.

Gotanda, Neil. "Failure of the Color-Blind Vision: Race, Ethnicity, and the California Civil Rights Initiative." *Hastings Constitutional Quarterly*, 1996, vol. 23, p. 1135. The California Civil Rights Initiative (CCRI) was successful in ending affirmative action in California through its 1995 ballot measure, Proposition 209; the author explores the notion of color-blindness, which the CCRI called for.

Graglia, Lino. "Affirmative Action in Admission to Institutions of Higher Education." *UWLA Law Review*, 1996, vol. 27, p. 347. In the wake of recent anti–affirmative action decisions, the author explores the future of affirmative action in higher education.

———. "The 'Affirmative Action' Fraud." *Washington University Journal of Urban & Contemporary Law*, 1998, vol. 54, p. 31. The author explores the deceptive concepts and arguments that have centered on the affirmative action debate.

———. "Affirmative Action: Have Race- and Gender-Conscious Remedies Outlived Their Usefulness? Yes: Reverse Discrimination Serves No One." *ABA Journal*, May 1995, p. 40. The author argues vigorously against affirmative action on the grounds that it is actually reverse discrimination.

———. "'Affirmative Action,' Past, Present, and Future." *Ohio Northern University Law Review*, 1996, vol. 22, p. 1207. The author, a staunch opponent of affirmative action, reviews the policy's history and future prospects.

———. "Affirmative Action: Today and Tomorrow." *Ohio Northern University Law Review*, 1996, vol. 22, p. 1353. The author, strongly critical of affirmative action, explores the history and current status of the policy.

———. "'Hate-Speech' Codes, and 'Political Correctness': Fruit of 'Affirmative Action.'" *Northern Kentucky Law Review*, 1996, vol. 23, p. 505. See also Michael L. Principe, "A Response to Professor Graglia's Essay on Political Correctness." *Northern Kentucky Law Review*, 1996, vol. 23, p. 515. Graglia, who opposes affirmative action, explains that this problematic policy has now led to unconstitutional restrictions of free speech in the form of hate-speech codes and political correctness. Graglia's article is followed by a response that defends the notion of racial and gender sensitivity embodied in the notion of political correctness.

———. "*Hopwood v. Texas*: Racial Preferences in Higher Education Upheld and Endorsed." *Journal of Legal Education*, 1995, vol. 45, p. 79. The author, a strong critic of affirmative action, looks at the case of *Hopwood* and its bearing on racial preferences. Although the *Hopwood* case eventually overturned the use of race-based criteria at the University of Texas, the author is writing at an earlier time, when it looked as though race might be upheld as one factor in law school admissions decisions.

———. "*Hopwood:* A Plea to End the "Affirmative Action" Fraud." *Texas Forum on Civil Liberties & Civil Rights,* 1996, vol. 2, p. 105. The author, a vigorous opponent of affirmative action, analyzes the *Hopwood* decision—which ended affirmative action at the University of Texas—as calling for a national end to the policy.

———. "*Podberesky, Hopwood,* and *Adarand:* Implications for the Future of Race-Based Programs." *Northern Illinois University Law Review,* 1996, vol. 16, p. 287. The author analyzes three major affirmative action cases and explores their implications for the policy's future.

Graves, Kathleen A. "Affirmative Action in Law School Admissions: An Analysis of Why Affirmative Action Is No Longer the Answer . . . Or Is It?" *Southern Illinois University Law Journal,* 1998, vol. 23, p. 149. The author explains why affirmative action may still be a viable and/or useful policy for law school admissions.

Green, Roger Craig. "Interest Definition in Equal Protection: A Study of Judicial Technique." *Yale Law Journal,* 1998, vol. 108, p. 439. The question of how interests are defined in affirmative action has been central to many cases; the author analyzes this aspect of affirmative action policy.

Gregory, John. "Diversity Is a Value in American Higher Education, But It Is Not a Legal Justification for Affirmative Action." *Florida Law Review,* 2000, vol. 52, p. 929. The author responds to the efforts of affirmative action supporters to defend the policy on the grounds of educational diversity, per Justice Lewis Powell's 1978 decision in *Bakke v. Regents of the University of California;* the author supports educational diversity but finds it unconvincing as a defense of affirmative action.

Greve, Michael S. "*Hopwood* and Its Consequences." *Pace Law Review,* 1996, p. 1. A discussion of *Hopwood v. Texas,* the decision that ended affirmative action at the University of Texas.

Griffith, Thomas D. "Diversity and the Law School." *Southern California Law Review,* 2000, vol. 74, p. 169. Diversity has been cited in many affirmative action cases as the rationale for race-based criteria in law school and other admissions decisions, ever since Justice Lewis Powell first cited educational diversity as a constitutionally permissible reason to consider race in his 1978 decision in *Bakke v. Regents of the University of California.* Griffith explores the role of diversity in law schools.

Guinier, Lani. "Reframing the Affirmative Action Debate." *Kentucky Law Journal,* 1997/1998, vol. 86, p. 505. Guinier, a leading supporter of affirmative action and a widely read writer on the topic, suggests a new way of looking at the debate. Guinier was the focus of an affirmative action controversy in 1993 when President Bill Clinton put forward her name for a position in the Justice Department, then withdrew it in response to conservatives who called her a "quota queen." She is the coauthor, with Susan Sturm, of a book on the notion of merit and affirmative action.

Hardtke, Erin M. "Elimination of Race as a Factor in Law School Admissions: An Analysis of *Hopwood v. Texas.*" *Marquette Law Review*, 1997, vol. 80, p. 1135. The author explores the consequences of the *Hopwood* case, which eliminated race as a factor in admissions to the University of Texas law school.

Harrington, James C. "Civil Rights." *Texas Tech Law Review*, 1997, vol. 28, p. 367. A look at the role of affirmative action in the civil rights movement.

Henry, John A., Jr. "*Hopwood v. Texas.*" *Race & Ethnic Ancestry Law Digest*, 1997, vol. 3, p. 97. A look at the landmark case that ended affirmative action at the University of Texas.

Holley, Danielle, and Delia Spencer. "The Texas Ten Percent Plan." *Harvard Civil Rights–Civil Liberties Law Review*, 1999, vol. 34, p. 245. When the *Hopwood* case prevented the University of Texas from using race as a criterion for admissions, the state responded with a plan to admit the top 10 percent of every high school class to Texas public colleges and universities. The authors review the plan and its effects.

Holley, Michael C. "More Repercussions from *Hopwood:* The Availability of Money Damages under Title VI." *Thurgood Marshall Law Review*, 1998, vol. 24, p. 77. The plaintiffs in *Hopwood* called for money damages as part of their claim that the University of Texas law school had discriminated against them. The author considers that aspect of the case.

Howard, Roscoe C., Jr. "Getting It Wrong: *Hopwood v. Texas* and Its Implications for Racial Diversity in Legal Education and Practice." *New England Law Review*, 1997, vol. 31, p. 831. In response to the *Hopwood* suit, the University of Texas argued for the need for racial diversity in both legal education and the legal profession; the author considers those implications of the *Hopwood* case.

Hueser-Stubbs, Courtney A. "*Hopwood v. Texas:* Ramifications and Options for University Affirmative Action Programs." *UMKC Law Review*, 1996, vol. 65, p. 143. *Hopwood* was one of the most significant recent cases with regard to university affirmative action programs; this article considers what the ruling entails and what options remain open to university admissions committees.

Inouye, Michelle M. "The Diversity Justification for Affirmative Action in Higher Education: Is *Hopwood v. Texas* Right?" *Notre Dame Journal of Law*

Ethics & Public Policy, 1997, vol. 11, p. 385. The University of Texas used the principle of educational diversity to justify its position in *Hopwood* and its affirmative action programs; this article explores the merits and demerits of its position.

Issacharoff, Samuel. "Can Affirmative Action Be Defended?" *Ohio State Law Journal*, 1998, vol. 59, p. 669. The author, a law professor at the University of Texas during the *Hopwood* case and a strong defender of affirmative action, explores the future action in legal education.

Jenkins, Alan. "Foxes Guarding the Chicken Coop: Intervention as of Right and the Defense of Civil Rights Remedies." *Michigan Journal of Race & Law*, 1999, vol. 4, p. 263. Intervention is the legal method by which additional parties can claim their interest in a case and be added to a suit, and it was a key feature of the affirmative action trials at the University of Michigan, *Gratz v. Bollinger* and *Grutter v. Bollinger*. The author takes a closer look at intervention in affirmative action cases.

Joyner, Kevin. "The Use of Race in the Admissions Programs of Higher Educational Institutions—A Violation of the Equal Protection Clause?" *Campbell Law Review*, 1997, vol. 19, p. 489. The keystone of affirmative action cases is the equal protection clause of the Fourteenth Amendment; although this clause was originally intended to protect the rights of African Americans, it has lately been used by white people as grounds for objecting to affirmative action. The author explores the equal protection clause in more detail.

Killenbeck, Mark R. "Pushing Things up to Their First Principles: Reflections on the Values of Affirmative Action." *California Law Review*, 1999, vol. 87, p. 1299. An exploration of affirmative action and its basis in legal principle.

Knickmeier, Amy L. "Blind Leading the 'Colorblind:' The Evisceration of Affirmative Action and a Dream Still Deferred." *Northern Illinois University Law Review*, 1997, vol. 17, p. 305. The author writes a critique of the ways that affirmative action is being undermined and its impact on civil rights.

Kostka, Kent. "Higher Education, *Hopwood*, and Homogeneity: Preserving Affirmative Action and Diversity in a Scrutinizing Society." *Denver University Law Review*, 1996, vol. 74, p. 265. The author explores the implications for higher education and diversity of the *Hopwood* decision, which abolished affirmative action in the Texas university system.

Lauer, Robert A. "*Hopwood v. Texas:* A Victory for 'Equality' That Denies Reality." *St. Mary's Law Journal*, 1996, vol. 28, p. 109. Although the premise of the *Hopwood* case was that white people had been discriminated against by affirmative action, the author argues that in fact, the decision denies the reality of racial discrimination.

Annotated Bibliography

Lee, John E. "The Rise (and Fall?) of Race-Conscious Remedies and 'Benign' Racial Discrimination in Public Education." *Suffolk University Law Review*, 1996, vol. 30, p. 153. A look at the stormy history of race-conscious remedies from a writer who is skeptical about their supposedly benign intent.

Levinson, Sanford. "1999 Owen J. Roberts Memorial Lecture: Diversity." *University of Pennsylvania Journal of Constitutional Law*, 2000, vol. 2, p. 573. Diversity has been the central notion in most cases on affirmative action in education; the author explores the nature of this concept and its implication for jurisprudence.

———. "*Hopwood*: Some Reflections on Constitutional Interpretation by an Inferior Court." *Texas Forum on Civil Liberties & Civil Rights*, 1996, vol. 2, p. 113. The author explores the implications of the *Hopwood* decision, which banned affirmative action in admissions decisions by the University of Texas law school.

Liddle, Keith. "Affirmative Action for Certain Non-black Minorities and Recent Immigrants—'Mend It or End It?'" *Georgetown Immigration Law Journal*, 1997, vol. 11, p. 835. Most of the debate about affirmative action focuses on African Americans and Latinos; this article considers its implications and possible uses for other ethnic groups.

Liu, Goodwin. "Affirmative Action in Higher Education: The Diversity Rationale and the Compelling Interest Test." *Harvard Civil Rights–Civil Liberties Law Review*, 1998, vol. 33, p. 381. The key concepts in affirmative action law have been diversity and compelling interest; the author explores the role of these principles in educational policy.

Loeb, Harlan A. "Equal Opportunity in Higher Education: An Affirmative Response," *Pace Law Review*, 1996, vol. 7, p. 27. The author explores the importance of equal opportunity in higher education.

Lorenzo, Marty B. "Race-Conscious Diversity Admissions Programs: An Empirical Analysis of the Consequences of Abandoning Race as a Factor in Law School Admissions Decisions." *Michigan Journal of Race & Law*, 1997, vol. 2, p. 361. The abandonment of affirmative action by many institutions of higher education has had dramatic consequences as far as minority enrollment and recruitment. This author offers an empirical analysis of some of the consequences of ending affirmative action in law school admissions.

Margolis, Emanuel. "Affirmative Action: Déjà Vu All Over Again?" *Southwestern University Law Review*, 1997, vol. 27, p. 1. A provocative look at the recurring themes of affirmative action.

Mateja, Bill. "Scattershooting on Diversity." *Texas Business Journal*, 1997, vol. 60, p. 1051. The question of how to achieve educational diversity is central to many affirmative action debates; this author joins the discussion with his own thoughts on the matter.

Maxwell, Susan M. "Racial Classifications under Strict Scrutiny: Policy Considerations and the Remedial-Plus Approach, *Texas Law Review*, 1998, vol. 77, p. 259. The questions of strict scrutiny and remedial approaches are central to many affirmative action debates, but they become especially problematic when looked at in light of racial classification.

McMahan, T. Vance, and Don R. Willett, "Hope from *Hopwood:* Charting a Positive Civil Rights Course for Texas and the Nation." *Stanford & Policy Review*, 1999, vol. 10, p. 163. The authors find a hopeful approach to the *Hopwood* decision, which ended affirmative action at the University of Texas.

Mease-White, Alexandra D. "*Hopwood v. Texas:* Challenging the Use of Race as a Proxy for Diversity in America's Public Universities." *Connecticut Law Review*, 1997, vol. 29, p. 1293. The justification for race-based criteria in admissions decisions has long been educational diversity; Mease-White disagrees with the use of race to substitute for more meaningful kinds of diversity.

Moeser, Jeremy. "*Hopwood v. Texas:* The Beginning of the End for Racial Preference Programs in Higher Education." *Mercer Law Review*, 1997, vol. 48, p. 941. Like many observers, this author sees the *Hopwood* decision, which ended affirmative action at the University of Texas, as the beginning of the end for racial preference programs in education nationwide.

Moran, Rachel F. "Diversity and Its Discontents: The End of Affirmative Action at Boalt Hall." *California Law Review*, 2000, vol. 99, p. 2241. A look at the end of affirmative action at the UC Berkeley's Boalt Law School.

Murphy, Tanya Y. "An Argument for Diversity-Based Action in Higher Education." *Annual Survey of American Law*, 1995, vol. 95, p. 515. Diversity has long been the cornerstone of affirmative action policy; this author calls for "diversity-based action."

Neuser, Mark A. "FCC's C Block Auction in the Wake of *Adarand:* Harbinger or Hoax?" *Wisconsin Law Review*, 1996, vol. 1996, p. 821. A look at Federal Communications Commission (FCC) policies of assisting minority-owned businesses in the wake of the 1995 *Adarand* decision, which barred set-asides for minority businesses.

Olivas, Michael A. "Constitutional Criteria: The Social Science and Common Law of Admissions Decisions in Higher Education." *University of Colorado Law Review*, 1997, vol. 68, p. 1065. A look at the constitutional basis for making admissions decision to colleges and universities.

———. "Higher Education Admissions and the Search for One Important Thing." *University of Arkansas Little Rock Review*, 1999, vol. 21, p. 993. A closer look at the issues involved in affirmative action in higher education.

Olson, Scott L. "The Case against Affirmative Action in the Admissions Process." *University of Pittsburgh Law Review*, 1997, vol. 58, p. 991. The author reviews the arguments against using affirmative action to make college and university admissions decisions.

Orentlicher, David. "Affirmative Action and Texas' Ten Percent Solution: Improving Diversity and Quality." *Notre Dame Law Review*, 1998, vol. 74, p. 181. In response to the *Hopwood* decision ending affirmative action at the University of Texas, the state implemented a "10 percent" policy, admitting the top 10 percent of every high school graduating class. This article explores the effects of that decision.

Padilla, Laura M. "Intersectionality and Positionality: Situating Women of Color in the Affirmative Action Dialogue." *Fordham Law Review*, 1997, vol. 66, p. 843. A focus on how affirmative action particularly affects women of color.

Patorious, Emily V. "The Erosion of Affirmative Action: The Fifth Circuit Contradicts the Supreme Court on the Issue of Diversity." *Golden Gate University Law Review*, 1997, vol. 27, p. 459. When the Fifth Circuit Court of Appeals ruled in *Hopwood*, it explicitly tossed out the argument made by the Supreme Court in *Bakke* for educational diversity as a constitutionally permissible basis for race-based criteria in admissions. Patorious explores the reasons why the Fifth Circuit seemed to rule in contradiction to the 1978 Supreme Court decision.

Portales, Marco. "*Hopwood*, Race, *Bakke* and the Constitution." *Texas Hispanic Journal of Law & Policy*, 1998, p. 29. A look at the ways that *Hopwood* seems to contradict *Bakke*.

Portinga, Andy. "Racial Diversity as a Compelling Governmental Interest." *University of Detroit Mercy Law Review*, 1997, vol. 75, p. 73. The use of racial diversity as a reason for race-based affirmative action policy has been discussed since Justice Powell's use of the term in the 1978 *Bakke* case. This author goes into more detail about the notion of diversity.

Powell, Cedric Merlin. "*Hopwood: Bakke II* and Skeptical Scrutiny." *Seton Hall Constitutional Law Journal*, 1999, vol. 9, p. 811. A look at the apparent contradictions between *Hopwood* and *Bakke*, focusing on the concept of strict versus skeptical scrutiny.

Powell, John A., and Marguerite L. Spencer. "Remaking the Urban University for the Urban Student: Talking about Race." *Connecticut Law Review*, 1998, vol. 30, p. 1247. A look at affirmative action decisions in higher education, with particular focus on the urban university and the multiracial urban population.

Pratt, Carla D. "In the Wake of *Hopwood:* An Update on Affirmative Action in the Education Arena, *Howard Law Journal*, 1999, vol. 42, p. 451. An analysis of how the *Hopwood* decision has affected affirmative action policy nationwide.

Rosman, Michael E. "The Error of *Hopwood's* Error." *Journal of Law and Education*, 2000, vol. 29, p. 355. A critical review of *Hopwood v. Texas*.

Rush, Sharon Elizabeth. "Sharing Space: Why Racial Goodwill Isn't Enough." *Connecticut Law Review*, 2000, vol. 32, p. 1. A look at the debate over whether goodwill or particular policies are needed to preserve the rights of different races and ethnicities.

Russell, Thomas D. "Law School Affirmative Action: An Empirical Study: The Shape of the Michigan River as Viewed from the Land of *Sweatt v. Painter* and *Hopwood*." *Law & Social Inquiry*, 2000, vol. 25, p. 507.

Scanlan, Laura C. "*Hopwood v. Texas*: A Backward Look at Affirmative Action in Education." *New York University Law Review*, 1996, vol. 71, p. 1580. The author considers the impact of *Hopwood v. Texas* on affirmative action policy in light of the history of affirmative action.

Sealing, Keith E. "The Myth of a Color-Blind Constitution." *Washington University Journal of Urban & Contemporary Law*, 1998, vol. 54, p. 157. Despite the conservative Supreme Court justices' call for color-blindness in interpreting constitutional law, this author is skeptical about the role of race in the Constitution.

Seamon, Richard H. "Damages for Unconstitutional Affirmative Action: An Analysis of the Monetary Claims in *Hopwood v. Texas*." *Temple Law Review*, 1998, vol. 71, p. 839. A lesser-known aspect of *Hopwood* is the plaintiffs' request for damages, a claim examined here.

Seaton, Richard H. "Affirmative Action at the Crossroads." *Washburn Law Journal*, 1997, vol. 36, p. 248. In light of the many anti–affirmative action decisions of recent years, the author considers the future of the controversial policy.

Sedler, Robert A. "The Constitution and Racial Preference in Law School Admissions." *Michigan Business Journal*, 1996, vol. 75, p. 1160. A focus on the question of affirmative action in admissions to law schools.

Selmi, Michael. "The Life of *Bakke*: An Affirmative Action Retrospective." *Georgetown Law Journal*, 1999, vol. 87, p. 981. The author returns to *Bakke*, the original decision regarding affirmative action in education.

Sirman, John. "Symposium on Excellence in the Profession with a Focus on Diversity." *Texas Business Journal*, 1997, vol. 60, p. 1044. The questions of excellence and diversity are often opposed in affirmative action debates; the author revisits the question.

Stanley, Richard C., and Thomas M. Flanagan. "Constitutional Law." *Loyola Law Review*, 1996, vol. 42, p. 491. A discussion of constitutional law as it pertains to affirmative action.

Straub, Stephanie E. "The Wisdom and Constitutionality of Race-Based Decision-Making in Higher Education Admission Programs: A Critical Look at *Hopwood v. Texas*." *Case Western Reserve Review*, 1997, vol. 48, p. 133. *Hopwood v. Texas* ended race-based decision making in admissions at the University of Texas; the author considers what effect it may have on other institutions of higher learning.

Sturm, Susan, and Lani Guinier. "The Future of Affirmative Action: Reclaiming the Innovative Deal." *California Law Review*, 1996, vol. 84, p. 953. A look at the future of affirmative action from two of its staunchest defenders; the two are also coauthors of a book exploring various approaches to measuring excellence.

Sullivan, Barbara Phillips. "The Gift of *Hopwood:* Diversity and the Fife and Drum March Back to the Nineteenth Century." *Georgia Law Review*, 1999, vol. 34, p. 291. An unusual look at the *Hopwood* decision, which eliminated affirmative action at the University of Texas.

Sullivan, Teresa. "Beyond Affirmative Action: Algorithmic versus Holistic Approaches to College Admissions." *Research in Social Stratification & Mobility*, 1999, vol. 17, p. 319. An innovative approach to college admissions in light of recent attacks on affirmative action.

Swain, Carol M., Robert R. Rodgers, and Bernard W. Silverman. "Life After *Bakke:* Where Whites and Blacks Agree: Public Support for Fairness in Educational Opportunities." *Harvard Blackletter Journal*, 2000, vol. 16, p. 147. A discussion of fairness from the point of view of different racial groups.

Terenzini, Patrick T., Alberto F. Cabrera, Carol L. Colgeck, Stefani A. Bjorklund, and John M. Parente. "Racial and Ethnic Diversity in the Classroom: Does It Promote Student Learning?" *Journal of Higher Education*, vol. 72, no. 5. September/October 2001, pp. 509–31. A study of affirmative action reveals that diversity in the classroom may indeed promote student learning, but not necessarily in a simple, direct way.

Turner, Michael A. B. "Should Race Be a Factor in Law School Admissions? A Study of *Hopwood v. Texas* and How the Equal Protection Clause Makes Race-Based Classifications Unconstitutional." *University of Baltimore Law Review*, 1998, vol. 27, p. 395. A review of the constitutional issues in *Hopwood v. Texas*, which eliminated race-based considerations from admissions to the University of Texas law school.

Walbourn, Jason. "Strict in Theory, but Not Fatal in Fact: *Hunter v. Regents of the University of California* and the Case for Educational Research as a New Compelling State Interest." *Minnesota Law Review*, 1998, vol. 83, p. 183. A look at a key affirmative action case at the University of California.

Ware, Leland. "Affirmative Action in Higher Education: Turning Back the Clock: The Assault on Affirmative Action." *Washington University Journal of Urban & Contemporary Law*, 1998, vol. 54, p. 3. An analysis that views the attacks on affirmative action as a step backward, away from the move toward racial equality and the full achievement of civil rights.

————. "Tales from the Crypt: Does Strict Scrutiny Sound the Death Knell for Affirmative Action in Higher Education?" *Journal of College & University Law*, 1996, vol. 23, p. 43. "Strict scrutiny" was the basis on which conservative justices began to rule against affirmative action cases, and this author explores whether the notion might indeed mean the end for that policy's role in higher education.

Weeden, L. Darnell. "Yo, *Hopwood*, Saying No to Race-Based Affirmative Action Is the Right Thing to Do from an Afrocentric Perspective." *Cumberland Law Review*, 1996–97, vol. 27, p. 533. An Afrocentric view arguing that race-based criteria are actually bad for African Americans and supporting the *Hopwood* decision ending affirmative action at the University of Texas.

Welch, Susan, and John Gruhl. "*Bakke* in the Admissions Office and the Courts: Does *Bakke* Matter? Affirmative Action and Minority Enrollments in Medical and Law Schools." *Ohio State Law Journal*, 1998, vol. 59, p. 697. *Bakke* has a mixed legacy: although the 1978 decision struck down an affirmative action program at the University of California, Davis medical school, the decision also seemed to support certain types of race-based admissions decisions. These authors review the effects of *Bakke* on medical and law schools.

Wolff, Jeffrey B. "Affirmative Action in College and Graduate School Admissions—The Effects of *Hopwood* and the Actions of the U.C. Board of Regents on Its Continued Existence." *SMU Law Review*, 1997, vol. 50, p. 627. A look at the future of affirmative action in the wake of *Hopwood*, the 1996 decision ending affirmative action at the University of Texas, along with the 1995 decision of the University of California regents to end that policy on California public campuses.

Wright, Victor V. "*Hopwood v. Texas:* The Fifth Circuit Engages in Suspect Compelling Interest Analysis in Striking Down an Affirmative Action Admissions Program." *Houston Law Review*, 1997, vol. 34, p. 871. A critique of the Fifth Circuit Court of Appeals use of the compelling interest analysis in *Hopwood v. Texas*, the decision that ended affirmative action at the University of Texas.

Yin, Tung. "A Carbolic Smoke Ball for the Nineties: Class-Based Affirmative Action." *Loyola Louisiana Law Review*, 1997, vol. 31, p. 213. A caustic look at affirmative action in the 1990s.

Zahler, Joanna R. "Lessons in Humanity: Diversity as a Compelling State Interest in Public Education." *Boston College Law Review*, 1999, vol. 40, p. 995. This article considers the question of whether diversity is a compelling interest that permits race-based criteria to ensure diversity on state campuses.

Zirkel, Perry A. "Introduction: *Bakke—Hopwood:* Errors or Exaggerations?" *Journal of Law & Education,* 2000, vol. 29, p. 53. An analysis of the relationship between the *Bakke* and the *Hopwood* decisions.

ARTICLES

GENERAL INTEREST

Abel, David. "Harvard Dispute Declared Settled; Black Professors Still Eyeing Options." *Boston Globe,* January 5, 2002, p. A1. After Harvard University president Lawrence H. Summers allegedly criticized Professor Cornel West and failed to support affirmative action, a controversy with the university's Afro-American studies department erupted; this article reports that the controversy has apparently subsided with an apology from Summers.

———. "Harvard 'Dream Team' Roiled Black Scholars, Summers, in Rift." *Boston Globe,* December 22, 2001, p. A1. A report on the controversy that erupted between Harvard University president Lawrence H. Summers, who had been in conflict with the school's renowned Afro-American studies department over his alleged criticism of Professor Cornel West and failure to support affirmative action.

Aleinikoff, T. Alexander. "A New Sort of Multiracial America." *Washington Post,* September 18, 1998, p. A29. A look at the report to be released by the advisory board of President Clinton's Race Initiative. The author points out that immigration from Asia and Latin America has complicated the "color problem" of "black and white," and reminds readers that "immigration history shows that racial categories are not fixed and unchangeable."

"Anti-Affirmative Action Petition Has Enough Signatures for Court Review." *Miami Herald,* August 31, 1999, p. 9B. Petitions seeking a ballot initiative to abolish affirmative action in Florida have 43,000 signatures—enough to warrant review by the State Supreme Court.

"Appeals Court Throws Out Race-Conscious Admissions Policy at UGA." *Black Issues in Higher Education,* vol. 18, no. 15. September 13, 2001, p. 15. Coverage of the court decision that ruled against a race-based admissions program at the University of Georgia.

Applebome, Peter. "Affirmative Action Ban Changes at Law School." *New York Times,* July 2, 1997, p. A14. In the wake of *Hopwood,* the University of Texas law school must drop affirmative action in its admissions policies, leading to a host of changes.

————. "In Shift, U.S. Tells Texas It Can't Ignore Court Ruling Barring Bias in College Admissions." *New York Times*, April 15, 1997, p. A20. Although the *Hopwood* ruling ended affirmative action at the University of Texas, the school was still subject to an Office of Civil Rights ruling requiring the school to overcome a history of segregation.

————. "Seeking New Approaches for Diversity." *New York Times*, April 23, 1997, p. B7. In the wake of *Hopwood*, which ended affirmative action at the University of Texas, the university seeks new ways to recruit minority students.

————. "Texas Is Told to Keep Affirmative Action in Universities or Risk Losing Federal Aid." *New York Times*, March 26, 1997, p. B11. Even though *Hopwood* ended affirmative action at the University of Texas, the school is still subject to federal guidelines requiring integration.

————. "Universities Report Less Minority Interest after Action to Ban Preferences." *New York Times*, March 19, 1997, p. B12. When *Hopwood* ended affirmative action at the University of Texas, minority students became far less interested in enrolling there.

Arellano, Amber. "GM Backs U-M Affirmative Action; Carmaker Files Brief in Support of Policy." *Detroit Free Press*, July 18, 2000, p. 2B. As the University of Michigan faces lawsuits seeking to end affirmative action in its undergraduate admissions and its law school acceptances, General Motors files amicus briefs in support of affirmative action.

Artze, Isis. "Colleges Find New Ways to Diversify." *Hispanic*, September 2001, vol. 14, no. 9, p. 64. In the wake of attacks on affirmative action, colleges and universities are finding that their minority enrollments have dropped dramatically, so schools are seeking new ways of ensuring a minority presence on campus.

Asher, Ed. "City Proposes Settling Academy Race Lawsuit." *Houston Chronicle*, October 2, 2001, p. 1. City attorneys recommend that Houston's City Council approve an out-of-court settlement on a reverse-discrimination lawsuit that would eliminate race as a factor in choosing police and fire academy cadets.

Bartindale, Becky. "Affirmative-Action Policies Repealed." *San Jose Mercury News*, May 16, 2001, p. 1A. The University of California regents rescind their 1995 ban on affirmative action policies that use race as one factor in considering admissions, despite the ongoing ban on affirmative action in California under Proposition 209.

————. "Latino Group Asks UC to End Affirmative-Action Ban." *San Jose Mercury News*, May 15, 2001, p. 17A. A group of 18 prominent Latino faculty members at the University of California ask the board of regents to drop its 1995 ban on affirmative action. Matters are complicated by the ongoing ban on affirmative action in California under Proposition 209.

————. "UC Drafts Symbolic Shift on Admissions: Regents' Goal: Be Race-Neutral but Welcoming." *San Jose Mercury News*, May 10, 2001 p. 1A. Regent Judith Hopkinson offers a consensus proposal on a new admissions policy for the University of California, meant to effect a compromise between Ward Connerly, the Sacramento lawyer who proposed a 1995 ban on affirmative action, and William Bagley, a San Francisco lawyer who has been fighting to overturn the ban.

Becker, Jo. "Connerly Hopes to Gain Support of Both Bushes." *St. Petersburg Times*, June 25, 1999, p. 13A. Florida governor Jeb Bush has repudiated Ward Connerly's efforts to end affirmative action in Florida, while Texas governor George W. Bush has asked Connerly's help in raising money for his presidential campaign.

Bennett, Brad. "Affirmative Action Battle Starts in State." *Miami Herald*, July 5, 1999, p. 1A. The conservative African-American businessman who got successful anti–affirmative action measures on the ballot in California and Washington State has begun a similar effort in Florida; in only four months Ward Connerly gathered half of the signatures required to put an initiative on the state ballot.

————. "Affirmative-Action Foe Gets 43,000 Signatures." *Miami Herald*, July 31, 1999, p. 4B. In only four months, Ward Connerly has collected thousands of signatures to get an anti–affirmative action measure on the Florida ballot, despite opposition from both local Democrats and Republican governor Jeb Bush, who has his own anti–affirmative action measure in the works.

————. "Affirmative Action Supporters Rally, Raise Money in Miami." *Miami Herald*, August 31, 1999, pp. 1D. Floridians Representing Equity and Equality (FREE) meet to oppose the efforts of Florida governor Jeb Bush and anti–affirmative action activist Ward Connerly to end affirmative action in Florida.

————. "Ballot Initiative Called Misleading: Foes Line Up against Proposal to Scrap Affirmative Action." *Miami Herald*, August 22, 1999, p. 1BR. Supporters of affirmative action charge that the language of a petition to put an anti–affirmative action measure on the Florida ballot is intentionally misleading.

————. "Bush to Look at Affirmative Action Plan." *Miami Herald*, August 14, 1999, p. 1B. Florida governor Jeb Bush is concerned about the efforts of activist Ward Connerly to get a measure on the Florida ballot that would abolish affirmative action, even as the governor is seeking his own anti–affirmative action measure, known as One Florida; Bush considers Connerly's plan "divisive."

————. "Poll: Affirmative Action Would Die If Put to a Vote." *Miami Herald*, November 8, 1999, p. 1A. A poll by the *Miami Herald* and the

St. Petersburg Times shows that Florida voters would support the ending of race and gender preferences by a margin of more than two to one; when the words "affirmative action" are used, the margin of opposition is more than four to one.

Bernstein, Richard. "Law School Calls Bias Ruling a Victory." *New York Times*, August 21, 1994, p. 26. Initially, the University of Texas looked as though it were winning the *Hopwood* case; a report on that phase of the court proceedings.

———. "Racial Discrimination or Righting Past Wrongs?" *New York Times*, July 13, 1994, p. B8. While the white students suing the University of Texas in *Hopwood* considered that they had been the victims of a new kind of racial discrimination, the law school considered that its affirmative action policies were the best way to overcome a long history of discrimination against African Americans and Latinos.

Birkland, Dave. "Gateses' $1 Billion to Fulfill Minorities' College Dream." *Seattle Times*, September 16, 1999, p. A1. Bill and Melinda Gates donate $1 billion to fund scholarships for minority college students with the goal of producing "a new generation of leaders."

Biskupic, Joan. "Diverse or Discriminatory? Affirmative Action in Education Remains Popular, Despite Setbacks." *USA Today*, October 10, 2001, p. D9. Despite numerous legal attacks on affirmative action, polls show that more people support such programs today (56 percent) than in 1995 (49 percent).

"Black Politicians Denounce Bush's Affirmative Action Plan." *Miami Herald*, November 16, 1999, p. 5B. African-American politicians express their outrage at Florida governor Jeb Bush's plan to end affirmative action in the state.

Borrego, Anne Marie. "Coalition Aims to Raise College-Going Rates of Minority and Low-Income Students." *Chronicle of Higher Education*, December 7, 2000. A coalition of foundations, colleges, and government agencies create the Pathways of College Network to increase access to higher education for minority and low-income students.

———. "Bush Returns Fire on Critics; Initiative to End Quotas Defended; Senator Rebuked." *Miami Herald*, November 19, 1999. Florida governor Jeb Bush responds angrily to those who have criticized his efforts to end affirmative action in Florida.

Bousquet, Steve, and Karen Branch. "As Black Leaders Blast Diversity Plan, Task Force Chairman Quits." *Miami Herald*, November 16, 1999, p. 4N. Florida state senator Daryl Jones resigns an appointment by Governor Jeb Bush and criticizes the governor's efforts to end affirmative action in Florida.

Brewer, Steve. "Black Officials Chastise Rulings in Hopwood Case." *Houston Chronicle*, April 12, 1997, p. 45. African American officials chastised

U.S. education officials for reversing their opinion on whether Texas colleges should consider race as part of their admissions decisions. When the *Hopwood* decision held that race could not be a criteria in admissions, Texas attorney general Dan Morales understood this as a ban on using race in admissions and scholarships in all Texas schools; the assistant secretary for civil rights in the education department, Norma Cantu, had originally said Morales's response was too broad, but later she agreed that the *Hopwood* decision was binding.

Bronner, Ethan. "Study Backs Affirmative-Action Policies." [Albany] *Times-Union.* September 9, 1998, p. A4. A new study spanning thousands of students and 20 years at the nation's top colleges and universities finds that affirmative action helped to create the black middle class and educated students of all races about living together.

————. "U. of Washington Will End Race-Conscious Admissions." *New York Times,* November 7, 1998, p. A12. In response to the passage of I-200, a referendum banning affirmative action in Washington State, the University of Washington regretfully suspends its 30-year-old affirmative action policies.

Brown, Christopher M., II, Saran Donahoo, and Roynelle D. Bertrand. "The Black College and the Quest for Educational Opportunity." *Urban Education,* vol. 36, no. 5, November 2001, pp. 553–571. The authors consider how affirmative action law will affect historically black colleges and universities.

Brown, Justin. "A Family Who Cries 'Foul'; Despite Title IX, Some Say Female High School Athletes Aren't Getting a Fair Shake." *Christian Science Monitor,* October 24, 2001, p. 12. In some schools, the wish to comply with Title IX, requiring equal athletic opportunities for men and women, has led to the cancellation of some men's programs rather than expansion of opportunities for women. Yet discrimination against women continues as well.

Brune, Tom. "I-200 Supporters Diversify Leadership." *Seattle Times,* June 16, 1998, p. B1. Although the leadership of the I-200 campaign had been Made up of only white men, an African-American Republican woman, Mary Radcliffe, has become the campaign's spokeswoman. I-200 is a ballot measure that would end affirmative action in Washington state.

————. "Can You Prove You're a Minority?" *Seattle Times,* May 26, 1998, p. A1. An analysis of the difficulty of proving oneself a minority, an inevitable accompaniment to affirmative action programs.

————. "Microsoft Elects to Fight I-200." *Seattle Times,* August 28, 1998, p. B3. Microsoft donates $25,000 to the campaign to defeat I-200, the ballot measure that seeks to end affirmative action in Washington State.

———. "Now That I-200 Is Law, What's Next?" *Seattle Times*, November 5, 1998, p. A1. An analysis of what is likely to happen in Washington State now that I-200—a measure banning affirmative action statewide—is law.

———. "Poll Indicates I-200 Passage Was Call for Reform." *Seattle Times*, November 4, 1998, p. A1. According to a *Seattle Times* poll done on the eve of election day, Washington State voters approved Initiative 200—a measure ending affirmative action statewide—"more to mend affirmative action than to end it."

Brune, Tom, and Joe Heim. "New Battle Begins: Interpreting I-200." *Seattle Times*, November 4, 1998, p. B1. A report on the possible implications of the passage of I-200, the statewide measure that banned affirmative action in Washington.

Brune, Tom, and David Postman. "Early Support Fueled by Thirst for 'Reform.'" *Seattle Times*, July 12, 1998, p. A8. Most Washington voters believe that discrimination against women and minorities still exists, but they do not think that affirmative action as currently practiced is the way to end it, according to a *Seattle Times* poll concerning I-200, a ballot measure that would end affirmative action statewide.

———. "Blethen Starts Ads against I-200." *Seattle Times*, September 1, 1998, p. B1. The publisher of the *Seattle Times* launches his own campaign of newspaper ads against I-200, the ballot measure that would end affirmative action in Washington State.

———. "Women Are Likely Targets of Campaign." *Seattle Times*, July 13, 1998, p. A1. Women's response seems to be central to the campaign for I-200, a ballot measure that would end affirmative action in Washington State.

Burdman, Pamela. "Complaint Hits UC's Admission Policies." *San Francisco Chronicle*, January 11, 1997, p. A1. Civil rights lawyers are trying to reinstate affirmative action in California, despite the state's ban on the program via Proposition 209; lawyers have argued that because most graduate students work as employees, they should be covered by the affirmative action plan that the university must maintain as a federal contractor.

Burress, Charles. "UC Protest Rips Policy on Minorities." *San Francisco Chronicle*, March 9, 2001, p. A19. Some 2,000 high school and college students join a protest at the campus of the University of California, Berkeley, demanding a repeal of the 1995 ban on affirmative action within the university system.

Carlson, Margaret. "Alienable Rights." *Time*, vol. 144, no. 18, October 31, 1994, p. 39. A column criticizing California governor Pete Wilson and his support of Proposition 187, a California initiative that would deny illegal immigrants public services and require teachers and health care workers to turn in any child suspected of being an illegal immigrant.

Annotated Bibliography

Chapman, Stephen. "Affirmative Action Unhinges a Nation." *Chicago Tribune*, March 31, 1996, p. 19C. A look at the impact of affirmative action decisions on U.S. education.

Chavez, Linda. "We Need Another *Brown v. Board of Education*." *Wall Street Journal*, August 31, 2000, p. A8. The author, president of the Center for Equal Opportunity in Washington, D.C., calls for the Supreme Court to "straighten out the mess" that is current affirmative action law by handing down another courageous civil-rights decision like the one that abolished school segregation in 1954.

Clark, Lesley. "Individuals Join Campaign to Ban Affirmative Action." *Miami Herald*, July 14, 1999. A small number of retirees and a wealthy group of contractors are supporting Ward Connerly's efforts to get an anti–affirmative action measure on the ballot in Florida.

Clayton, Mark. "Michigan Affirmative Action Case Will Reverberate Widely." *Christian Science Monitor*, October 23, 2001, p. 14. An analysis of the two University of Michigan cases, which the Supreme Court had been scheduled to hear on October 23. The hearing was postponed until December 6 to allow all nine justices to hear the arguments.

Coeyman, Marjorie. "Harvard's President in the Hot Seat; Afro-American Studies Professors Throw Down the Gauntlet on Affirmative Action." *Christian Science Monitor*, January 8, 2002, p. 13. Controversy ensued when Harvard University president Lawrence H. Summers allegedly rebuked Professor Cornel West for unprofessional activities and failed to support affirmative action; this article reports on the progress of the dispute.

Cohen, Adam. "The Next Great Battle over Affirmative Action." *Time*, November 10, 1997, p. 52. An exploration of the legal landscape of affirmative action, focusing on the anti–affirmative action lawsuits against the University of Michigan, sponsored by the conservative public-interest law firm, Center for Individual Rights (CIR).

Cohen, Carl. "Race Preference and the Universities—A Final Reckoning?" *Commentary*, vol. 112, no. 2, September 2001, pp. 31–39. Cohen, a philosopher and the author of *Naked Racial Preference: The Case against Affirmative Action*, a 1995 critique of race-based preferences as morally indefensible, looks at the prospects for the Supreme Court making a definitive ruling on affirmative action in higher education in its 2001–02 term. Cohen points out that not since 1978 has the Court ruled on affirmative action in college admissions, and the time is ripe for a new decision.

Cohen, Jodi S. "Affirmative Action on Trial: Law School Policy Defended." *Detroit News*, January 19, 2001, p. 1. An account of *Grutter v. Bollinger*, the lawsuit seeking to end affirmative action in admissions decisions to the University of Michigan law school.

————. "U-M Regent Election Key to Race Policy; Board Will Make Pivotal Decisions on Minority Admissions." *Detroit News*, October 3, 2000, p. 1. A look at the regents' election at the University of Michigan, which is in the midst of two lawsuits challenging affirmative action in undergraduate education and at the law school.

Coleman, Trevor. "OSU Joins U-M's Team in Support of Affirmative Action." *Detroit Free Press*, August 21, 2000. Although Ohio State University (OSU) and the University of Michigan are historic rivals, the two are joining forces: OSU is supporting the University of Michigan in defending affirmative action against two lawsuits.

Collier, Willyerd R., Sr. "Not Your Average Affirmative Action Program." *Black Issues in Higher Education*, vol. 18, no. 18, October 25, 2001, p. 160. Legal attacks in several states to abolish affirmative action in higher education are discussed, with the author arguing that diversity must now be achieved through other means than strictly race-based programs.

Connerly, Ward. ". . . but First, Let's End the Preference Paradigm." *Los Angeles Times*, December 19, 2000, p. B11. The founder of the anti–affirmative action movement in California calls on newly designated president George W. Bush to put race at the top of his presidential agenda, given than 90 percent of black voters favored Bush's rival, Vice President Al Gore. Connerly acknowledges that "black people often see events . . . through different lenses," and calls for a new unity based on the principle of equality.

————. "Losing the Soul of the GOP." *National Review*, vol. 53, no. 19. October 1, 2001, pp. 42–44. The founder of the anti–affirmative action movement in California analyzes the developments in the affirmative action issue and the Republican Party over the previous five years.

"Contractors Urged to Stop Connerly Plan." *Miami Herald*, June 26, 1999. South Florida's general contractors are being urged to repudiate Ward Connerly's efforts to end affirmative action in Florida; Connerly is trying to get a measure on the ballot that would ban affirmative action.

Cooper, Kenneth J. "'A Certain Distance' from 1960s in Georgia: Leaders in a State That Once Fought Civil Rights Movement Rise to Defend University's Approach to Affirmative Action." *Washington Post*, January 3, 2001, p. A3. The leaders of Georgia state government, who once pledged "massive resistance" to civil rights, have now risen in bipartisan defense of affirmative action in response to a court challenge to affirmative action at the University of Georgia.

————. "University of Georgia to Appeal Ruling against Affirmative Action." *Washington Post*, August 16, 2000, p. A10. The University of Georgia announces plans to appeal a federal court ruling that struck down the school's affirmative action policy.

Annotated Bibliography

Cotter, Holland. "Beyond Multiculturalism, Freedom?" *New York Times,* July 29, 2001, p. 2.1. The author analyzes the 1990s phenomenon known as multiculturalism, suggesting that the movement had a function but may have outlived its usefulness.

"Court Lifts Affirmative Action Injunction." *Washington Post,* December 22, 2000, p. A20.

Darity, William, Jr. "Give Affirmative Action Time to Act." *Chronicle of Higher Education,* December 1, 2000, p. B18. The author, a professor of economics and sociology at the University of North Carolina at Chapel Hill, and a professor of public policy, African-American studies, and economics at Duke, points out that black Americans' income per capita is only 59 percent of white Americans' income—the same percentage estimated to be the case in 1880. To be effective, he argues, affirmative action will need time.

Denniston, Lyle. "High Court Declines to Rule on Race-Based Government Programs." *Boston Globe,* November 28, 2001, p. A2. A look at the Supreme Court's decision not to review the *Adarand* case, despite expectations that the ruling would bring new clarity to affirmative action law.

———. "High Court Test Looms for Affirmative Action: Mich. Case Highlights Demands for Review." *Boston Globe,* March 30, 2001, p. A2. An analysis of the Michigan court case in which a federal judge banned race as a factor in admissions to the law school; the article considers the implications of this decision for affirmative action as a whole.

Diamond, Laura. "One Florida Plan Taking Flak: Education Department to Monitor Enrollment." *Florida Times-Union,* February 26, 2000. The U.S. Department of Education has expressed "severe concern" regarding the One Florida Initiative, an effort to end the use of racial and ethnic preferences in state university admissions.

DiGiovanni, Aimee. "I-200: Equal Opportunity Will Yield Qualified Applicants." *Seattle Times,* July 26, 1998, p. B5. The writer expresses her support for affirmative action and explains that "there is a difference between affirmative action, set-asides and double standards."

"The Diversity Dilemma." *Commonweal,* vol. 128, no. 5, March 9, 2001, pp. 5–6. An analysis of the two cases challenging affirmative action in admissions to the University of Michigan. The article calls on public universities to recognize their "social and moral obligations" and suggests that affirmative action "will not compromise the academic integrity of the institution, but will actually contribute to its improvement."

Dorse, Bob. "Education Is the Best Affirmative Action." *Seattle Times,* July 30, 1998, p. B5. A column in support of Washington state's I-200, a ballot initiative that would abolish affirmative action statewide. Dorse argues that improving public schools and boosting the educational performance of disadvantaged youth is the best form of affirmative action.

Duran, Estella. "VMI Women Are Worthy but Still Not Welcome." *Boston Globe*, June 13, 1998, p. A5. A report on the status of women at Virginia Military Institute (VMI) one year after the first female cadets are admitted to the formerly all-male school as the result of a Supreme Court case.

Dworkin, Ronald. "Race and the Uses of Law." *New York Times*, April 13, 2001, p. A17. The liberal legal analyst asks why affirmative action in universities is so unpopular when it seems to be working so well, pointing out that studies show that the policy has "improved racial diversity not only in the classrooms but later in life, in business and the professions, as well, and contributed to improved understanding among the races."

Editorial Board. "*Adarand* Nondecision." *Denver Post*, November 29, 2001, p. B10. The *Post* laments the Supreme Court's failure to address *Adarand*, which would have brought new clarity to affirmative action law.

————. "Adarand, again." *Denver Post*. August 13, 2001, p. B7. The *Adarand* case makes its third appearance before the Supreme Court; the decision involves federally required set-asides for minority contractors, and the editorial stresses its importance to affirmative action policy.

Editorial Board. "Affirmative Reaction." *Washington Post*. April 16, 2001, p. A36. The editorial takes a moderate position on affirmative action, holding that "Nobody should be comfortable with government's making distinctions according to race, even for laudable purposes," while also lamenting the court's "simplistic" denial of all programs designed to ensure diversity.

Editorial Board. "Bakke's Elegant Compromise." *St. Louis Post-Dispatch*, September 2, 2001, p. B3. The editorial analyzes the impact of three court decisions involving lawsuits challenging affirmative action at three state universities, in Georgia, Michigan, and Texas. "When the Supreme Court finally re-examines the issue," the editorial concludes, "it should remember that a couple of decades of affirmative action can't wipe out the effects of centuries of slavery and segregation."

Editorial Board. "Balancing the Scales; A Court Ruling Confirms What's Obvious: Any System That Offers Advantages Based on Race Is Unconstitutional." *Atlanta Journal Constitution*, August 29, 2001, p. A20. The editorial distinguishes between affirmative action and systems that automatically give preference to people because of their race, in response to the 11th Circuit Court of Appeal's latest ruling on a lawsuit challenging race-based admissions criteria at the University of Georgia.

Editorial Board. "Bush's Soft Spot." *Los Angeles Times*, August 15, 2001, p. B12. The editorial considers President George W. Bush's mixed responses to affirmative action.

Editorial Board. "Confusion on Affirmative Action." *New York Times,* June 4, 2001, p. A16. The editorial board discusses the many contradictory Supreme Court rulings on affirmative action in the wake of the Court's declining to review cases involving affirmative action at the law schools of the University of Washington and the University of Texas.

Editorial Board. "Diversity Dilemmas." *Boston Globe,* October 25, 2001, p. A18. A response to the Nellie Mae Education Foundation report that New England colleges do practice affirmative action—but without lowering the bar for minority students.

Editorial Board. "Georgia on Our Mind." *Wall Street Journal,* August 30, 2001, p. A12. An analysis of race-based preferences in college admissions in light of the latest court decision, which ruled against affirmative action programs at the University of Georgia. However, affirmative action law is far from clear, and the Supreme Court has not ruled on this issue since 1978. The editorial calls on the Supreme Court to hand down a decision that will finally resolve the confusion.

Editorial Board. "Identity Politics." *Christian Science Monitor,* August 29, 2001, p. 10. The editorial considers the ironies of Secretary of State Colin Powell not attending a United Nations conference on racism because of an Arab campaign to equate Zionism with racism, while a federal court rules that race-based admissions programs at the University of Georgia cannot ensure diversity.

Editorial Board. "In Search of Diversity." *Denver Post,* September 4, 2001, p. B6. Regardless of what happens with affirmative action, say the writers, self-destructive issues in the black community such as teen pregnancy, drug use, and anti-intellectual youth culture are also important barriers to minority enrollment.

Editorial Board. "Initiative 200: Wrong Direction for This State." *Seattle Times,* April 5, 1998, B6. According to the editorial, I-100 would be just as bad for Washington as its predecessor, Proposition 209, was for California, where the number of black and Latino students entering state universities has fallen drastically.

Editorial Board. "Jury Still Out on Talented 20." *South Florida Sun-Sentinel,* August 14, 2001, p. 18A. The board feels that it is still too early to evaluate Governor Jeb Bush's Talented 20 plan, which replaced race-based criteria with a blanket guarantee of college admissions to all students ranking in the top 20 percent of their high school graduating classes.

Editorial Board. "Legal Guidance." *Fort Worth Star Telegram,* June 27, 2001, p. 12. The board calls on the Supreme Court to "provide clarity on affirmative action," in the wake of its refusal to rule on *Hopwood v. Texas,* a 1996 case that ended affirmative action at the University of Texas.

Editorial Board. "UGA Not Root of Diversity Problem." *Atlanta Journal Constitution*, September 4, 2001, p. A10. The editors argue that affirmative action is the wrong way to achieve racial equality.

Editorial Board. "Poor Timing, Good Policy." *Los Angeles Times*, November 25, 2001, p. M4. The editorial reviews the University of California Regents' recent decision to use "comprehensive review" in admissions—a policy that allows a student's overcoming of personal hardship to be a factor in admissions decisions. Critics have charged that the policy is a backdoor way of allowing race to be a factor, despite the 1996 passage of Proposition 209, which outlawed affirmative action in the state.

Editorial Board. "Wrongheaded on Race." *Washington Post*, July 2, 2001, p. A16. The Washington, D.C., Circuit Court of Appeals recently declined to review an opinion that struck down the Federal Communications Commissions equal opportunity rules for the broadcasters it licenses; the editorial board opposes this decision.

Egelko, Bob. "Court Overturns Laws on Minority Job Goals; Statutes Didn't Include Quotas, But Treated Races Differently." *San Francisco Chronicle*, September 5, 2001, p. A3. A state appellate court strikes down California laws that set goals for increasing women and minorities in state jobs and contracts.

———. "Suit against Contra Costa Dismissed." *San Francisco Chronicle*, November 30, 2001, p. A25. A judge rules that the Contra Costa County policy on awarding construction contracts shows no evidence of discrimination, though discriminatory effects may result. The ruling is in response to a 1998 suit brought by women and minority contractors.

Ely, Jane. "In Need of Face-Value Talk on Race Relations." *Houston Chronicle*, April 15, 1997, p. 32. The author calls for more open, honest communications about race.

Ervin, Keith. "Parents Challenge Seattle District on Racial 'Tiebreaker.'" *Seattle Times*, July 19, 2000, p. B1. Parents challenge a school-choice plan in Seattle that uses race as a tiebreaker to determine where students shall be sent when they cannot get into their first-choice schools, claiming that the plan is illegal under I-200, the ballot measure that abolished affirmative action statewide in 1998.

Ettlin, David Michael. "Judge Says Race Not Factor in Rejection by UM Medical School; Lawyer Plans Appeal." *Baltimore Sun*, August 16, 2001, p. 1B. A white applicant named Robert Farmer is charging that racial discrimination led to his rejection by the University of Maryland School of Medicine; his lawsuit was dismissed by a federal judge in Baltimore.

Everett, Jana. "PC: Do the Demands of Political Correctness Create Community—Or Corrupt It?" *Denver Post*, August 26, 2001, p. D1. The author defends political correctness as part of a politics of inclusion that can build community.

Fairchild, Denise G. "Commentary: Affirmative Action Is Good for the State's Economy." *Los Angeles Times*, December 10, 2000, p. M5. The author, founder and president of the Los Angeles–based Community Development Technologies Center, argues that there is strong evidence that excluding "minority businesses from mainstream opportunities threatens the Southern California economy."

Fairchild, Halford H. "Commentary: SAT's 'Halo Effect' Casts a Long Shadow." *Los Angeles Times*, February 26, 2001, p. B7. The author, a professor of psychology and black studies at Pitzer College, argues that the SAT is "a poorly defined test that reflects racial and economic privileges . . . [and] reproduces sex, race, and class inequalities."

"Fewer Black Freshmen Enter University of Florida." *Jet*, vol. 100, no. 12, September 3, 2001, p. 40. Since Governor Jeb Bush has banned affirmative action in public university admissions in Florida, the number of black freshmen has dropped by almost half; from almost 12 percent of the freshman class in 2000 to about 6 or 7 percent in 2001. California and Texas also saw steep declines in minority enrollment after affirmative action programs were ended.

Fields, Gary. "Bush Delays Offensive against Affirmative Action." *Wall Street Journal*, August 13, 2001, p. A14. The Bush administration has asked the Supreme Court to uphold a federal minority set-aside program; despite the administration's general distaste for affirmative action, the administration is legally bound to uphold existing federal law.

Filaroski, P. Douglas. "All Eyes on One Florida's Effect on Campaign." *Florida Times-Union*, March 11, 2000. An analysis of Governor Jeb Bush's efforts to abolish affirmative action in Florida.

Finefrock, Don. "Judge Refuses to Stop Minority Set-Asides." *Miami Herald*, October 5, 1999. U.S. District Judge William Hoeveler refuses to grant a preliminary injunction halting a Miami-Dade County affirmative action program for minority architects and engineers, despite the request of two Coral Gables firms.

Finn, Chester E., Jr. "The Cost of College Sports." *Commentary*, October 2001, vol. 112, no. 3, pp. 53–57. College sports are involved with both the "shoddy quality" of U.S. education and the "rocky terrain of affirmative action," in this critique by a writer in the conservative magazine *Commentary*.

Finn, Peter. "School's First Female 'Rats' Talk of Intimidating Rituals." *Houston Chronicle*, May 18, 1998, p. 18. A report on the status of women at Virginia Military Institute (VMI), one year after female "rats"—first-year students—are first admitted to the formerly all-male school.

Firestone, David. "U. of Georgia Cannot Use Race in Admission Policy, Court Rules." *New York Times*, August 27, 2001, p. A1. A federal appeals court panel finds that the University of Georgia's race-based preferences in admissions are unconstitutional.

"First Female Cadets 'Breakout' at VMI." *The Chronicle of Higher Education*, vol. 44, no. 29, March 27, 1998, p. A8. A report on the experience of the first female students at the formerly all-male Virginia Military Institute (VMI) after women have "broken out" of the intensive hazing meted out to all first-year students.

Fish, Stanley. "Reverse Racism: Or How the Pot Got to Call the Kettle Black." *Atlantic Monthly*, vol. 272, no. 5, November 1993, p. 128. A respected literary critic argues against the concept of reverse racism, pointing out that "When the deck is stacked against you in more ways than you can even count, it is small consolation to hear that you are now free to enter the game and take your chances."

Fix, Sybil. "Citadel Ends Year with Big Changes." *Charleston Post and Courier*, May 17, 1997. The Citadel, a formerly all-male school, announces big changes in its Fourth Class (first-year) system, as a result of the problems that occurred when the first four women students entered in fall 1996; two of the women left the school in January 1997, charging sexual harassment and physical abuse at the hands of fellow students.

———. "Citadel, Justice Reach Agreement." *Charleston Post and Courier*, May 18, 1997. The U.S. Justice Department and the Citadel reach agreement on a plan for more successful assimilation of incoming female students. The Citadel, a formerly all-male school, admitted four female students in August 1996; two of the students left the school in January 1997, charging sexual harassment and physical abuse at the hands of fellow students.

Fletcher, Michael A. "Michigan Admissions Policy Rejected: Ruling Muddles Legal Status of Affirmative Action at Colleges." *Washington Post*, March 28, 2001, p. A2. A federal judge rejects the use of race in admissions at the University of Michigan law school, even though a December 2000 ruling had allowed race to be considered in admissions to the undergraduate school.

Foer, Franklin. "Best Intentions." *New Republic*, vol. 223, no. 13, October 2, 2000, pp. 26–29. An analysis of the contradictions in President George W. Bush's positions on race and civil rights; while the president portrays himself as supportive of civil rights, there are several disturbing features of his actual political record.

Freedberg, Louise. "Why the GOP Can't End Affirmative Action." *San Francisco Chronicle*, May 17, 1998, p. 7. The author analyzes why Congress has repeatedly voted against attempts to end affirmative action on a national scale despite vocal Republican opposition to affirmative action from Newt Gingrich and others.

Garrow, David J. "The Path to Diversity? Different Differences." *New York Times*, September 2, 2001, p. 4. A look at the impact of the court decision that struck down the University of Georgia's affirmative action program.

Gearan, Anne. "Justices Admit Confusion in Affirmative Action Case; Colorado Firm Claims It Has Lost Business Due to Discriminatory Policy." *St. Louis Post-Dispatch*, November 1, 2001, p. A12. Coverage of the Supreme Court hearing of the *Adarand* case, which the Supreme Court justices found confusing despite their previous agreement to hear the case.

Gehring, John. "Eyeing Campus Diversity." *Education Week*, vol. 20, no. 43, August 8, 2001, pp. 42–45. An exploration of the effects of *Hopwood v. Texas*, the court case that ruled against affirmative action at the University of Texas; the author questions the effectiveness of the race-neutral means colleges have been using to boost minority enrollment in place of affirmative action.

George, Maryanne. "Expert: Asians 'Pawns' in U-M Admissions Case." *Detroit Free Press*, February 13, 2001. Howard University law professor Frank Wu testifies that the achievements of Asian Americans have been misused to discredit the abilities of African Americans; Wu was speaking at the trial engendered by a challenge to affirmative action at the University of Michigan's law school.

———. "U-M Goes to Court Today to Defend Its Affirmative Action; Admissions Outcome Could Set a Precedent." *Detroit Free Press*, November 16, 2000. Reporting on the beginning of the federal trial to determine whether the University of Michigan law school can use race as one factor in determining admissions.

———. "U-M Law School Admissions Stall: Injunction Appealed While Applicants Wait during a Busy Season." *Detroit Free Press*, March 29, 2001. University of Michigan lawyers prepare to appeal the ruling banning race as a factor in admissions to the law school; meanwhile, the application process for the law school has stalled.

Gose, Ben, and Peter Schmidt. "Ruling against Affirmative Action Could Alter Legal Debate and Admissions Practices." *Chronicle of Higher Education*, vol. 48, no. 2, September 7, 2001, p. A36. An analysis of the U.S. Circuit Court of Appeals' ruling against the University of Georgia's affirmative action policies.

Gottlieb, Jeff. "Orange County; UCI Gets Grant to Hire, Retain More Women" *Los Angeles Times*, October 10, 2001, p. B3. The University of California, Irvine, gets a $3.45 million five-year grant to hire and retain female professors in the sciences, engineering, and the school of management.

Graves, Rachel, and Lori Rodriguez. "Candidates' Rhetoric Rises in Affirmative Action Debate; Bell, Brown Support City's Program; Sanchez's Stance Vacillates." *Houston Chronicle*, August 20, 2001, p. A17. City Councillor Orlando Sanchez is the sole opponent of affirmative action among the three major candidates for mayor of Houston.

Greenhouse, Linda. "In a New Climate of Unity, Justices Face Divisive Issues." *New York Times*, October 1, 2001, p. 16. Greenhouse looks at the upcoming Supreme Court season, which will include a major case on affirmative action.

———. "Justices to Revisit Affirmative Action in a Test Case for Bush." *New York Times*, March 27, 2001, p. A15. The Supreme Court accepts a constitutional challenge to a federal contracting law that sets aside a certain number of opportunities for minority-owned businesses; the case will be a test for the Bush administration, which opposes affirmative action but is legally bound to defend federal law.

———. "Making the Supreme Decision." *New York Times Upfront*, October 1, 2001, pp. 16–18. In an article for teenagers, Greenhouse reviews the upcoming Supreme Court season, including an important case on affirmative action.

Guinier, Lani. "The Real Bias in Higher Education." *New York Times*, June 24, 1997, p. A19. An op-ed piece by a renowned supporter of affirmative action, claiming that the real bias in higher education is not against white people, as the recent spate of affirmative-action suits have claimed.

Guinier, Lani, and Gerald Torres. "Credit Bush Doesn't Deserve." *New York Times*, August 8, 2000, p. A27. Commentators who support affirmative action argue that presidential candidate George W. Bush does not deserve the credit he is getting for being a moderate in race relations.

Hatfield, Larry D. "Top Court Sidesteps Affirmative Action Case; Ruling Stands That Texas Program Hurts Whites." *San Francisco Chronicle*, June 25, 2001, p. A1. The U.S. Supreme Court refuses to rule in *Hopwood v. Texas*, a 1996 case that abolished a University of Texas affirmative action program on the grounds that it discriminated against white people.

Healy, Patrick. "Affirmative Action Is Found Strong at Colleges in N.E." *Boston Globe*, October 16, 2001, p. A1. Coverage of the Nellie Mae Foundation study, which found a widespread use of affirmative action at northeastern colleges—and which also found that institutions in no way "lowered the bar" for minority students.

———. "Conflicting Court Rulings." *Chronicle of Higher Education*, vol. 42, no. 35, May 10, 1996, p. A35. An analysis of *United States v. Fordice*, a 1992 court ruling that required 19 states, including Texas, to wipe out traces of segregation in their public-college systems; this ruling would seem to conflict with the Supreme Court ruling in *Hopwood v. Texas*

(1996), which found that the affirmative action program at the University of Texas at Austin's law school discriminated against white applicants.

――――. "Judge Throws Out Race-Based Admissions: On Michigan Campus, Two Distinct Policies." *Boston Globe*, March 28, 2001, p. A3. A federal judge rules against race-based admissions to the University of Michigan's law school, despite a previous ruling in December 2000 permitting the undergraduate school to take account of race.

――――. "Low, High Marks for Grade Inflation." *Boston Globe*, October 7, 2001, p. A33. Harvard professor Harvey C. Mansfield charges that grade inflation began in the late 1960s when professors gave unduly high grades to new black students in order to boost the students' self-esteem; his remark provokes a controversy.

Healy, Thomas. "Old Policy Trumps New in Affirmative Action; Bush Administration Finds Itself Defending Clinton-era Program." *Baltimore Sun*, August 14, 2001, p. 1A. The Bush administration's decision to defend a federal contracting program that gives racial preferences to minorities puzzled some observers; but many lawyers believe that the move reflects a long-standing policy that the Justice Department must defend all federal laws before the Supreme Court, regardless of whether it agrees with them.

Hebel, Sara. "Education Department Releases Final Version of Guide on Use of Test Scores in Admissions." *Chronicle of Higher Education*, vol. 47, no. 17, January 5, 2001, p. A31. A report on the final version of a guidebook issues by the U.S. Education Department's Office for Civil Rights on the use of standardized tests; the guidebook supports "the fair use of tests."

――――. "U. of Georgia Won't Appeal Affirmative-Action Case to Supreme Court." *Chronicle of Higher Education*, vol. 48, no. 13, November 23, 2001, p. A23. A report on the University of Georgia's decision to accept an appeals court ruling that forbids the school from using race as a factor in admissions decisions for undergraduates.

Higginbotham, A. Leon, Jr., "Breaking Thurgood Marshall's Promise." *New York Times*, January 18, 1998, p. F28. An editorial lamenting the decline in the Supreme Court's support of civil rights since the retirement of civil rights pioneer Justice Thurgood Marshall.

Himelstein, Linda, with Stephanie Anderson Forest. "Breaking Through: How Do Some Companies Help Women Get Ahead While So Many Miss the Boat?" *Business Week*, February 17, 1997, p. 64. An analysis of the different approaches to women executives and managers among various U.S. corporations and businesses.

Holder, Eric, and Neal Kayal. "The Strong Case for Campus Diversity." *Washington Post*, June 27, 2001, p. A25. Holder, a former U.S. deputy attorney general and U.S. attorney; and Kayal, a Georgetown University law professor, argue that campus diversity is an important goal. They decry the "constitutional confusion" caused by the Supreme Court's declining to review two federal appeals court cases: one that allows the University of Washington law school to maintain its affirmative action program; the other that bans affirmative action at the University of Texas.

Holland, Gina. "Bush Defends Racial Set-Asides." [Albany] *Times-Union*, August 12, 2001, p. A3. In a renewal of the *Adarand* case before the Supreme Court, the Bush administration defends the use of racial preferences in a highway program, not because Bush supports affirmative action, but because he is bound to support existing federal law.

———. "Court to Tackle Business Issues; Rulings Will Involve Affirmative Action, Identity Theft; Others." *Detroit News*, October 1, 2001, p. 6. A look at the upcoming Supreme Court season, which will include a major affirmative action case.

———. "No Affirmative Action Ruling; Supreme Court Drops Plans to Decide High-Profile Case." *Houston Chronicle*, November 28, 2001, p. 9. Coverage of the Supreme Court decision not to decide *Adarand*, a major affirmative action case that might have helped define nationwide policy.

Holzer, Harry J., and David Neumark. "Assessing Affirmative Action." *Journal of Economic Literature*, vol. 38, 2000, pp. 483–595. A comprehensive review of more than 200 scientific studies of affirmative action, showing that affirmative action policies have produced tangible benefits for the economy as a whole, as well as for women and minorities.

———. "What Does Affirmative Action Do?" *Industrial and Labor Relations Review*, vol. 53, no. 2, January 2000, p. 240. A key study analyzing the economic effects of affirmative action, showing that such policies produce tangible benefits for women and minority business owners, workers, and students, as well as measurable benefits for the economy as a whole.

Hong, Peter Y. "Diversity Driven by the Dollar." *Los Angeles Times*, May 26, 1998, p. 1. A Toyota dealership in southern California features a diverse sales force—not out of principle, but due to economic necessity: the company needs sales agents who can speak Mandarin, Spanish, and Tagalog to appeal to the area's diverse population.

Hoppe, Christy. "High Court Declines to Address *Hopwood*; Race Still Can't Be Factor in College Admissions." *Dallas Morning News*, June 26, 2001, p. 1A. The U.S. Supreme Court declines to hear the *Hopwood* case, in which the University of Texas was barred from using race as a factor in admissions.

———. "Affirmative Action Ruling Allowed to Stand; UT Hopes Justices Will Restore Race to Admissions." *Dallas Morning News*, May 30, 2001,

p. 15A. The U.S. Supreme Court has let stand a decision allowing the University of Washington law school to use affirmative action; officials at the University of Texas hope that someday they, too, may be able to reinstate affirmative action, which was ruled unconstitutional in a 1996 Fifth Circuit Court of Appeals case, *Hopwood v. Texas.*

Hull, Dana. "Thousands at UC-Berkeley Rally for Affirmative Action." *San Jose Mercury News,* March 9, 2001. Thousands of students rally at the University of California, Berkeley, to demand that the university system reverse its 1995 ban on affirmative action.

Hunt, Albert R. "A Persuasive Case for Affirmative Action." *Wall Street Journal,* February 3, 2001, p. A23. A column supporting affirmative action for college admissions on the grounds that they promote diversity.

Jones, Mondella S. "Who's Qualified?" *Black Issues Book Review,* vol. 3, no. 5, September/October 2001, p. 10. A review of *Who's Qualified?* by Lani Guinier and Susan Sturm; the book questions traditional means of measuring merit and supports affirmative action as pointing the way toward new definitions of "being qualified."

Jost, Kenneth. "The Issues: Affirmative Action." *CQ Researcher,* vol. 11, no. 32, September 21, 2001, p. 21. An analysis of affirmative action.

Kaminer, Wendy. "Politics of Identity." *American Prospect,* vol. 12, no. 17. September 24–October 8, 2001, pp. 32–33. The liberal author suggests that liberals learn from President George W. Bush's affirmative action program, which illustrates the shortcomings of identity politics.

Kazin, Michael. "Cybercapitalism's Manifesto: Policy for a Brave New World." *New York Observer,* October 8, 2001, p. 10. A review of *The Radical Center: The Future of American Politics,* by Ted Halstead and Michael Lind, a book that calls for equal funding for all the nation's schoolchildren and other universal safety nets that would replace affirmative action's notion of race with a more generally applicable notion of class.

Kiefer, Peter. "SAG Report Finds There's Still Plenty of Room Left for Diversity." *Hollywood Reporter,* August 14, 2001. Despite the gains of minority actors in theater and television, more than three-quarters of all the roles in Hollywood go to white performers, according to a newly released Screen Actors Guild (SAG) report.

King, Marsha. "Business Leaders in Poll Stress Need for Diversity Education." *Seattle Times,* September 17, 1998, p. B4. Most business leaders in Washington State believe that U.S. society is growing apart, but that college courses about diversity can help bring people together. The poll was undertaken even as I-200, the initiative that would ban affirmative action statewide, was slated for a November vote.

———. "California Regent Enlists in Local Anti-preference Initiative." *Seattle Times,* August 5, 1997, p. B1. Ward Connerly, who spurred a successful anti–affirmative action campaign in California, is beginning a similar campaign in Washington State.

Kinsley, Michael. "Commentary: What Happened to Advice and Consent?" *Los Angeles Times*, July 1, 2001, p. M5. The liberal columnist questions the conservative effort to limit the Senate's "advice and consent" role in judicial nominations.

Krauthammer, Charles. "Affirmative Action Fails Again." *Washington Post*, July 13, 2001, p. A21. Krauthammer, a noted conservative critic of affirmative action, decries the "shibboleth of diversity" that is leading the University of California to seek what he calls "backdoor" methods of reintroducing affirmative action after it was banned in California in 1996 by Proposition 209.

Lane, Charles. "Supreme Court: On the Sidelines for Now." *Washington Post*, September 30, 2001, p. A5. As a new Supreme Court season begins, the *Adarand* case promises to offer new rulings on affirmative action.

Lederman, Douglas. "Texas Asks High Court to Uphold Legality of Affirmative Action." *Chronicle of Higher Education*, vol. 42, no. 35, May 10, 1996, p. A35. A report on the Texas university system's efforts to overturn *Hopwood*, a circuit court ruling that found the university's use of affirmative action in admissions to be unconstitutional.

"Legally Blind to the Problem." *San Francisco Chronicle*, September 7, 2001, p. A24. The State Court of Appeals unanimously denies state agencies the tools needed to identify and change racially skewed hiring patterns, ruling that five state laws designed to help women and minorities learn about and compete for state jobs and contracts are invalid under Proposition 209, the 1996 initiative that ended affirmative action in California.

Lewis, Diane E. "Student Finds Views of Race Diverge." *Boston Globe*, January 20, 2002, p. K2. A study released by an institute associated with Rutgers University finds that African Americans have considerably lower expectations of how they will be treated by employers than do their white counterparts.

Lewis, Neil. "Administration Backs Affirmative Action Plan." *New York Times*, August 11, 2001, p. A11. The Bush administration asks the Supreme Court to uphold a Transportation Department program that was intended to help minority contractors.

Lichtblau, Eric. "Bush Changes Stance on Affirmative Action; Position Hailed by Civil Rights Activists." *Houston Chronicle*, August 11, 2001, p. 2. In a Supreme Court case, the Bush administration defends a federal program that sets aside contracts for minority-owned enterprises, not because of a commitment to affirmative action, but because of an obligation to defend existing federal law.

Annotated Bibliography

Locke, Michelle. "Admission Policy Would Weight Hardships; Some Say Proposal in Calif. to Revive Affirmative Action." *Boston Globe*, November 15, 2001, p. A2. Coverage of the University of California regents' decision to adopt a policy known as comprehensive review, which takes into account the personal hardships a student had to overcome. Critics of the policy charge that it is a way of evading the 1996 proscription against using race as a criterion in admissions decisions.

———. "Minority College Enrollment Rising." Associated Press. April 4, 2001. African-American and Latino admissions to the University of California seem to have rebounded from a sharp decline after the 1995 ban on affirmative action within the state university system. However, fewer minorities are enrolling at the system's top campuses but instead are attending less prestigious universities.

———. "UC Regents Repeal Ban on Racial Preferences: It Doesn't End Prop. 209 But Sends a Welcoming Message, Advocates Say." Associated Press Online, May 17, 2001. Regents of the University of California unanimously repeal their 1995 ban on using racial preferences to help determine college admissions, despite the ongoing ban on racial and gender preferences in California under Proposition 209.

Lords, Erik. "Expert: Aptitude Tests Are Biased; He Says U-M's Policy Can Correct Imbalance." *Detroit Free Press*, February 7, 2001. Standardized tests for college and law school admissions are inherently biased against women and minority applicants according to Martin Shapiro, a testing specialist and psychology professor at Emory University and an expert witness in the federal trail to determine the constitutionality of race-based criteria for admission to the University of Michigan's law school.

———. "Expert: Colleges Must Fight Racism; Witness for U-M Says Its Policy Can Help Heal." *Detroit Free Press*, January 25, 2001. Professor and civil rights leader John Hope Franklin calls for affirmative action and antiracist measures as a way to heal divisions among all races; Franklin was testifying at the trial resulting from a challenge to the University of Michigan's affirmative action program.

———. "Michigan's Affirmative Action Cases to Be Heard by a Full Circuit Court." *Black Issues in Higher Education*, vol. 18, no. 19, November 8, 2001, p. 10. An analysis of the upcoming Supreme Court hearing of two landmark University of Michigan court cases concerning affirmative action in admissions policies.

Lords, Erik, and Maryanne George. "Affirmative Action Debated; Judge Hears Arguments from U-M Lawyers, Critics." *Detroit Free Press*, November 17, 2000. U.S. District Judge Patrick Duggan says that he might be able to decide one of two legal questions in the University of Michigan affirmative action case without a complete trial; both the plaintiffs and the defendants had asked for a ruling without a trial.

————. "Jackson Leads Protest over U-M Case: He Says Students Should Fight Court's Decision." *Detroit Free Press*, March 30, 2001. Nearly 1,000 students gather to hear civil rights leader Reverend Jesse Jackson call for protest over a court decision that race cannot be a factor in admissions to the University of Michigan's law school.

————. "Trial on U-M Race Rule Is Done; Students Get Last Word; Judge's Ruling Awaited." *Detroit Free Press*, February 17, 2001. A group of affirmative action supporters testifies at the trial resulting from a challenge to affirmative action in admissions at the University of Michigan's law school.

————. "U-M Law School's Race Policy Rejected." *Detroit Free Press*, March 28, 2001. A federal judge rejects race as a factor in admissions at the University of Michigan law school despite a 2000 case that allowed race to be taken into account in undergraduate admissions.

Lords, Erik, and Mary Owen. "Students Express Surprise: Achieving Diversity in Future, Effect on Morale and Theme." *Detroit Free Press*, March 28, 2001. Students respond to the federal court ruling that race cannot be a factor in admissions to the University of Michigan law school; they are particularly surprised in the wake of a December 2000 decision allowing race as a factor in undergraduate admissions.

Lum, Lydia. "Black Students' Struggles to Integrate Cause Doubts of Acceptance." *Houston Chronicle*, August 25, 1997, p. 6. A look at the historical context of the 1996 *Hopwood* case, which banned affirmative action at the University of Texas; the article describes the experience of the first black students to attend the University of Texas, Austin, after it formally desegregated in 1950.

————. "Difference of Opinion about *Hopwood;* U.S Official Backs Race-Based Stances." *Houston Chronicle*, March 26, 1997, p. 1. U.S. Department of Education assistant secretary for civil rights Norma Cantu writes to Texas attorney general Dan Morales, chastising him for taking too broad an interpretation of *Hopwood*. The *Hopwood* decision held that race could not be a factor in admissions in Texas public colleges and universities.

————. "Freshman Fallout." *Houston Chronicle*, August 24, 1997, p. 1. A look at the minority freshmen choosing not to attend the University of Texas in the wake of the 1996 *Hopwood* decision, which banned affirmative action in the university's admissions decisions.

————. "Law Schools Want State to Allocate More Money for Recruitment of Minorities." *Houston Chronicle*, September 6, 1998, p. 33. Texas law school deans ask the state legislature for funds to recruit more minority students, in response to the 1996 *Hopwood* court case, which ended affirmative action in university admissions.

————. "Minorities Heading Out of State for Professional Schools." *Houston Chronicle*, August 25, 1997, p. 1. The 1996 *Hopwood* ban on affirmative action in Texas university admissions has seemed to spur an exodus of minority students, who are choosing to attend law schools and medical schools located out of state.

————. "Minority Enrollment: How to Stop the Hemorrhaging." *Houston Chronicle*, August 24, 1997, p. 19. Educators in Texas struggle to stop the flow of minority students out of state in response to the 1996 *Hopwood* decision, banning affirmative action in university admissions.

————. "Minority Rolls Cut by Hopwood; Undergrad Level at UT Posts Hike." *Houston Chronicle*, September 16, 1997, p. A15. Black and Latino enrollment at Texas's largest university has fallen because of the drop in minorities at the university's law and graduate schools; meanwhile, the number of black and Latino freshmen at the University of Texas, Austin, rose slightly. Officials are unsure of what caused the increase in freshmen, but attribute the drop in older students to the 1996 *Hopwood* case, which ended affirmative action in Texas's public university system.

————. "Proposals Seek More Minorities at UT, A&M." *Houston Chronicle*, October 5, 1998, p. 1. Two years after the *Hopwood* decision ended affirmative action in Texas university admissions, the Texas legislature seeks to attract minority students by increasing financial aid.

————. "Texas A&M Enrolls Fewer Minorities: University Officials Cite Hopwood Case." *Houston Chronicle*, September 20, 1997, p. 30. Enrollment of black and Latino freshmen at Texas A&M University is down sharply, apparently in response to the 1996 *Hopwood* decision ended affirmative action in state university admissions.

————. "University Applications by Minorities Down: State's Largest Universities See Drop in Wake of Hopwood Case." *Houston Chronicle*, April 8, 1997, p. 1. The 1996 *Hopwood* decision banning affirmative action in state university admissions decisions had led to a dramatic drop in the number of minorities applying to attend the system's largest universities.

————. "UT Faculty Supports Diversity: Minority Numbers Likely to Stagnate." *Houston Chronicle*, August 28, 1997, p. 41. University of Texas law school faculty fear that the 1996 affirmative action ban resulting from the *Hopwood* case will cause the number of minority students to remain at its current low level.

Mabin, Connie. "School Drops Efforts to Use Affirmative Action in Admissions; Texas University Will Not Appeal." *Boston Globe*, November 28, 2001, p. A9. The University of Texas decides to drop all further possible appeals in the *Hopwood* case in light of a June 2001 decision by the U.S. Supreme Court not to hear the case. The university could have appealed some minor portions of the case but chooses not to.

Mailman, Stanley. "California's Proposition 187 and Its Lessons." *New York Law Journal*, January 3, 1995, p. 3. An analysis of California's Proposition 187, the legislation that denies illegal immigrants public services and requires doctors and health care workers to report children whose parents are suspected of being in the United States illegally.

Malveaux, Julianne. "Reparations and Affirmative Action: What You Owe Me." *Black Issues in Higher Education*, vol. 18, no. 16, September 27, 2001, p. 47. An exploration of the issues of reparations for slavery and affirmative action; the author argues that ongoing discrimination against people of color is ignored while the spurious issue of reverse discrimination is promoted.

Mann, Judy. "Just Say Yes to Affirmative Action." *Washington Post*, October 20, 2000, p. C11. An editorial supporting affirmative action in the context of the Bush-Gore presidential debate over the topic.

Marshall, William. "Commentary: Preferences for the Rich Grease the Way to College." *Los Angeles Times*, May 21, 2001, p. B11. The author, a law professor at the University of North Carolina at Chapel Hill and the former deputy White House counsel under President Clinton, challenges opponents of affirmative action to join him in criticizing "wealth preferences," whereby students receive preferred treatment by colleges on the basis of wealth.

McAllister, Bill. "High Court to Rehear Colorado Bias Case: Fate of Affirmative Action May Be at Stake." *Denver Post*, October 1, 2001, p. A1. A look ahead at the Supreme Court's term, which will include a look at *Adarand*, a case that could redefine the future of affirmative action.

McCarthy, Rebecca. "UGA Enrolls Fewer Blacks; Ruling on Admissions Policy Cited." *Atlanta Journal Constitution*, August 29, 2001, p. A1. As soon as the University of Georgia's affirmative action policy was ruled unconstitutional, the school saw a 20 percent drop in new African-American freshmen and a 40 percent drop in applications from African-American high school seniors.

———. "UGA: No More Hedging: Admissions Factors Limited to Academics." *Atlanta Journal-Constitution*, November 30, 2001, p. A1. A look at how University of Georgia admissions are affected now that affirmative action in admissions has been banned at that school.

McCarthy, Rebecca, and Bill Rankin. "Court Rejects UGA Effort to Enroll More Minorities." *Atlanta Journal Constitution*, August 28, 2001, p. A1. A report on the federal appeals court ruling on the University of Georgia's affirmative action policy.

McCormick, Richard. "Race and the University: Why Social Justice Leads to Academic Excellence." *Seattle Times*, March 19, 2000, p. B7. The author reports that I-200, which outlawed affirmative action in Washington in 1998, had led to a sharp decline in the numbers of minority freshmen enrolled at the University of Washington. In the author's view, the lack of racial diversity has seriously compromised the academic excellence of the state educational system.

McWhorter, John. "Commentary: Why I Don't Want Reparations for Slavery." *Los Angeles Times*, July 15, 2001, p. 5. The author, an associate professor of linguistics at UC Berkeley, and the author of *Losing the Race: Self Sabotage in Black America*, explains that "the only way for human beings to succeed is through individual initiative," so as an African-American man, he feels offended by the notion of reparations.

Meyer, Eugene L. "Williams Diversifying College Faculty; Goal Is to Reflect County Population." *Washington Post*, August 23, 2001, p. PGE9. President Ronald A. Williams sees the resignation of 25 veteran faculty and staff from Prince George's Community College as a great opportunity to diversify the predominantly white faculty, many of whom had been hired when the majority of the student body was white; now, most students at the school are black.

Morain, Dan. "5 State Laws Fall Victim to Prop. 209, Affirmative Action: An Appeals Court Strikes Down Statutes Aimed at Helping Women and Minorities Win Jobs and Contracts." *Los Angeles Times*, September 5, 2001, p. B1. A state appellate court strikes down major affirmative action laws in California, on the grounds that they violate Proposition 209, the initiative that ended affirmative action in California in 1996.

Moritz, John. "Cornyn Asks That High Court Review College Admissions Case." *Fort Worth Star-Telegram*, April 17, 2001, p. 1. Texas attorney general John Cornyn asked the U.S. Supreme Court to review the *Hopwood v. Texas* case, in which race was barred as a factor in admissions at a Texas law school; the Supreme Court had refused to hear the case in 1996.

Murakami, Kery. "King County Makes Changes to Conform with I-200." *Seattle Times*, December 4, 1998, p. B3. King County in Washington State will end its policy of requiring that women and minorities be interviewed for any job that becomes open, in response to the passage of I-200, a ballot measure that ended affirmative action in the state.

Nakashima, Ellen. "Bush Weighs Help for Minority Firms; New Rules Would Ease Bidding for U.S. Jobs Being Privatized." *Washington Post*, September 6, 2001, p. A1. The Bush administration considers a significant change in contracting rules that would make it easier for women- and minority-owned businesses to get federal contracts.

Affirmative Action

Navarette, Ruben, Jr. "Bush Turning Out to Be Skillfully Unpredictable." *Chicago Tribune*, August 15, 2001, p. 21. The author, a columnist for the *Dallas Morning News*, argues that President George W. Bush is trying to have it both ways: He wants to make the Republican Party more welcoming to Latinos and African Americans, but he also opposes affirmative action, which most minorities support.

Nichols, Hans S., and Erin Condon. "Courts Continue to Move Away from Racial Preferences." *Insight on the News/Washington Times*, September 24, 2001, p. 6. A look at the 11th U.S. Circuit Court of Appeals decision that the University of Georgia's race-based admissions policies are unconstitutional.

Nickens, Tim. "Bush Backing Off Deal on Suit over Districts." *St. Petersburg Times*, August 19, 1999, p. 1A. Florida governor Jeb Bush is reconsidering a deal he had signed earlier that would have removed African-American voters from the south Florida congressional districts of two prominent black Democrats.

Nickens, Tim, and Peter Wallsten. "2000 Is Targeted for Vote on Race: Critics Denounce a California Businessman's Plans for a Florida Campaign against Affirmative Action." *St. Petersburg Times*, March 16, 1999, p. 1A. Ward Connerly, who got successful anti–affirmative action measures on the ballot in California and Washington State, has now begun a similar campaign in Florida, despite opposition from Florida Democrats.

Novoa, Jose. "At Times, the Problem Is Economics, Not Racism." *Los Angeles Times*, September 28, 1997, p. 2. The author argues that affirmative action has benefited middle-class people of color far more than working people and the poor.

O'Sullivan, John. "Preferred Members." *National Review*, vol. 53, no. 17, September 3, 2001, p. 19. The conservative journal looks at affirmative action and the upcoming *Adarand* case, a Supreme Court case that promises to have a major impact on affirmative action policies.

Page, Clarence. "The Never-Ending Tap Dance around Affirmative Action: What's with Bush's U-Turn on Racial Goals?" *Chicago Tribune*, August 15, 2001, p. I21. The author asserts that President George W. Bush is trying to "have it both ways" on affirmative action: He has not attacked it, but he has not been an advocate for it, either.

Parnes, Amie. "Enrollment Data Feed Rift on Florida Policy." *Boston Globe*, September 9, 2001, p. A19. A report on responses to the efforts of Florida governor Jeb Bush to end affirmative action in Florida.

Phillips, Melanie. "Home Truths." *Wall Street Journal*, August 28, 2001, p. A12. A review of *An Old Wife's Tale*, the autobiography of Midge Decter, who argues that modern feminism is a revolt against motherhood and womanhood itself; Decter also opposes affirmative action.

Pendleton, Randolph, and Thomas B. Pfanjuch. "Sit-in over Governor's Initiative: Lawmakers Ask Bush to Rescind One Florida." *Florida Times-Union*, January 19, 2000. Two African-American lawmakers stage a sit-in in Lieutenant Governor Frank Brogan's office saying that they will not leave until Governor Jeb Bush rescinds his plan to eliminate affirmative action in Florida.

"A Pleasant Normalcy." *St. Louis Post-Dispatch*, October 4, 2001, p. B6. A look at the new U.S. Supreme Court term, which will include another look at the *Adarand* case—a case that could determine the future of affirmative action.

Postman, David, and Lynda V. Mapes. "I-200 Lacks Lawmakers' Votes: It's Likely Headed for Ballot." *Seattle Times*, February 10, 1998, p. A1. Because the Washington state legislature will not pass I-200, the measure will probably go to the voters in November; I-200 would ban affirmative action statewide.

Pressley, Sue Anne. "Reno Vows 'Vigorous' Campaign, Ex-Attorney General Mutes Criticism of Jeb Bush—For Now." *Washington Post*, September 5, 2001, p. A3. Former U.S. attorney general Janet Reno enters the race for Florida governor as a Democratic candidate.

———. "Texas Students, Faculty Protest Racial Remarks: Rally Is Urged to Make Law Professor a 'Pariah.'" *Washington Post*, September 17, 1997, p. A03. A report on a racial incident at the University of Texas law school.

Price, Hugh B. "Merit Means More Than Test Scores." *Los Angeles Times*, May 15, 1996, p. B9. The president and chief executive officer of the National Urban League, a civil rights group, argues that the attack on affirmative action misses a key point: Qualities that make good workers, leaders, and entrepreneurs are not necessarily measured by test scores or other "objective" evaluations.

Pucci, Carol. "Minority Conventions Are Shunning Washington." *Seattle Times*, August 27, 2000, p. K1. The number of minority conventions in Washington has been "decimated" thanks to the passage of I-200, a ballot measure that ended affirmative action in Washington State in 1998.

"Racial Diversity at College." *Providence Journal*, January 27, 2001, p. A06. A criticism of affirmative action made in the context of the affirmative action policy at the University of Michigan and the lawsuit brought by Jennifer Gratz, the white undergraduate applicant who was unable to gain acceptance at the university's prestigious Ann Arbor campus.

Ratcliffe, R. G. "Senate Approves Bill Designed to Boost Minority Enrollments." *Houston Chronicle*, May 9, 1997, p. 1. The Texas Senate passes legislation that would replace affirmative action with a race-neutral system of boosting minority enrollment, namely, requiring state universities to automatically accept the top 10 percent of every high school graduating class, and maintaining an admissions policy that includes a number of subjective factors—but not race. The legislation is in response to the 1996 *Hopwood* decision, which found affirmative action in state college admissions to be unconstitutional.

Rayburn, Laurel. "Women to Watch: Caroline Wong." *Ms.*, October/November 2001, vol. 11, no. 6, pp. 10–11. Caroline Wong is a national outreach counselor for the Coalition to Defend Affirmative Action and Integration by Any Means Necessary (BAMN). She also encouraged a group of students to become independent defendants in an affirmative action case at the University of Michigan.

"Recent Actions Bring Affirmative Action to Foreground." *The Presidency*, winter 2001, vol. 4, no. 1, p. 11. Three recent court decisions have fueled debate about affirmative action: the federal appeals court decision upholding affirmative action in *Smith v. University of Washington;* the federal district court decision upholding affirmative action in *Gratz v. Bollinger;* and the justices reviewing *Hopwood v. Texas*, who found for the university on several points.

Reich, Robert B. "Commentary: Amid the Mess, It's the Same Ol' Same Ol'." *Los Angeles Times*, November 16, 2000, p. B11. The former secretary of labor, currently a professor at Brandeis University, argues that the new center of power in the United States lies with the moderates of both parties, and charges that the power to resolve any controversial issue—including affirmative action—will shift from the political parties to the federal courts.

Reinhard, Beth. "Broward GOP Leaders: Review County Policies." *Miami Herald*, November 11, 1999. The Broward County Republican Party applauds Florida governor Jeb Bush's plan to end affirmative action in Florida.

Riley, Jason L. "The 'Diversity' Defense." *Commentary*, vol. 111, no. 4, April 2001, pp. 24–27. Riley deplores the shortcut of assuming that race represents an individual's entire experience, an assumption that he argues is the foundation of affirmative action policies in educational admissions.

Ritter, Scott. "High Court Rejects Appeal Concerning Affirmative Action." *Wall Street Journal*, November 28, 2001, p. B2. A look at the Supreme Court's dismissal of the *Adarand* case, which had potentially been a major affirmative-action landmark decision. However, the Court decided not to rule on the matter.

Rivera, Ray. "UW Unveils Plan for Scholarships." *Seattle Times*, October 21, 2000, p. A11. The University of Washington plans a $65.6 million scholarship proposal to restore freshman minority numbers on campus to the levels that obtained before Initiative 200, the ballot initiative that abolished affirmative action statewide.

Roberts, David, and Marc Levin. "What Does Bush Owe Black Democrats? Nothing." *Houston Chronicle*, January 9, 2001, p. A17. The authors argue that the "wishy-washy" strategy on race promoted by both President George W. Bush and his brother, Florida governor Jeb Bush, failed to prevent an energized minority Democratic turnout and instead discouraged unionized voters in swing states from voting Republican.

Romano, Lois. "Positioned for a Call to Justice." *Washington Post*, July 10, 2001, p. C1. White House counsel Al Gonzales may become the first Latino to serve on the Supreme Court; meanwhile, he is reluctant to discuss affirmative action, which the Bush administration opposes. He says he supports equal opportunity but opposes "special treatment because of race" and "quotas," even though he himself "has probably been helped because of his race."

Rosenberg, Paul. "New Look at Perils of Testing: Affirmative Action Issues Prove Complex." *Denver Post*, September 16, 2001, p. K6. A review of *Who's Qualified*, a book by Lani Guinier and Susan Sturm, which defends affirmative action by criticizing the supposed norm of standardized testing, suggesting that such tests do not in fact measure performance very well. Guinier was an early Clinton nominee to head the Justice Department's civil rights division; her nomination was later withdrawn when conservatives labeled her the "quota queen" because of her support for affirmative action.

Sack, Joetta L. "Counsel Pick Seeks to Dispel Democrats' Doubts." *Education Week*, vol. 21, no. 2, September 12, 2001, p. 26. Despite criticism by congressional Democrats for his opposition to affirmative action, Brian W. Jones asserted that if confirmed as the Department of Education's general counsel, he would protect the rights of the disadvantaged in education.

Sanchez, Rene. "University of Calif. Broadens Admission Criteria." *Washington Post*, November 15, 2001, p. A8. Coverage of the University of California's decision to adopt the admissions policy called comprehensive review, which allows committees to take into account a student's history of overcoming personal hardship. Critics of the policy claim it is another race-based program, like those that were outlawed in California in 1996.

Satel, Sally. "How Racial Preferences Refuse to Die." *New York Post*, January 31, 2001. Commenting on the case of Robert Farmer, a rejected white applicant to the University of Maryland's medical school who claimed that he had been discriminated against, Satel takes issue with using race-based criteria to determine admissions. Satel is a psychiatrist, author of *PC, MD—How Political Correctness Is Corrupting Medicine* (Basic Books, 2001), and an expert witness in Farmer's case.

Saunders, Jim. "Protestors Await Bush." *Florida Times-Union,* March 7, 2000. Thousands of protestors gather to send the message that Governor Jeb Bush's plan to eliminate affirmative action could devastate women and minorities. Protestors include U.S. Representative Corrine Brown, a Jacksonville Democrat.

———. "Regents Unanimous for One Florida." *Florida Times-Union,* February 18, 2000. The Florida Board of Regents approves Governor Jeb Bush's One Florida initiative, a move to end affirmative action in the state.

Savage, David G. "Adarand Didn't Add Up." *ABA Journal,* vol. 88, no. 26, January 2002, p. 26. The end of the *Adarand* case is analyzed, with an eye toward the case's impact on affirmative action.

———. "Court Lets Stand Ruling against Race Preference." *Los Angeles Times,* July 2, 1996, p. 1 The Supreme Court refused to hear an appeal of the *Hopwood* case, causing confusion among many observers, who had expected the Court to rule on the case and set a national precedent. The lower court's ruling had found unconstitutional the state university's use of affirmative action in admissions.

———. "Unlikely Backer of Affirmative Action Emerges; Race: Conservative Solicitor General Defends Clinton-Era Policy. U.S. Hiring Efforts Are under Supreme Court Review." *Los Angeles Times,* November 1, 2001, p. A26. Ironically, Theodore B. Olson, the attorney who brought the *Hopwood* suit, is now solicitor general and so acts to defend Clinton-era affirmative action policies before the Supreme Court.

Schevitz, Tanya. "Critics Say Plan Fails to Counter Image of Bias." *San Francisco Chronicle,* May 16, 2001, p. A4. An analysis of the debate around the University of California Board of Regents' attempt to lift its 1995 ban on using race as one factor in admissions decisions; the regents' decision is complicated by the ongoing ban on affirmative action in California under Proposition 209.

———. "Illegal Scholarships Costly to UC Diego; Audit Finds Campus Needs Extra $1 Million to Pay for Violating Affirmative Action Ban." *San Francisco Chronicle,* September 11, 2001, p. A3. An internal audit for the University of California says that the University of California, San Diego, must raise an extra $1 million to pay for obligations incurred in a now-canceled scholarship program that, according to the attorneys, illegally targeted underrepresented minorities.

———. "Protesters Slam UC Admissions Policy: Noisy UCLA Crowd Storms Hall, Calls for Reversal of Affirmative Action Ban." *San Francisco Chronicle,* March 15, 2001, p. A3. An angry crowd of University of California students demand that a 1995 ban on affirmative action in university admissions be rescinded; their noisy protest forces the cancellation of a mayoral debate and wins support from various politicians.

———. "UC Regents Ask for Research on Admission Plan; Some See Threat to Standards." *San Francisco Chronicle*, October 18, 2001, p. A19. The University of California Board of Regents is considering a plan to institute comprehensive review, which allows admissions committees to take into account a student's overcoming of personal hardship. This article about the regents' exploration of the plan includes a great deal of helpful background information on the policy, which was eventually adopted.

———. "UC San Diego Told Scholarships May Be Illegal Under Prop. 209." *San Francisco Chronicle*, July 23, 2001, p. A6. The University of California, San Diego, has been warned by its lawyers that its Millennium Scholarships, which are privately funded, may be illegal because they are designed to attract minority students to the school; Proposition 209, passed in 1996, outlawed all forms of affirmative action in California.

———. "UC Widens Chance of Gaining Admission; Policy Approved to Aid Minorities, Disadvantaged." *San Francisco Chronicle*, July 20, 2001, p. A1. The University of California Board of Regents approves a dual admissions program expected to dramatically increase the number of minority and disadvantaged students at the school. Since affirmative action in California was banned by Proposition 209 in 1996, officials have sought various avenues to attract underrepresented students.

Schmidt, Peter. "Opposing Sides Argue Their Cases in Key Affirmative-Action Suit." *Chronicle of Higher Education*, vol. 48, no. 16, December 14, 2001, p. A24. A report on the federal appeals court hearing of affirmative action cases relating to the University of Michigan's law school and undergraduate programs.

Schrag, Peter. "Backing off *Bakke*." *Nation*, vol. 262, no. 16, April 22, 1996, p. 11. A look at the 1996 ballot initiative to end affirmative action in California, led by the California Civil Rights Initiative.

Segal, David. "Putting Affirmative Action on Trial; D.C. Public Interest Law Firm Scores Victories in War on Preferences." *Washington Post*, February 20, 1998, p. A1. Coverage of the Committee for Individual Rights (CIR), a Washington, D.C.–based public interest law firm that seeks candidates for class-action suits against affirmative action.

Selingo, Jeffrey. "U. of Texas at Austin Ends Minority-Hiring Program." *Chronicle of Higher Education*, vol. 45, no. 19, January 15, 1999, p. A38. The University of Texas, Austin, ends a $300,000-a-year program aimed at recruiting minority professors, fearing that it might be barred by the *Hopwood* decision, which led the university to abandon affirmative action in admissions.

Sharlot, M. Michael, and Herma Hill Kaybym. "Affirmative Action Was a Success: Public Law Schools Must Be More Creative to Keep Attracting Minority Students." *Los Angeles Times*, August 29, 1997, p. B9. The deans of the UC Berkeley and University of Texas schools of law analyze how affirmative action policy has affected their institutions.

Simmons, Kelly. "Considering 'Legacies' in Admissions Attacked." *Atlanta Constitution*, September 5, 2001, p. B1. African-American leaders argue that if affirmative action is outlawed, then legacies—the preference given to children of alumni—should also be ended.

Sowell, Thomas. "Slavery Reparations Create Black Victims." *Detroit News*, August 5, 2001, p. 12. According to black conservative economist Thomas Sowell, "Blacks have already been the first victims of the campaign to get reparations for slavery," because reparations will never happen, while the vast majority of black people lose the good will of the larger society as the campaign for reparations progresses.

Steinberg, Jacques. "At Odds with Harvard President, Black-Studies Stars Eye Princeton." *New York Times*, December 29, 2001, p. A1. A report on the controversy between Harvard University president Lawrence Summers and the school's Afro-American studies department, which had clashed over Summers's alleged lack of support for affirmative action and reported criticism of Professor Cornel West.

———. "Defending Affirmative Action with Social Science." *New York Times*, December 17, 2000, A41. An analysis of affirmative action in light of developments in the University of Michigan case.

———. "Redefining Diversity." *New York Times*, August 29, 2001, p. A14. The ban on affirmative action in admissions at the University of Georgia calls upon colleges to expand their notions of diversity to go beyond race as a general category and look at every applicant as an individual—a process that may be beyond the means of large public universities. Affirmative action at elite private colleges, on the other hand, may remain intact.

———. "U.S. Appeals Court Hears Debate over Race-Based Admissions." *New York Times*, December 7, 2001, p. A27. A report on the appeals court hearing of arguments over the affirmative action programs at the University of Michigan's undergraduate and law schools.

Sturrock, Carrie. "Cal Activists: Can the Ban." *Contra Costa Times*, March 2, 2001. Students organize to overturn a 1995 ban on affirmative action in the University of California system.

———. "Connerly Starts Push to End Tracking Race: UC Regent Begins Gathering Signatures to Ensure the Measure Will Appear on Ballot in 2002." *Contra Costa Times*, April 14, 2001, p. A01. Ward Connerly, a University of California regent, has begun collecting signatures on an initiative to outlaw keeping statistics by race in university admissions, school district composition, and a host of other areas. Connerly fought successfully for a 1995 ban on affirmative action by the University of California Board of Regents, and he chaired the committee for the 1996 ballot measure, Proposition 209, that ended affirmative action in the state. Connerly is attempting to get his new initiative on the ballot in March 2002.

———. "New Debate on UC Race Preference: Regents Likely Will Approve a Compromise That Doesn't Repeat But 'Replaces' the Ban on Affirmative Action." *Contra Costa Times*, May 13, 2001. Coverage of the debate surrounding the likelihood that regents of the University of California will repeal their 1995 ban on using racial preferences to help determine college admissions, despite the ongoing ban on racial and gender preferences in California under Proposition 209.

———. "Regents Rally for Diversity. Repeal of the 1995 Ban on Racial Preferences Would Be a 'Symbolic Step' toward Making UC More Accessible, Advocates Say." *Contra Costa Times*, February 18, 2001. Coverage of the efforts among regents of the University of California to overturn their 1995 ban on affirmative action at the university.

———. "UC Makes the Grade for Minority Students: System Credits Program for Accepting Top Applicants Regardless of SAT Scores, Outreach for Increases; State Natives' Acceptance Is Up." *Contra Costa Times*, April 4, 2001. The percentage of minority students at the University of California has now nearly reached affirmative action levels, thanks to outreach efforts and a new program that admitted the top 4 percent of each high school graduating class regardless of SAT scores.

Timberg, Craig. "Judge Ends U.S. Oversight of VMI Coeducation Efforts." *Washington Post*, December 8, 2001, p. B5. A report on the ending of the federal oversight of the Virginia Military Institute (VMI) effort to integrate women into the formerly all-male school.

Traub, James. "The Class of Prop. 209." *New York Times*, May 2, 1999, p. F44. The education reporter for *The New Yorker* reports on the results of California's ending of affirmative action at public colleges and universities.

Trounson, Rebecca, and Kenneth R. Weiss. "Numbers of Blacks, Latinos Admitted to UC System Rise. Education: Outreach Efforts Are Paying Off, Official Says, 'But We Have a Long Way to Go.' Levels Still Lag at UCLA, Berkeley." *Los Angeles Times*, April 4, 2001, p. A3. After a drop in minority enrollment due to a 1995 ban on affirmative action, African-American and Latino admissions to the University of California have begun to increase dramatically. However, minority enrollment still lags at the system's top schools, UCLA and Berkeley.

Tucker, Cynthia. "Ruling Ignores Importance of Diversity." *Denver Post*, September 2, 2001, p. E5. A look at the court decision to overturn the University of Georgia's affirmative action policies.

Tucker, Cynthia. "UGA Ruling Sets Back Hopes for Racially Diverse Campuses." *Atlanta Journal-Constitution*, August 29, p. A20. The author takes issue with the ruling of judges in the University of Georgia affirmative-action case, in which the judges banned race as a factor in admissions while claiming that a black suburban student might not contribute to on-campus diversity. The author accuses the judges of imagining that afflu-ent black and white teenagers growing up in the same suburb share a common experience—but, she argues, they do not; racism eventually confronts every person of color, no matter how wealthy.

Van Slambrouck, Paul. "View of Post–Affirmative Action America." *Christian Science Monitor,* April 2, 1998, p. 1. The University of California reports a dramatic drop in minorities admissions now that affirmative action has been ended in California as a result of the 1996 initiative known as Proposition 209.

Vandenabeele, Janet Naylor, and Jodi S. Cohen. "U-M Race Policy Declared Illegal." *Detroit News,* March 28, 2001. The University of Michigan appeals a federal court ruling banning race as a factor in admissions to the law school; this article examines the implications of the ruling for the University of Michigan.

———. "U-M Suits Head to Court; Cases Center on College's Race-Based Admissions Policy." *Detroit News,* September 9, 2001, p. C1. Lawyers will argue the University of Michigan's affirmative action suit before the sixth U.S. Circuit Court in Cincinnati on October 23.

Varner, Lynne K. "Blacks Feeling Unease about I-200." *Seattle Times,* October 23, 1998, p. A1. Tension is high among the 3.4 percent of Washington voters who are African American; they have a wide variety of feelings about I-200, the measure that would end affirmative action statewide.

———. "Jackson; I-200 Not Minority Issue." *Seattle Times,* September 2, 1998, p. B1. Reverend Jesse Jackson says that if every person who had ever benefited from affirmative action voted against I-200—the ballot measure that would ban affirmative action statewide—the measure would be defeated.

Verhovek, Sam Howe. "For 4 Whites Who Sued University, Race Is the Common Thread." *New York Times,* March 23, 1996, p. A6. A look at the four white students who sued the University of Texas in the *Hopwood* case.

Wallsten, Peter. "Quotas Foe Will Fight in Florida: Californian Ward Connerly Says His Polls Show the State Is Ready for a Ballot Initiative Effort to End Affirmative Action." *St. Petersburg Times,* March 14, 1999, p. 1A. Ward Connerly, who led successful initiatives in California and Washington State to end affirmative action, is beginning a similar campaign in Florida.

Walsh, Edward. "Affirmative Action's Confusing Curriculum: Ruling against University of Georgia's System Is Latest in Series of Conflicting

Annotated Bibliography

Court Decisions." *Washington Post,* September 4, 2001, p. A2. An analysis of the court decision overturning affirmative action at the University of Georgia, as well as other recent legal decisions.

———. "Rulings Could Further Muddle Affirmative Action for Colleges." *Houston Chronicle,* September 12, 2001. An analysis of where affirmative action now stands in the wake of the court decision on the University of Georgia's race-based admissions policies.

Walsh, Mark. "Appeals Court Rejects Preferences at U. of Ga." *Education Week,* vol. 21, no. 1, September 5, 2001, p. 4. An analysis of the federal court decision striking down affirmative action at the University of Georgia.

Washington, Wayne. "Ashcroft Supports Affirmative Action Rule; Files a Brief Backing Policy in Colorado Case." *Boston Globe,* August 11, 2001, p. A3. U.S. Attorney General John Ashcroft files a brief supporting federal affirmative action policy in the *Adarand* case as it comes before the Supreme Court; the Bush administration does not support affirmative action but feels bound to uphold federal law.

Weinstein, Michael M. "A Reassuring Scorecard for Affirmative Action." *New York Times,* October 17, 2000, p. A30. An editorial reporting on a review of over 200 studies of affirmative action, published in the *Journal of Economic Literature,* showing that affirmative action "produces tangible benefits for women, for minority entrepreneurs, students and workers, and for the overall economy."

Weiss, Kenneth R. "Applications to UC Hit a Record High: But the Number of African Americans and Latinos Seeking Admission Falls for Second Year in a Row." *Los Angeles Times,* February 5, 1997, p. 3. Weiss reports on the decline in minority applicants to the University of California system two years after Proposition 209 ended affirmative action in the state.

———. "Minority Applications to UC Rise. Education: Blacks and Latinos Post Double-Digit Percentage Increases. *Los Angeles Times,* January 31, 2001, p. 3. Record numbers of African-American and Latino students are applying to the University of California, suggesting that diversity in the University of California system has returned after declining in the wake of the regents' 1995 ban on affirmative action.

Werner, Erica. "'Minority' Has Uncertain Future." Associated Press. May 8, 2001. An analysis of the changing racial and ethnic composition of California, in the wake of census figures revealing that non-Hispanic whites make up only 47 percent of the state's population; the first time whites were not in the majority since accurate census reports were available.

Wheat, Jack. "Bush Plan Aids College Skills, Educators Say." *Miami Herald,* November 12, 1999. Higher education officials applaud portions of Florida governor Jeb Bush's plan to end affirmative action, saying that the governor's plan attacks "head on" the problem of too few minority students having the skills and background to gain admission to and succeed in college.

Wieberg, Steve. "Bush's Pick to Enforce Title IX Raises Concerns." *USA Today*, September 27, 2001, p. C2. President Bush appointed Gerald Reynolds, a staunch opponent of affirmative action and former president of the conservative Center for New Black Leadership, to serve as the U.S. Department of Education's assistant secretary for civil rights.

Wilgoren, Jodi. "Judge May Rule in Admissions Case without Trial." *New York Times*, November 17, 2000, p. A16. Continuing coverage of the federal trial over whether race-based criteria can be used in admissions decisions at the University of Michigan law school.

———. "Law School Wins Reprieve on Admissions Policy." *New York Times*, April 6, 2001, p. A16. A federal appeals panel allows the University of Michigan's law school to continue using affirmative action in admissions, pending the appeal of a lower court ruling.

———. "U.S. Court Bars Race as Factor in School Entry." *New York Times*, March 28, 2001, p. A1. A federal judge in Detroit rules against the race-conscious system of admissions to the University of Michigan's law school, contradicting a parallel case in December 2000 that upheld affirmative action in undergraduate admissions.

Will, George. "Affirmative Action Out of Control." *Washington Post*, March 1, 2001, p. A19. The conservative columnist argues that affirmative action was originally supposed to be a remedial and temporary measure, not—as current supporters argue—a means of achieving diversity on campus. The danger with the current rationale, Will argues, is that it makes affirmative action in higher education "a potentially permanent servant of institutions' interests rather than a theoretically temporary assistance for blacks."

Williams, John. "Same-Sex Benefits Put on November Ballot." *Houston Chronicle*, September 27, 2001, p. 1. Houston City Council put a referendum on the November 6 ballot to ban same-sex benefits; the referendum would also ban affirmative action benefiting gay men and lesbians.

Woodward, Calvin. "Diversity Means Many Things to Bush." Associated Press. March 29, 2001. President Bush has a broad notion of diversity that goes beyond simply hiring women and minorities, according to administration official Clay Johnson; the president also likes diverse opinions among his staff.

Wooten, Jim. "UGA Case Ideal: Chance to Reinforce Ruling Challenging Diversity Rates." *Atlanta Journal-Constitution*, August 29, 2001, p. A20. The author argues that the University of Georgia affirmative action case raises the central issue of whether race ensures diversity and whether that is a worthy goal; he hopes that the Supreme Court will use this case to make a ruling that could determine national policy.

Young, Cathy, and Michael Lynch. "Internal Constraints." *Reason*, October 2001, vol. 33, no. 5, pp. 36–41. A profile of John McWhorter, author of the controversial *Losing the Race: Self-Sabotage in Black America*, an African-American author highly critical of affirmative action.

Zernike, Kate. "Black Scholars Mending a Rift with Harvard." *New York Times*, January 4, 2002, p. A1. A report on the apparent end to the controversy between Harvard president Lawrence Summers and the school's Afro-American studies department, which resulted from Summers's alleged failure to declare support for affirmative action and reported criticism of Professor Cornel West.

WEB DOCUMENTS

Affirmative Action. Available online. URL: http://www.africana.com/Articles.tt_606.htm. Downloaded on April 14, 2002. A useful summary, chronology, and history of affirmative action.

Affirmative Action and Diversity Project: A Web Page for Research. Available online. URL: http://www.aad.english.ucsb.edu. Downloaded on April 14, 2002. An incredibly comprehensive website put together by supporters of affirmative action; includes articles from many U.S. newspapers dating back to 1996, along with a chronology of affirmative action events for each year; focused coverage and news reports on events at the University of Michigan; coverage and news reports on Proposition 209 and I-200; bibliographies; commentary; pending state and federal legislation; information on court cases; and a great deal of other useful information.

Beyond Self-Interest: APAs toward a Community of Justice. Available online. URL: http://www.sscnet.ucla.edu/aasc/policy/index.html. Downloaded on April 14, 2002. This analysis of affirmative action by Four "Asian Pacific American" (APA) law professors, was prepared by UCLA's Asian-American Studies Center.

California Votes No! on 209; California Votes No! on CCRI: Available online. URL: http://www.ajdj.com/noccri/. Downloaded on April 14, 2002. The website of a coalition of groups originally dedicated to defeating California ballot measure Proposition 209, now dedicated to overturning it. Proposition 209 was the initiative sponsored by the California Civil Rights Initiative, led by Ward Connerly, that resulted in the banning of affirmative action statewide. The website has news updates on affirmative action issues in California, as well as links to other groups.

Chronicle of Higher Education. Available online. URL: http://chronicle. merit.edu. Downloaded on April 14, 2002. The *Chronicle of Higher Education* is available at this site, with the latest news on all issues affecting higher education, including affirmative action.

The Disability Rights Activist. Available online. URL: http://www. disrights.org. Downloaded on April 14, 2002. A newsletter with extensive information about disability rights.

Doctorate Recipients from United States Universities: Summary Report 1998. Available online. URL: http://www.nsf.gov/sbe/srs/srs00410/. Downloaded on April 14, 2002. An online version of a report on the recipients of doctorate-level degrees from U.S. universities.

A History and Timeline of Affirmative Action. Available online. URL: http://www.infoplease.com/spot/affirmative.htm. Downloaded on April 14, 2002. A useful summary of basic information about affirmative action, including a time line and details about affirmative action history.

Hopwood. Available online. URL: http://www.law.utexas.edu/hopwood. Downloaded on April 14, 2002. A pro–affirmative action site, created by the University of Texas, with information about *Hopwood v. Texas*, the landmark case in which the University of Texas law school was sued by Cheryl Hopwood, a white applicant, for discriminating against her on the basis of race. In response, the law school created this site with background information about the case, news stories from the *Houston Chronicle*, research, statistics, a bibliography, and other resources.

Ito, Robert. "Going Anti-Native: Affirmative Action Foes Are Putting Programs to Help Native Hawaiians on Trial." *Mother Jones* Available online. URL: www.motherjones.com/web_exclusives/features/news/hawaii.html. Downloaded on April 14, 2002. Efforts to create "race-neutral" policies in Hawaii are challenging programs designed to help native Hawaiians.

Social Psychology. Available online. URL: http://www.socialpsychology. org/affirm.htm. Downloaded on April 14, 2002. The article "10 myths about Affirmative Action" is available at this address.

Thomas: Legislative Information on the Internet. Available online. URL: http://thomas.loc.gov. Downloaded on April 14, 2002. A service of the Library of Congress, this comprehensive search engine offers information on federal legislation, congressional committee activity, and congressional legislation. To find out the latest federal development on affirmative action, key in "affirmative action" to the search engine.

Annotated Bibliography

Townhall.com. Available online. URL: http://www.townhall.com/columnists. Downloaded on April 14, 2002. The archives and current writing of more than 60 conservative columnists on a wide variety of topics, including affirmative action. Columnists include such prominent conservatives as Mona Charen, Linda Chavez, Ann Coulter, and Charles Krauthammer.

CHAPTER 8

ORGANIZATIONS AND AGENCIES

The organizations and agencies in this section represent a broad range of groups and institutions. Listed here are government agencies charged with oversight of various affirmative action policies; legal and political organizations that concern themselves with affirmative action as one aspect of a broader political agenda; membership and advisory groups designed to educate personnel officers and other officials on affirmative action policy; and organizations specifically focused on affirmative action issues. Every effort has been made to include groups on all sides of the issue, as well as to include the major figures in the legal and political arenas.

American Association for Affirmative Action
1600 Duke Street
Suite 700
Alexandria, VA 22314
Tel: (800) 252-8952 or (703) 299-9285
Fax: (703) 299-8822
URL: http://www.affirmative action.org.
The American Association for Affirmative Action is an association of professionals involved in human resources programs, including programs involving affirmative action, equal opportunity, and diversity. Its website features primarily information about the organization itself, but

there is an excellent page of links to government websites and the sites of other organizations. A good starting place for someone researching affirmative action regulations and policy, or for someone trying to enter the field of human resources.

American Civil Liberties Union
125 Broad Street
18th Floor
New York, NY 10004-2400
URL: www.aclu.org
This civil liberties group is also dedicated to civil rights and affirmative action and has joined in several court cases on affirmative action, civil rights, and discrimination.

American Civil Rights Institute
P.O. Box 188350
Sacramento, CA 95818
Tel: (916) 444-2278
Fax: (916) 444-2279
URL: http://www.acri.org/
The group headed by anti–affirmative action pioneer Ward Connerly, who helped to abolish affirmative action in California and Washington State. The group is dedicated to ending affirmative action nationwide. The website has information about the group's own activities as well as updates on legislation and other developments regarding affirmative action.

Americans against Discrimination and Preferences (AADAP)
c/o California Civil Rights Initiative/Prop. 209 (CCRI)
1537 4th Street #231
San Rafael, CA 94901
Tel: (415) 453-2347
Fax: (415) 721-0674
E-mail: cadap-209@microweb.com
URL: http://www.cadap.org; www.aadap.org
AADAP is the national organization that grew out of the California Civil Rights Initiative (CCRI), the group founded by Ward Connerly to overturn affirmative action in California via Proposition 209, the anti–affirmative action measure that passed in 1996. Their extensive website has news, updates, information, and analysis on a wide variety of affirmative action–related topics.

By Any Means Necessary (BAMN)
Coalition to Defend Affirmative Action & Integration and Fight for Equality by Any Means Necessary
BAMN c/o MSA Office
3909 Michigan Union
530 South State Street
Ann Arbor, MI 48109-1439

Coalition to Defend Affirmative Action and Integration and Fight for Equality by Any Means Necessary (BAMN)
ASUC Box 155
UC Berkeley
Berkeley, CA 94720-4510
Fax: 530-618-6867
URL: http://www.bamn.com
The website of the Coalition to Defend Affirmative Action and Integration and Fight for Equality by Any Means Necessary (BAMN) has a wide variety of materials, including an online version of the group's journal, *Liberator;* information about affirmative action fights in Michigan and Berkeley, California (the two places where the group is based); news of protest demonstrations; and other information about "fighting racism and sexism on campus."

Campaign for a Color-Blind America
P.O. Box 321
Aldie, VA 20105
E-mail: raceblind@aol.com
Tel: (703) 327-4533
Fax: (603) 925-2956

URL: http://www.equalrights.
com
A group dedicated to abolishing affirmative action and all race-based
preferences; the group includes
self-proclaimed civil rights activists
as well as social scientists and legal
scholars.

Center for Equal Opportunity
14 Pidgeon Hill Drive
Suite 500
Sterling, VA 20165
Tel: (703) 421-5443
Fax: (703) 421-6401
E-mail: comment@ceousa.org
URL: http://www.ceousa.org
A group dedicated to ending race-
based preferences and affirmative
action nationwide, founded in
1995 by prominent conservative
Linda Chavez.

Center for Individual Rights
1233 20th Street, NW
Suite 300
Washington, DC 20036
Tel: (202) 833-8400
Fax: (202) 833-8410
E-mail: cir@mail.wdn.com
URL: http://www.cir-usa.org
The Center for Individual Rights is
a public interest law firm specializ-
ing in anti–affirmative action cases;
it spurred the lawsuits against the
University of Michigan, among
other landmark cases.

Citizens' Commission
on Civil Rights
2000 M Street, NW
Suite 400

Washington, DC 20036
Phone: (202) 659-5565
Fax: (202) 223-5302
URL: http://www.cccr.org
This group is dedicated to "the revi-
talization of a progressive civil rights
agenda at the national level," on the
theory that "such an agenda benefits
the entire country, not just particular interest groups." The group is
committed to equal opportunity in
education, employment, and housing; "political and economic empowerment"; and "equal treatment
in the administration of justice,"
through "vigorous civil rights enforcement as a duty and obligation
of the federal government."

Civilrights.org, the Online
Social Justice Network
Leadership Conference
on Civil Rights
1629 K Street, NW
Suite 1010
Washington, D.C. 20006
Tel: (202) 466-3311
Fax: (202) 466-3435
URL: http:www.civilrights.org.
A "social justice network" supportive of affirmative action; the site includes a wide variety of links and
information, providing access to research, Supreme Court cases, other
civil rights groups, news and events,
and a host of other information resources.

College and University
Professional Association
for Human Resources
(CUPA-HR)

1233 20th Street, NW
Suite 1650
Washington, DC 20036-1250
Tel: (202) 429-0311
URL: http://www.cupahr.org/
feedback.htm
This group, founded more than 50
years ago, serves more than 6,500
human-resource administrators at
nearly 1,700 colleges and universities
as well as others interested in human
resources in higher education, including students and institutions.

Council for Disability Rights
205 West Randolph
Suite 1650
Chicago, IL 60606
Tel: (312) 444-9484
TDD: (312) 444-1967
Fax: (312) 444-1977
URL: http://www.disabilityrights.
org
A council devoted to equal rights for
the disabled, with assistance and in-
formation on the Americans with
Disabilities Act, special education,
and a host of other civil rights issues.

**Equal Employment Opportunity
Commission**
1801 L Street, NW
Washington, DC 20507
Tel: (202) 663-4900
TTY: (202) 663-4494
URL: http://www.eeoc.gov
The U.S. agency charged with
overseeing equal employment and
affirmative action under the 1964
Civil Rights Act. Their website offers information on how to file a
suit with the EEOC, the latest policy developments, and a great deal
of background information on federal policies, current lawsuits,
EEOC court briefs, and other
legal/legislative matters.

**Feminist Majority/Feminist
Majority Foundation**
1600 Wilson Boulevard
Suite 801
Arlington, VA 22209
Tel: (703) 522-2214
Fax: (703) 522-2219
E-mail: femmaj@feminist.org
or
8105 West Third Street
Los Angeles, CA 90048
Tel: (323) 651-0495
Fax: (323) 653-2689
URL: http://www.feminist.org
The website of the Feminist Major-
ity Foundation, offering informa-
tion about affirmative action on a
state and federal level.

**Labor Relations Reporter
Bureau of National Affairs**
1231 25th Street, NW
Washington, DC 20037
Tel: (800) 372-1033
E-mail: customercare@bna.com
URL: http://www.bna.com//rr
The Labor Relations Reporter is a
comprehensive source of labor and
employment law information; the
group is a division of the Bureau of
National Affairs.

**Legal Information Institute
Cornell Law School
Myron Taylor Hall**

Ithaca, NY 14853
E-mail: lii@lii.law.cornell.edu
URL: http://www.law.cornell.edu.
One of the best resources for affirmative law—or any other kind of law—available online. The LII offers access to Supreme Court cases and some lower court cases, as well as pages focusing on legislation regarding civil rights, equal protection, and employment discrimination.

The National Center for Public Policy Research
777 North Capitol Street, NE
Suite 803
Washington, DC 20002
Tel: (202) 371-1400
Fax: (202) 408-7773
E-mail: info@nationalcenter.org
URL: http://www.nationalcenter. org
A conservative policy and research institute whose areas of interest includes affirmative action; the website provides commentary, information about legislation, and links to a wide variety of other anti–affirmative action sites.

National Council of Women's Organizations
733 15th Street, NW
Suite 1011
Washington, DC 20005
Tel: (202) 393-7122
Fax: (202) 387-7915
E-mail: info@womens organizations.org
URL: http://www.womens organizations. org

A coalition of more than 100 women's groups, representing some 6 million members nationwide, this group is devoted to preserving affirmative action, among other issues.

National Association for the Advancement of Colored People (NAACP)
4805 Mt. Hope Drive
Baltimore, MD 21215
Tel: (410) 521-4939
URL: http:// www.naacp.org
The oldest civil rights group in the country supports affirmative action as part of its civil rights program.

National Minority Supplier Development Council
1040 Avenue of the Americas
2nd floor
New York, NY 10018
Tel: (212) 944-2430
Fax: (212) 719-9611
URL: http:// www.nmsdcus.org
An organization dedicated to developing strong business relationships between minority-owned businesses and corporate America; represents many businesses that receive or have received minority set-asides under government affirmative-action programs.

National Urban League
120 Wall Street
New York, NY 10025
URL: http//www.nul.org
This major civil rights organization fights for affirmative action

230

as part of its overall civil rights program.

**NOW Legal Defense
and Education Fund**
395 Hudson Street
New York, NY 10014
Tel: (212) 925-6635
Fax: (212) 226-1066
The National Organization for Women's Legal Defense and Education Fund focuses on issues of concern to women, including affirmative action.

**U.S. Department of Labor
Office of Federal Contract
Compliance Programs**
Room C-3325
200 Constitution Avenue, NW
Washington, DC 20210
Tel: (202) 693-0101
Office of the Ombudsperson
1 (888) 37-OFCCP
**URL: http://www.dol.gov/dol/
esa/public/ofcp_org.htm.**
The office of Federal Contract Compliance Programs monitors compliance with affirmative action according to executive orders and federal legislation and regulations. Its website has a great deal of information and statistics on employment opportunity and programs.

**Office of Small Business and
Minority Affairs**
Room C-2318

200 Constitution Avenue, NW
Washington, DC 20210
Tel: (202) 219-9148
Fax: (202) 219-9167
URL: http://www.dol.gov/osbma
The Office of Small Business and Minority Affairs deals with small and minority-owned businesses; minority- and female-owned businesses have been the recipients of affirmative action programs, while white-owned small businesses have often brought suit against race- and gender-based federal programs.

Pathways to College Network
330 Stuart Street
Boston, MA 02116-5237
**URL: http://www.pathwaysto
college.net**
This coalition, launched in 2000, of foundations, nonprofit organizations, educational institutions, and the U.S. Department of Education is committed to improving college access and success for "low-income, underrepresented minority, and first-generation students."

People for the American Way
2000 M Street, NW
Suite 400
Washington, DC 20036
Tel: (202) 467-4999
or (800) 326-7329
URL: http://www.pfaw.org
A liberal organization dedicated to civil liberties and civil rights; one of its particular fields of interest is affirmative action.

Society for Human Resource
Management
1800 Duke Street
Alexandria, VA 22314
Tel: (703) 548-3440
Fax: (703) 535-6490
URL: http://www.shrm.org
An organization of human-resource
professionals who manage affirma-
tive action in corporations and
other institutions.

Public Information Officer
Supreme Court of
the United States
Washington, DC 20543
Supreme Court
URL:http://www.supreme
courtus.gov.
The official website of the U.S.
Supreme Court, with the latest in-
formation about the Court's activi-
ties as well as archives of past cases
and other information.

Tarlton Law Library
Jamail Center for Legal
Research
University of Texas School of
Law
727 E. Dean Keeton Street
Austin, TX 78705
Tel: (512) 471-7726
E-mail: refdesk@mail.law.
utexas.edu
URL: http//www.law.utexas.edu
This law library site has a great deal
of information on *Hopwood v. Texas*,
the landmark affirmative action
case that ended affirmative action
in Texas.

United States Commission on
Civil Rights (USCCR)
624 Ninth Street, NW
Washington, DC 20425
For information about
publications, contact: Library,
USCCR (202) 376-8128
For congressional inquiries,
contact: Congressional Affairs
Unit, USCCR (202) 376-8317
For press inquiries, contact:
Public Affairs Unit, USCCR
(202) 376-8312
URL: http://www.usccr.gov
The commission is an independent,
bipartisan, fact-finding agency of
the executive branch, first established under the Civil Rights Act of
1957. On November 30, 1983, a
new commission was established
under the Civil Rights Act of 1983
(P.L. 98-183). The commission's
duties include collecting information on discrimination and serving
as a national clearinghouse for information about discrimination.

U.S. Census Bureau
Postal Address:
U.S. Census Bureau
Washington DC 20233
or
Street address:
4700 Silver Hill Road
Suitland, MD 20746
Email on population, including
historical figures: pop@
census.gov
Email on income, poverty,
housing, labor force,

occupations: hhes-info@
census.gov
URL: http//www.census.gov
A website offering Census 2000
data among other statistical information on employment, education,
and other information relating to
affirmative action.

United States Department of
Justice, Civil Rights Division
950 Pennsylvania Avenue, NW
Washington, DC 20530-0001
Tel: (202) 353-1555
The federal agency charged with
overseeing civil rights issues, in-
cluding affirmative action.

PART III

APPENDICES

APPENDIX A

CONSTITUTIONAL AMENDMENTS

The following constitutional amendments form the basis of affirmative action law. Most often cited in the court cases are the Fifth and the Fourteenth Amendments. However, the Thirteenth and the Fifteenth Amendments are part of the post–Civil War effort to extend equality to African Americans who were formerly slaves, while the Twenty-fourth Amendment represents the civil rights movement of the 1950s and 1960s, in which legal barriers to African-American equality were gradually struck down.

The Nineteenth Amendment guarantees women's right to vote. Passed in 1920 after nearly 75 years of agitation and protest on the part of women's groups, it remains the only constitutional reference to women's legal status. Although feminist groups of that time began to press for an equal rights amendment that would guarantee U.S. women full legal equality with men, in 2002 the ERA languishes just two states shy of ratification, with little expectation as of this writing that it will be passed any time in the near future.

AMENDMENT V

No person shall be held to answer for a capital, or otherwise infamous crime, unless on a presentment or indictment of a grand jury, except in cases arising in the land or naval forces, or in the militia, when in actual service in time of war or public danger; nor shall any person be subject for the same offense to be twice put in jeopardy of life or limb; nor shall be compelled in any criminal case to be a witness against himself, nor be deprived of life, liberty, or property, without due process of law; nor shall private property be taken for public use, without just compensation.

AMENDMENT XIII

Section 1. Neither slavery nor involuntary servitude, except as a punishment for crime whereof the party shall have been duly convicted, shall exist within the United States, or any place subject to their jurisdiction.

Section 2. Congress shall have power to enforce this article by appropriate legislation.

AMENDMENT XIV

Section 1. All persons born or naturalized in the United States, and subject to the jurisdiction thereof, are citizens of the United States and of the state wherein they reside. No state shall make or enforce any law which shall abridge the privileges or immunities of citizens of the United States; nor shall any state deprive any person of life, liberty, or property, without due process of law; nor deny to any person within its jurisdiction the equal protection of the laws.

Section 2. Representatives shall be apportioned among the several states according to their respective numbers, counting the whole number of persons in each state, excluding Indians not taxed. But when the right to vote at any election for the choice of electors for President and Vice President of the United States, Representatives in Congress, the executive and judicial officers of a state, or the members of the legislature thereof, is denied to any of the male inhabitants of such state, being twenty-one years of age, and citizens of the United States, or in any way abridged, except for participation in rebellion, or other crime, the basis of representation therein shall be reduced in the proportion which the number of such male citizens shall bear to the whole number of male citizens twenty-one years of age in such state.

Section 3. No person shall be a Senator or Representative in Congress, or elector or President and Vice President, or hold any office, civil or military, under the United States, or under any state, who, having previously taken an oath, as a member of Congress, or as an officer of the United States, or as a member of any state legislature, or as an executive or judicial officer of any state, to support the Constitution of the United States, shall have engaged in insurrection or rebellion against the same, or given aid or comfort to the enemies thereof. But Congress may by a vote of two-thirds of each House, remove such disability.

Section 4. The validity of the public debt of the United States, authorized by law, including debts incurred for payment of pensions and bounties for services in suppressing insurrection or rebellion, shall not be questioned. But neither the United States nor any state shall assume or pay any debt or obligation incurred in aid of insurrection or rebellion against the United States, or any claim for the loss or emancipation of any slave; but all such debts, obligations and claims shall be held illegal and void.

Section 5. The Congress shall have power to enforce, by appropriate legislation, the provisions of this article.

AMENDMENT XV

Section 1. The right of citizens of the United States to vote shall not be denied or abridged by the United States or by any state on account of race, color, or previous condition of servitude.

Section 2. The Congress shall have power to enforce this article by appropriate legislation.

AMENDMENT XIX

Section 1. The right of the citizens of the United States to vote shall not be denied or abridged by the United States or by any State on account of sex.

Section 2. Congress shall have power to enforce this article by appropriate legislation.

AMENDMENT XXIV

Section 1. The right of citizens of the United States to vote in any primary or other election for President or Vice President, for electors for President or Vice President, or for Senator or Representative in Congress, shall not be denied or abridged by the United States or any state by reason of failure to pay any poll tax or other tax.

Section 2. The Congress shall have power to enforce this article by appropriate legislation.

APPENDIX B

SUPREME COURT CASES

A great deal of affirmative action law has been hammered out in court decisions, particularly decisions of the U.S. Supreme Court. Questions of affirmative action in educational admissions, hiring, layoffs, seniority, and the awarding of business to minority-owned enterprises were all determined by Supreme Court decisions. Following are the syllabi (summaries) of some of the key Supreme Court decisions in this field. More extensive discussions of each case, as well as discussions of other important cases, can be found in chapter 2; cases that precede *Regents of the University of California v. Bakke* (1978) are discussed in chapter 1.

REGENTS OF THE UNIV. OF CAL. V. BAKKE (1978)

Regents of the University of California v. Bakke (1978) established the premise that "educational diversity" might be a legitimate goal of admissions policies—but that actual quotas were not constitutionally permissible.

SYLLABUS

The Medical School of the University of California at Davis (hereinafter Davis) had two admissions programs for the entering class of 100 students—the regular admissions program and the special admissions program. Under the regular procedure, candidates whose overall undergraduate grade point averages fell below 2.5 on a scale of 4.0 were summarily rejected. About one out of six applicants was then given an interview, following which he was rated on a scale of 1 to 100 by each of the committee members (five in 1973 and six in 1974), his rating being based on the interviewers' summaries, his overall grade point average, his science courses grade point average, his Medical College Admissions Test (MCAT) scores, letters of recommendation, extracurricular activities, and other biographical data, all of which resulted in a total "benchmark score." The full admissions committee then made offers of admission on the basis of their review of the applicant's file and his score, considering and acting upon applications as they were received. The committee chairman was responsible for placing names on the waiting list and had discretion to include persons with "special skills." A separate committee, a majority of whom were members of minority groups, operated the special admissions program. The 1973 and 1974 application forms, respectively, asked candidates whether they wished to be considered as "economically and/or educationally disadvantaged" applicants and members of a "minority group" (blacks, Chicanos, Asians, American Indians). If an applicant of a minority group was found to be "disadvantaged," he would be rated in a manner similar to the one employed by the general admissions committee. Special candidates, however, did not have to meet the 2.5 grade point cutoff and were not ranked against candidates in the general admissions process. About one-fifth of the special applicants were invited for interviews in 1973 and 1974, following which they were given benchmark scores, and the top choices were then given to the general admissions committee, which could reject special candidates for failure to meet course requirements or other specific deficiencies. The special committee continued to recommend candidates until 16 special admission selections had been made. During a four-year period, 63 minority students were admitted to Davis under the special program and 44 under the general program. No disadvantaged whites were admitted under the special program, though many applied. Respondent, a white male, applied to Davis in 1973 and 1974, in both years being considered only under the general admissions program. Though he had a 468 out of 500 score in 1973, he was rejected, since no general applicants with scores less than 470 were being accepted after respondent's application, which was filed late in the year, had been processed and completed. At that time, four special admission slots were still unfilled. In 1974 respondent applied early, and though he had a total score of 549 out of 600, he was again rejected. In neither year was his name placed on the discretionary waiting list. In both years, special applicants were admitted with significantly lower scores than respondent's. After his second rejection, respondent filed this action in state court for mandatory, injunctive, and declaratory relief to compel his admission to Davis, alleging that the special admissions program operated to exclude him on the basis of his race in violation of the Equal Protection Clause of the Fourteenth Amendment, a provision of the California Constitution, and §601 of Title VI of the Civil

Rights Act of 1964, which provides, *inter alia*, that no person shall on the ground of race or color be excluded from participating in any program receiving federal financial assistance. Petitioner cross-claimed for a declaration that its special admissions program was lawful. The trial court found that the special program operated as a racial quota, because minority applicants in that program were rated only against one another, and 16 places in the class of 100 were reserved for them. Declaring that petitioner could not take race into account in making admissions decisions, the program was held to violate the Federal and State Constitutions and Title VI. Respondent's admission was not ordered, however, for lack of proof that he would have been admitted but for the special program. The California Supreme Court, applying a strict scrutiny standard, concluded that the special admissions program was not the least intrusive means of achieving the goals of the admittedly compelling state interests of integrating the medical profession and increasing the number of doctors willing to serve minority patients. Without passing on the state constitutional or federal statutory grounds, the court held that petitioner's special admissions program violated the Equal Protection Clause. Since petitioner could not satisfy its burden of demonstrating that respondent, absent the special program, would not have been admitted, the court ordered his admission to Davis.

Held: The judgment below is affirmed insofar as it orders respondent's admission to Davis and invalidates petitioner's special admissions program, but is reversed insofar as it prohibits petitioner from taking race into account as a factor in its future admissions decisions.

MR. JUSTICE POWELL concluded:

1. Title VI proscribes only those racial classifications that would violate the Equal Protection Clause if employed by a State or its agencies.

2. Racial and ethnic classifications of any sort are inherently suspect and call for the most exacting judicial scrutiny. While the goal of achieving a diverse student body is sufficiently compelling to justify consideration of race in admissions decisions under some circumstances, petitioner's special admissions program, which forecloses consideration to persons like respondent, is unnecessary to the achievement of this compelling goal, and therefore invalid under the Equal Protection Clause.

3. Since petitioner could not satisfy its burden of proving that respondent would not have been admitted even if there had been no special admissions program, he must be admitted.

MR. JUSTICE BRENNAN, MR. JUSTICE WHITE, MR. JUSTICE MARSHALL, and MR. JUSTICE BLACKMUN concluded:

242

1. Title VI proscribes only those racial classifications that would violate the Equal Protection Clause if employed by a State or its agencies.

2. Racial classifications call for strict judicial scrutiny. Nonetheless, the purpose of overcoming substantial, chronic minority underrepresentation in the medical profession is sufficiently important to justify petitioner's remedial use of race. Thus, the judgment below must be reversed in that it prohibits race from being used as a factor in university admissions.

MR. JUSTICE STEVENS, joined by THE CHIEF JUSTICE, MR. JUSTICE STEWART, and MR. JUSTICE REHNQUIST, being of the view that whether race can ever be a factor in an admissions policy is not an issue here; that Title VI applies; and that respondent was excluded from Davis in violation of Title VI, concurs in the Court's judgment insofar as it affirms the judgment of the court below ordering respondent admitted to Davis.

UNITED STEELWORKERS OF AMERICA, AFL-CIO-CLC V. WEBER (1979)

United Steelworkers of America v. Weber (1979) held that Title VII of the 1964 Civil Rights Act, despite its prohibition against racial discrimination in employment, did not prohibit race-conscious affirmative action plans if they were private and voluntary.

SYLLABUS

In 1974, petitioners United Steelworkers of America (USWA) and Kaiser Aluminum Chemical Corp. (Kaiser) entered into a master collective bargaining agreement covering terms and conditions of employment at 15 Kaiser plants. The agreement included an affirmative action plan designed to eliminate conspicuous racial imbalances in Kaiser's then almost exclusively white craft work forces by reserving for black employees 50% of the openings in in-plant craft training programs until the percentage of black craft workers in a plant is commensurate with the percentage of blacks in the local labor force. This litigation arose from the operation of the affirmative action plant at one of Kaiser's plants where, prior to 1974, only 1.83% of the skilled craft workers were black, even though the local workforce was approximately 39% black. Pursuant to the national agreement,

Affirmative Action

Kaiser, rather than continuing its practice of hiring trained outsiders, established a training program to train its production workers to fill craft openings, selecting trainees on the basis of seniority, with the proviso that at least 50% of the trainees were to be black until the percentage of black skilled craft workers in the plant approximated the percentage of blacks in the local labor force. During the plan's first year of operation, seven black and six white craft trainees were selected from the plant's production workforce, with the most senior black trainee having less seniority than several white production workers whose bids for admission were rejected. Thereafter, respondent Weber, one of those white production workers, instituted this class action in Federal District Court, alleging that, because the affirmative action program had resulted in junior black employees' receiving training in preference to senior white employees, respondent and other similarly situated white employees had been discriminated against in violation of the provisions of §§ 703(a) and(d) of Title VII of the Civil Rights Act of 1964 that make it unlawful to "discriminate . . . because of . . . race" in hiring and in the selection of apprentices for training programs. The District Court held that the affirmative action plan violated Title VII, entered judgment in favor of the plaintiff class, and granted injunctive relief. The Court of Appeals affirmed, holding that all employment preferences based upon race, including those preferences incidental to bona fide affirmative action plans, violated Title VII's prohibition against racial discrimination in employment.

Held:

1. Title VII's prohibition in §§ 703(a) and (d) against racial discrimination does not condemn all private, voluntary, race-conscious affirmative action plans.

(a) Respondent Weber's reliance upon a literal construction of the statutory provisions and upon *McDonald v. Santa Fe Trail Transp. Co.*, 427 U.S. 273, which held, in a case not involving affirmative action, that Title VII protects whites as well as blacks from certain forms of racial discrimination, is misplaced, since the Kaiser-USWA plan is an affirmative action plan voluntarily adopted by private parties to eliminate traditional patterns of racial segregation. "[A] thing may be within the letter of the statute and yet not within the statute, because not within its spirit, nor within the intention of its makers," *Holy Trinity Church v. United States*, 143 U.S. 457, 459, and, thus, the prohibition against racial discrimination in §§ 703(a) and (d) must be read against the background of the legislative history of Title VII and the historical context from which the Act arose.

(b) Examination of those sources makes clear that an interpretation of §§ 703(a) and (d) that forbids all race-conscious affirmative action would bring about an end completely at variance with the purpose of the statute, and must be rejected. Congress' primary concern in enacting the prohibition against racial discrimination in Title VII was with the plight of the Negro in our economy, and the prohibition against racial discrimination in employment was primarily addressed to the problem of opening opportunities for Negroes in occupations which have been traditionally closed to them. In view of the legislative history, the very statutory words intended as a spur or catalyst to cause employers and unions to self-examine and to self-evaluate their employment practices and to endeavor to eliminate, so far as possible, the last vestiges of an unfortunate and ignominious page in this country's history, *Albemarle Paper Co. v. Moody*, 422 U.S. 405, 418, cannot be interpreted as an absolute prohibition against all private, voluntary, race-conscious affirmative action efforts to hasten the elimination of such vestiges.

(c) This conclusion is further reinforced by examination of the language and legislative history of § 703(j) of Title VII, which provides that nothing contained in Title VII shall be interpreted to require any employer . . . to grant preferential treatment . . . to any group because of the race . . . of such . . . group on account of a *de facto* racial imbalance in the employer's workforce. Had Congress meant to prohibit all race-conscious affirmative action, it could have provided that Title VII would not require or permit racially preferential integration efforts. The legislative record shows that § 703(j) was designed to prevent § 703 from being interpreted in such a way as to lead to undue federal regulation of private businesses, and thus use of the word "require," rather than the phrase "require or permit," in § 703(j) fortifies the conclusion that Congress did not intend to limit traditional business freedom to such a degree as to prohibit all voluntary, race-conscious affirmative action.

2. It is not necessary in these cases to define the line of demarcation between permissible and impermissible affirmative action plans; it suffices to hold that the challenged Kaiser-USWA plan falls on the permissible side of the line. The purposes of the plan mirror those of the statute, being designed to break down old patterns of racial segregation and hierarchy, and being structured to open employment opportunities for Negroes in occupations which have been traditionally closed to them. At the same time, the plan does not unnecessarily trammel the interests of white employees, neither requiring the discharge of white workers and their replacement with new black hires, nor creating an absolute bar to the advancement of white employees, since half of those trained in the program will be white. Moreover, the plan is a temporary measure, not intended to maintain racial balance, but simply to eliminate a manifest racial imbalance. BRENNAN, J., delivered the opinion of the Court, in which

STEWART, WHITE, MARSHALL, and BLACKMUN, JJ., joined. BLACKMUN, J., filed a concurring opinion. BURGER, C.J., filed a dissenting opinion. REHNQUIST, J., filed a dissenting opinion, in which BURGER, C.J., joined. POWELL and STEVENS, JJ., took no part in the consideration or decision of the cases.

FULLILOVE V. KLUTZNICK (1980)

Fullilove v. Klutznick (1980) found that set-asides that guaranteed to minority-owned businesses a tiny percentage of government contracting business were indeed constitutional.

Syllabus

The "minority business enterprise" (MBE) provision of the Public Works Employment Act of 1977 (1977 Act) requires that, absent an administrative waiver, at least 10% of federal funds granted for local public works projects must be used by the state or local grantee to procure services or supplies from businesses owned by minority group members, defined as United States citizens "who are Negroes, Spanish-speaking, Orientals, Indians, Eskimos, and Aleuts." Under implementing regulations and guidelines, grantees and their private prime contractors are required, to the extent feasible, in fulfilling the 10% MBE requirement, to seek out all available, qualified, bona fide MBE's, to provide technical assistance as needed, to lower or waive bonding requirements where feasible, to solicit the aid of the Office of Minority Business Enterprise, the Small Business Administration, or other sources for assisting MBE's in obtaining required working capital, and to give guidance through the intricacies of the bidding process. The administrative program, which recognizes that contracts will be awarded to bona fide MBE's even though they are not the lowest bidders if their bids reflect merely attempts to cover costs inflated by the present effects of prior disadvantage and discrimination, provides for handling grantee applications for administrative waiver of the 10% MBE requirement on a case-by-case basis if infeasibility is demonstrated by a showing that, despite affirmative efforts, such level of participation cannot be achieved without departing from the program's objectives. The program also provides an administrative mechanism to ensure that only bona fide MBE's are encompassed by the program, and to prevent unjust participation by minority firms whose access to public contracting opportunities is not impaired by the effects of prior discrimination.

Appendix B

Petitioners, several associations of construction contractors and subcontractors and a firm engaged in heating, ventilation, and air conditioning work, filed suit for declaratory and injunctive relief in Federal District Court, alleging that they had sustained economic injury due to enforcement of the MBE requirement, and that the MBE provision, on its face, violated, inter alia, the Equal Protection Clause of the Fourteenth Amendment and the equal protection component of the Due Process Clause of the Fifth Amendment. The District Court upheld the validity of the MBE program, and the Court of Appeals affirmed.

Held: The judgment is affirmed.

MR. CHIEF JUSTICE BURGER, joined by MR. JUSTICE WHITE and MR. JUSTICE POWELL, concluded that the MBE provision of the 1977 Act, on its face, does not violate the Constitution.

(a) Viewed against the legislative and administrative background of the 1977 Act, the legislative objectives of the MBE provision and of the administrative program thereunder were to ensure—without mandating the allocation of federal funds according to inflexible percentages solely based on race or ethnicity—that, to the extent federal funds were granted under the 1977 Act, grantees who elected to participate would not employ procurement practices that Congress had decided might result in perpetuation of the effects of prior discrimination which had impaired or foreclosed access by minority businesses to public contracting opportunities.

(b) In considering the constitutionality of the MBE provision, it first must be determined whether the objectives of the legislation are within Congress' power.

(i) The 1977 Act, as primarily an exercise of Congress' Spending Power under Art. I, § 8, cl. 1, "to provide for the . . . general Welfare," conditions receipt of federal moneys upon the receipt's compliance with federal statutory and administrative directives. Since the reach of the Spending Power is at least as broad as Congress' regulatory powers, if Congress, pursuant to its regulatory powers, could have achieved the objectives of the MBE program, then it may do so under the Spending Power.

(ii) Insofar as the MBE program pertains to the actions of private prime contractors, including those not responsible for any violation of antidiscrimination laws, Congress could have achieved its objectives under the Commerce Clause. The legislative history shows that there was a rational basis for Congress to conclude that the subcontracting practices of prime contractors could perpetuate the prevailing impaired access by minority businesses to public contracting opportunities, and that this inequity has an effect on interstate commerce.

(iii) Insofar as the MBE program pertains to the actions of state and local grantees, Congress could have achieved its objectives by use of its power under § 5 of the Fourteenth Amendment "to enforce, by appropriate legislation" the equal protection guarantee of that Amendment. Congress had abundant historical basis from which it could conclude that traditional procurement practices, when applied to minority businesses, could perpetuate the effects of prior discrimination, and that the prospective elimination of such barriers to minority-firm access to public contracting opportunities was appropriate to ensure that those businesses were not denied equal opportunity to participate in federal grants to state and local governments, which is one aspect of the equal protection of the laws. Cf., e.g., *Katzenbach v. Morgan*, 384 U.S. 641; *Oregon v. Mitchell*, 400 U.S. 112.

(iv) Thus, the objectives of the MBE provision are within the scope of Congress' Spending Power. Cf. *Lau v. Nichols*, 414 U.S. 563.

(c) Congress' use here of racial and ethnic criteria as a condition attached to a federal grant is a valid means to accomplish its constitutional objectives, and the MBE provision, on its face, does not violate the equal protection component of the Due Process Clause of the Fifth Amendment.

(i) In the MBE program's remedial context, there is no requirement that Congress act in a wholly "color-blind" fashion. Cf., e.g., *Swann v. Charlotte-Mecklenberg Board of Education*, 402 U.S. 1; *McDaniel v. Barresi*, 402 U.S. 39; *North Carolina Board of Education v. Swann*, 402 U.S. 43.

(ii) The MBE program is not constitutionally defective because it may disappoint the expectations of access to a portion of government contracting opportunities of nonminority firms who may themselves be innocent of any prior discriminatory actions. When effectuating a limited and properly tailored remedy to cure the effects of prior discrimination, such "a sharing of the burden" by innocent parties is not impermissible. *Franks v. Bowman Transportation Co.*, 424 U.S. 747, 777.

(iii) Nor is the MBE program invalid as being underinclusive in that it limits its benefit to specified minority groups, rather than extending its remedial objectives to all businesses whose access to government contracting is impaired by the effects of disadvantage or discrimination. Congress has not sought to give select minority groups a preferred standing in the construction industry, but has embarked on a remedial program to place them on a more equitable footing with respect to public contracting opportunities, and there has been no showing that Congress inadvertently effected an invidious discrimination by excluding from coverage an identifiable minority group that has been the victim of a degree of disadvantage and discrimination equal to or greater than that suffered by the groups encompassed by the MBE program.

Appendix B

(iv) The contention that the MBE program, on its face, is overinclusive in that it bestows a benefit on businesses identified by racial or ethnic criteria which cannot be justified on the basis of competitive criteria or as a remedy for the present effects of identified prior discrimination is also without merit. The MBE provision, with due account for its administrative program, provides a reasonable assurance that application of racial or ethnic criteria will be narrowly limited to accomplishing Congress' remedial objectives, and that misapplications of the program will be promptly and adequately remedied administratively. In particular, the administrative program provides waiver and exemption procedures to identify and eliminate from participation MBE's who are not "bona fide," or who attempt to exploit the remedial aspects of the program by charging an unreasonable price not attributable to the present effects of past discrimination. Moreover, grantees may obtain a waiver if they demonstrate that their best efforts will not achieve or have not achieved the 10% target for minority firm participation within the limitations of the program's remedial objectives. The MBE provision may be viewed as a pilot project, appropriately limited in extent and duration and subject to reassessment and reevaluation by the Congress prior to any extension or reenactment.

(d) In the continuing effort to achieve the goal of equality of economic opportunity, Congress has latitude to try new techniques such as the limited use of racial and ethnic criteria to accomplish remedial objectives, especially in programs where voluntary cooperation is induced by placing conditions on federal expenditures. When a program narrowly tailored by Congress to achieve its objectives comes under judicial review, it should be upheld if the courts are satisfied that the legislative objectives and projected administration of the program give reasonable assurance that the program will function within constitutional limitations.

MR. JUSTICE MARSHALL, joined by MR. JUSTICE BRENNAN and MR. JUSTICE BLACKMUN, concurring in the judgment, concluded that the proper inquiry for determining the constitutionality of racial classifications that provide benefits to minorities for the purpose of remedying the present effects of past racial discrimination is whether the classifications serve important governmental objectives and are substantially related to achievement of those objectives, University of *California Regents v. Bakke*, 438 U.S. 265, 359 (opinion of BRENNAN, WHITE, MARSHALL, and BLACKMUN, JJ., concurring in judgment in part and dissenting in part), and that, judged under this standard, the 10% minority set-aside provision of the 1977 Act is plainly constitutional, the racial classifications being substantially related to the achievement of the important and congressionally articulated goal of remedying the present effects of past racial discrimination.

249

Affirmative Action

MISSISSIPPI UNIVERSITY FOR WOMEN V. HOGAN (1982)

Mississippi University for Women v. Hogan (1982) held that a man who wanted to attend an all-female nursing program was legally entitled to do so under Title IX of the Education Amendments of 1972, which prohibited discrimination in educational institutions on the basis of sex.

SYLLABUS

Held: The policy of petitioner Mississippi University for Women (MUW), a state-supported university which has from its inception limited its enrollment to women, of denying otherwise qualified males (such as respondent) the right to enroll for credit in its School of Nursing violates the Equal Protection Clause of the Fourteenth Amendment.

(a) The party seeking to uphold a statute that classifies individuals on the basis of their gender must carry the burden of showing an "exceedingly persuasive justification" for the classification. *Kirchberg v. Feenstra,* 450 U.S. 455, 461; *Personnel Administrator of Mass. v. Feeney,* 442 U.S. 256, 273. The burden is met only by showing at least that the classification serves "important governmental objectives and that the discriminatory means employed" are "substantially related to the achievement of those objectives." *Wengler v. Druggists Mutual Insurance Co.,* 446 U.S. 142, 150. The test must be applied free of fixed notions concerning the roles and abilities of males and females.

(b) The single-sex admissions policy of MUW's School of Nursing cannot be justified on the asserted group that it compensates for discrimination against women and, therefore, constitutes educational affirmative action. A State can evoke a compensatory purpose to justify an otherwise discriminatory classification only if members of the gender benefited by the classification actually suffer a disadvantage related to the classification. Rather than compensating for discriminatory barriers faced by women, MUW's policy tends to perpetuate the stereotyped view of nursing as an exclusively woman's job. Moreover, the State has not shown that the gender-based classification is substantially and directly related to its proposed compensatory objective. To the contrary, MUW's policy of permitting men to attend classes as auditors fatally undermines its claim that women, at least those in the School of Nursing, are adversely affected by the presence of men. Thus, the State has fallen far short of establishing the "exceedingly persuasive justification" needed to sustain the gender-based classification.

(c) Nor can the exclusion of men from MUW's School of Nursing be justified on the basis of the language of § 901(a)(5) of Title IX of the Education Amendments of 1972, which exempts from § 901(a)'s general prohibition of gender discrimination in federally funded education programs the admissions policies of public institutions of undergraduate higher education "that traditionally and continually from [their] establishment [have] had a policy of admitting only students of one sex." It is not clear that, as argued by the State, Congress enacted the statute pursuant to its power granted by § 5 of the Fourteenth Amendment to enforce that Amendment, and thus placed a limitation upon the broad prohibitions of the Equal Protection Clause. Rather, Congress apparently intended, at most, to create an exemption from Title IX's requirements. In any event, Congress' power under § 5 is limited to adopting measures to enforce the guarantees of the Amendment; § 5 grants Congress no power to restrict, abrogate, or dilute these guarantees.

Katzenbach v. Morgan, 384 U.S. 641, 651, n. 10.

O'CONNOR, J., delivered the opinion of the Court, in which BRENNAN, WHITE, MARSHALL, and STEVENS, JJ., joined. BURGER, C.J., and BLACKMUN, J., filed dissenting opinions. POWELL, J., filed a dissenting opinion, in which REHNQUIST, J., joined.

WYGANT V. JACKSON BOARD OF EDUCATION (1986)

Wygant v. Jackson Board of Education (1986) found that a layoff provision designed to overrule seniority to some extent, so that a certain portion of African-American teachers would remain on the faculty, was unconstitutional.

SYLLABUS

The collective bargaining agreement between respondent Board of Education (Board) and a teachers' union provided that, if it became necessary to lay off teachers, those with the most seniority would be retained, except that at no time would there be a greater percentage of minority personnel laid off than the current percentage of minority personnel employed at the time of the layoff. After this layoff provision was upheld in litigation arising from the Board's noncompliance with the provision, the Board adhered to it, with the result that, during certain school years, nonminority teachers were laid off, while minority teachers with less seniority were retained. Petitioners, displaced nonminority teachers, brought suit in Federal District Court, alleging violations of the Equal Protection Clause and certain federal and state statutes. Dismissing the suit on cross-motions for summary judgment, the District Court upheld the constitutionality of the layoff provision, holding that the racial preferences granted by the Board need not be grounded on a finding of prior discrimination but were permissible under the Equal Protection Clause as an attempt to remedy societal discrimination by providing "role models" for minority schoolchildren. The Court of Appeals affirmed.

Held: The judgment is reversed.

JUSTICE POWELL, joined by THE CHIEF JUSTICE, JUSTICE REHNQUIST, and JUSTICE O'CONNOR, concluded that the layoff provision violates the Equal Protection Clause.

(a) In the context of affirmative action, racial classifications must be justified by a compelling state purpose, and the means chosen by the State to effectuate that purpose must be narrowly tailored.

(b) Societal discrimination alone is insufficient to justify a racial classification. Rather, there must be convincing evidence of prior discrimination by the governmental unit involved before allowing limited use of racial classifications to remedy such discrimination. The "role model" theory employed by the District Court would allow the Board to engage in discriminatory hiring and layoff practices long past the point required by any legitimate remedial purpose. Moreover, it does not bear any relationship to the harm caused by prior discriminatory hiring practices. Societal discrimination, without more, is too amorphous a basis for finding race-conscious state action and for imposing a racially classified remedy.

(c) If the purpose of the layoff provision was to remedy prior discrimination, as the Board claims, such purpose, to be constitutionally valid, would require the District Court to make a factual determination that the Board had a strong basis in evidence for its conclusion that remedial action was necessary. No such finding has ever been made.

JUSTICE POWELL, joined by THE CHIEF JUSTICE and JUSTICE REHNQUIST, concluded that, as a means of accomplishing purposes that otherwise may be legitimate, the layoff provision is not sufficiently narrowly tailored. Other, less intrusive means of accomplishing similar purposes—such as the adoption of hiring goals—are available.

JUSTICE WHITE concluded that respondent Board of Education's layoff policy has the same effect, and is equally violative of the Equal Protection Clause, as integrating a workforce by discharging whites and hiring blacks until the latter comprise a suitable percentage of the workforce.

JUSTICE O'CONNOR concluded that the layoff provision is not "narrowly tailored" to achieve its asserted remedial purpose, because it acts to maintain levels of minority hiring set by a hiring goal that has no relation to the remedying of employment discrimination.

POWELL, J., announced the judgment of the Court and delivered an opinion in which BURGER, C.J., and REHNQUIST, J., joined, and in all but Part IV of which O'CONNOR, J., Joined. O'CONNOR, J., filed an opinion concurring in part and concurring in the judgment. WHITE, J., filed an opinion concurring in the judgment. MARSHALL, J., filed a dissenting opinion in which BRENNAN and BLACKMUN, JJ., joined. STEVENS, J., filed a dissenting opinion.

UNITED STATES V. PARADISE (1987)

In *United States v. Paradise*, the Court found that a particularly egregious case of racial discrimination by the Alabama Department of Public Safety could indeed be remedied by a "one-for-one" promotions plan that temporarily required the department to promote one qualified African-American trooper for every white trooper promoted, so long as qualified candidates for promotion could be found.

SYLLABUS

In 1972, upon finding that, for almost four decades, the Alabama Department of Public Safety (Department) had systematically excluded blacks from employment as state troopers in violation of the Fourteenth Amendment, the District Court issued an order imposing a hiring quota and requiring the Department to refrain from engaging in discrimination in its employment practices, including promotions. By 1979, no blacks had attained the upper ranks of the Department. The court therefore approved a partial consent decree in which the Department agreed to develop within one year a procedure for promotion to corporal that would have no adverse impact on blacks and would comply with the Uniform Guidelines on Employee Selection Procedures (Guidelines), and thereafter to develop similar procedures for the other upper ranks (1979 Decree). As of 1981, however, more than a year after the 1979 Decree's deadline, no black troopers had been promoted. The court approved a second consent decree in which the parties agreed that the Department's proposed corporal promotion test would be administered to applicants, that the results would be reviewed to determine any adverse impact on blacks under the Guidelines, that the determination of a procedure would be submitted to the court if the parties were unable to agree thereon, and that no promotions would occur until the parties agreed or the court ruled upon the promotion method to be used (1981 Decree). Of the 60 blacks to whom the test was administered, only 5 (8.3%) were listed in the top half of the promotional register, and the highest ranked black was number 80. The Department then declared that it had an immediate need for between 8 and 10 new corporals, and stated its intention to elevate between 16 and 20 individuals before constructing a new list. The United States objected to any use of the list in making promotions. In 1983, the District Court held that the test had an adverse impact on blacks, and ordered the Department to submit a plan to promote at least 15 qualified candidates to corporal in a manner that would not have an adverse racial impact. The Department proposed to promote 4 blacks among the 15 new corporals, but the court rejected that proposal and ordered that "for a period of time," at least 50% of those promoted to corporal must be black, if qualified black candidates were available, and imposed a 50% promotional requirement in the other upper ranks, but only if there were qualified black candidates, if a particular rank were less than 25% black, and if the Department had not developed and implemented a promotion plan without adverse impact for the relevant rank. The Department was also ordered to submit a realistic schedule for the development of promotional procedures for all ranks above the entry level. Subsequently, the Department promoted eight blacks and eight whites under the court's order, and submitted its proposed corporal and sergeant promotional procedures, at which times the court suspended the 50% requirement for those ranks. The United States appealed the court's order on the ground that it violated the Fourteenth Amendment's equal protection guarantee. The Court of Appeals affirmed the order.

Held: The judgment is affirmed.

JUSTICE BRENNAN, joined by JUSTICE MARSHALL, JUSTICE BLACKMUN, and JUSTICE POWELL, concluded that, even under a strict scrutiny analysis, the one-black-for-one-white promotion requirement is permissible under the Equal Protection Clause of the Fourteenth Amendment.

1. The race-conscious relief ordered by the District Court is justified by a compelling governmental interest in eradicating the Department's pervasive, systematic, and obstinate discriminatory exclusion of blacks. The contention that promotion relief is unjustified because the Department has been found to have committed only hiring discrimination is without merit, since promotion, like hiring, has been a central concern of the District Court since the action's commencement. The Department's intentional hiring discrimination had a profound effect on the force's upper ranks by precluding blacks from competing for promotions. Moreover, the record amply demonstrates that the Department's promotional

254

procedure is itself discriminatory, resulting in an upper rank structure that totally excludes blacks.

2. The District Court's enforcement order is also supported by the societal interest in compliance with federal court judgments. The Department has had a consistent history of resistance to the District Court's orders, and relief was imposed only after the Department failed to live up to its court-approved commitments.

3. The one-for-one promotional requirement is narrowly tailored to serve its purposes, both as applied to the initial corporal promotions and as a continuing contingent order with respect to the upper ranks.

(a) The one-for-one requirement is necessary to eliminate the effects of the Department's long-term, open, and pervasive discrimination, including the absolute exclusion of blacks in the upper ranks; to ensure expeditious compliance with the 1979 and 1981 Decrees by inducing the implementation of a promotional procedure that would not have an adverse racial impact; and to eradicate the ill effects of the Department's delay in producing such a procedure. The option proffered by the Department—to promote 4 blacks and 11 whites as a stopgap measure, and to allow additional time for the development and submission of a nondiscriminatory procedure—would not have satisfied any of the above purposes. Furthermore, the heavy fines and fees suggested by the Government as an alternative were never actually proposed to the District Court; were likely to be ineffective, since the imposition of attorney's fees and costs in the past had not prevented delays; would not have compensated the plaintiffs for the delays; and would not have satisfied the Department's need to make 15 promotions immediately.

(b) The one-for-one requirement is flexible in application at all ranks, in that it applies only when the Department needs to make promotions and does not require gratuitous promotions. Furthermore, the requirement may be waived by the court if there are no qualified black troopers, and, in fact, this has already happened with respect to lieutenant and captain positions. Moreover, the requirement is temporary, its term being contingent upon the Department's successful implementation of valid promotional procedures. It was, in fact, suspended upon the timely submission of procedures for promotion to corporal and sergeant.

(c) The numerical relief ordered bears a proper relation to the percentage of nonwhites in the relevant work force, since the District Court ordered 50% black promotions until each rank is 25% black, whereas blacks constitute 25% of the relevant labor market. The one-for-one requirement is not arbitrary when compared to the 25% minority labor pool, since the 50% figure is not itself the goal, but merely represents the speed at which the 25% goal will be achieved, some promptness being justified by the Department's history of discrimination and delays. Although the 50% figure necessarily involves a degree of imprecision, it represents the District Court's informed attempt to balance the rights and interests of the plaintiffs, the Department, and white troopers.

(d) The one-for-one requirement does not impose an unacceptable burden on innocent white promotion applicants. The requirement is temporary and limited in nature, has only been used once, and may never be used again. It does not bar, but simply postpones, advancement by some whites, and does not require the layoff or discharge of whites or the promotion of unqualified blacks over qualified whites.

(e) District judges, having firsthand experience with the parties and the particular situation, are given broad discretion to fashion appropriate remedies to cure Fourteenth Amendment violations, and the exercise of that discretion is entitled to substantial respect.

JUSTICE STEVENS concluded that *Swann v. Charlotte-Mecklenburg Bd. of Education*, 402 U.S. 1, sets forth the appropriate governing standards for district court remedial orders in cases such as the present that involve racially discriminatory state actions violative of the Fourteenth Amendment. Because the record here discloses an egregious violation of the Equal Protection Clause, the District Court had broad and flexible authority to fashion race-conscious relief under the *Swann* standards. There has been no showing that the District Judge abused his discretion in doing so.

BRENNAN, J., announced the judgment of the Court and delivered an opinion in which MARSHALL, BLACKMUN, and POWELL, JJ., joined. POWELL, J., filed a concurring opinion, STEVENS, J., filed an opinion concurring in the judgment, WHITE, J., filed a dissenting statement, O'-CONNOR, J., filed a dissenting opinion, in which REHNQUIST, C.J., and SCALIA, J., joined.

CITY OF RICHMOND V. J. A. CROSON CO. (1989)

City of Richmond v. Croson (1989) established that the City of Richmond could not set aside 30 percent of the city's contracting business for so-called Minority Business Enterprises, despite *Fullilove v. Klutznick* (1980), which found such set-asides constitutional in an apparently similar case.

SYLLABUS

Appellant city adopted a Minority Business Utilization Plan (Plan) requiring prime contractors awarded city construction contracts to subcontract at least 30% of the dollar amount of each contract to one or more "Minority Business Enterprises" (MBE's), which the Plan defined to include a business from anywhere in the country at least 51% of which is owned and controlled by black, Spanish-speaking, Oriental, Indian, Eskimo, or Aleut citizens. Although the Plan declared that it was "remedial" in nature, it was adopted after a public hearing at which no direct evidence was presented that the city had discriminated on the basis of race in letting contracts, or that its prime contractors had discriminated against minority subcontractors. The evidence that was introduced included: a statistical study indicating that, although the city's population was 50% black, only 0.67% of its prime construction contracts had been awarded to minority businesses in recent years; figures establishing that a variety of local contractors' associations had virtually no MBE members; the city's counsel's conclusion that the Plan was constitutional under *Fullilove v. Klutznick*, 448 U.S. 448; and the statements of Plan proponents indicating that there had been widespread racial discrimination in the local, state, and national construction industries. Pursuant to the Plan, the city adopted rules requiring individualized consideration of each bid or request for a waiver of the 30% set-aside, and providing that a waiver could be granted only upon proof that sufficient qualified MBE's were unavailable or unwilling to participate. After appellee construction company, the sole bidder on a city contract, was denied a waiver and lost its contract, it brought suit under 42 U.S.C. § 1983, alleging that the Plan was unconstitutional under the Fourteenth Amendment's Equal Protection Clause. The Federal District Court upheld the Plan in all respects, and the Court of Appeals affirmed, applying a test derived from the principal opinion in *Fullilove, supra*, which accorded great deference to Congress' findings of past societal discrimination in holding that a 10% minority set-aside for certain federal construction grants did not violate the equal protection component of the Fifth Amendment. However, on appellee's petition for certiorari in this case, this Court vacated and remanded for further consideration in light of its intervening decision in *Wygant v. Jackson Board of Education*, 476 U.S. 267, in which the plurality applied a strict scrutiny standard in holding that a race-based layoff program agreed to by a school board and the local teachers' union violated the Fourteenth Amendment's Equal Protection Clause. On remand, the Court of Appeals held that the city's Plan violated both prongs of strict scrutiny, in that (1) the Plan was not justified by a compelling governmental interest, since the record revealed no prior discrimination by the city itself in awarding contracts, and (2) the 30% set-aside was not narrowly tailored to accomplish a remedial purpose.

Held: The judgment is affirmed.

Affirmative Action

JUSTICE O'CONNOR delivered the opinion of the Court with respect to Parts I, III-B, and IV, concluding that:

1. The city has failed to demonstrate a compelling governmental interest justifying the Plan, since the factual predicate supporting the Plan does not establish the type of identified past discrimination in the city's construction industry that would authorize race-based relief under the Fourteenth Amendment's Equal Protection Clause.

(a) A generalized assertion that there has been past discrimination in the entire construction industry cannot justify the use of an unyielding racial quota, since it provides no guidance for the city's legislative body to determine the precise scope of the injury it seeks to remedy, and would allow race-based decisionmaking essentially limitless in scope and duration. The city's argument that it is attempting to remedy various forms of past societal discrimination that are alleged to be responsible for the small number of minority entrepreneurs in the local contracting industry fails, since the city also lists a host of nonracial factors which would seem to face a member of any racial group seeking to establish a new business enterprise, such as deficiencies in working capital, inability to meet bonding requirements, unfamiliarity with bidding procedures, and disability caused by an inadequate track record.

(b) None of the "facts" cited by the city or relied on by the District Court, singly or together, provide a basis for a *prima facie* case of a constitutional or statutory violation by *anyone* in the city's construction industry. The fact that the Plan declares itself to be "remedial" is insufficient, since the mere recitation of a "benign" or legitimate purpose for a racial classification is entitled to little or no weight. Similarly, the views of Plan proponents as to past and present discrimination in the industry are highly conclusory, and of little probative value. Reliance on the disparity between the number of prime contracts awarded to minority business and the city's minority population is also misplaced, since the proper statistical evaluation would compare the percentage of MBE's in the relevant market that are qualified to undertake city subcontracting work with the percentage of total city construction dollars that are presently awarded to minority subcontractors, neither of which is known to the city. The fact that MBE membership in local contractors' associations was extremely low is also not probative, absent some link to the number of MBE's eligible for membership, since there are numerous explanations for the dearth of minority participation, including past societal discrimination in education and economic opportunities, as well as both black and white career and entrepreneurial choices. Congress' finding in connection with the set-aside approved in *Fullilove* that there had been nationwide discrimination in the construction industry also has extremely limited probative value, since, by including a waiver procedure in the national program, Congress explicitly recognized that the scope of the problem would vary from market area to market area. In any event, Congress was acting pursuant to its unique enforcement powers under § 5 of the Fourteenth Amendment.

(c) The "evidence" relied upon by JUSTICE MARSHALL's dissent—the city's history of school desegregation and numerous congressional reports—does little to define the scope of any injury to minority contractors in the city or the necessary remedy, and could justify a preference of any size or duration. Moreover, JUSTICE MARSHALL's suggestion that discrimination findings may be "shared" from jurisdiction to jurisdiction is unprecedented, and contrary to this Court's decisions.

(d) Since there is absolutely no evidence of past discrimination against Spanish-speaking, Oriental, Indian, Eskimo, or Aleut persons in any aspect of the city's construction industry, the Plan's random inclusion of those groups strongly impugns the city's claim of remedial motivation.

2. The Plan is not narrowly tailored to remedy the effects of prior discrimination, since it entitles a black, Hispanic, or Oriental entrepreneur from anywhere in the country to an absolute preference over other citizens based solely on their race. Although many of the barriers to minority participation in the construction industry relied upon by the city to justify the Plan appear to be race neutral, there is no evidence that the city considered using alternative, race-neutral means to increase minority participation in city contracting. Moreover, the Plan's rigid 30% quota rests upon the completely unrealistic assumption that minorities will choose to enter construction in lockstep proportion to their representation in the local population. Unlike the program upheld in *Fullilove*, the Plan's waiver system focuses upon the availability of MBE's, and does not inquire whether the particular MBE seeking a racial preference has suffered from the effects of past discrimination by the city or prime contractors. Given the fact that the city must already consider bids and waivers on a case-by-case basis, the city's only interest in maintaining a quota system, rather than investigating the need for remedial action in particular cases, would seem to be simply administrative convenience, which, standing alone, cannot justify the use of a suspect classification under equal protection strict scrutiny.

JUSTICE O'CONNOR, joined by THE CHIEF JUSTICE and JUSTICE WHITE, concluded in Part II that, if the city could identify past discrimination in the local construction industry with the particularity required by the Equal Protection Clause, it would have the power to adopt race-based legislation designed to eradicate the effects of that discrimination.

The principal opinion in *Fullilove* cannot be read to relieve the city of the necessity of making the specific findings of discrimination required by the Clause, since the congressional finding of past discrimination relied on in that case was made pursuant to Congress' unique power under § 5 of the Amendment to enforce, and therefore to identify and redress violations of, the Amendment's provisions. Conversely, § 1 of the Amendment, which includes the Equal Protection Clause, is an explicit constraint upon the power of States and political subdivisions, which must undertake any remedial efforts in accordance with the dictates of that section. However, the Court of Appeals erred to the extent that it followed by rote the *Wygant* plurality's ruling that the Equal Protection Clause requires a showing of prior discrimination by the governmental unit involved, since that ruling was made in the context of a race-based policy that affected the particular public employer's own workforce, whereas this case involves a state entity which has specific state law authority to address discriminatory practices within local commerce under its jurisdiction.

JUSTICE O'CONNOR, joined by THE CHIEF JUSTICE, JUSTICE WHITE, and JUSTICE KENNEDY, concluded in Parts III-A and V that:

1. Since the Plan denies certain citizens the opportunity to compete for a fixed percentage of public contracts based solely on their race, *Wygant's* strict scrutiny standard of review must be applied, which requires a firm evidentiary basis for concluding that the underrepresentation of minorities is a product of past discrimination. Application of that standard, which is not dependent on the race of those burdened or benefited by the racial classification, assures that the city is pursuing a remedial goal important enough to warrant use of a highly suspect tool, and that the means chosen "fit" this compelling goal so closely that there is little or no possibility that the motive for the classification was illegitimate racial prejudice or stereotype. The relaxed standard of review proposed by JUSTICE MARSHALL's dissent does not provide a means for determining that a racial classification is in fact "designed to further remedial goals," since it accepts the remedial nature of the classification before examination of the factual basis for the classification's enactment and the nexus between its scope and that factual basis. Even if the level of equal protection scrutiny could be said to vary according to the ability of different groups to defend their interests in the representative process, heightened scrutiny would still be appropriate in the circumstances of this case, since blacks comprise approximately 50% of the city's population and hold five of nine seats on the City Council, thereby raising the concern that the political majority may have acted to disadvantage a minority based on unwarranted assumptions or incomplete facts.

2. Even in the absence of evidence of discrimination in the local construction industry, the city has at its disposal an array of race-neutral devices to increase the accessibility of city contracting opportunities to small entrepreneurs of all races who have suffered the effects of past societal discrimination, including simplification of bidding procedures, relaxation of bonding requirements, training, financial aid, elimination or modification of formal barriers caused by bureaucratic inertia, and the prohibition of discrimination in the provision of credit or bonding by local suppliers and banks.

JUSTICE STEVENS, although agreeing that the Plan cannot be justified as a remedy for past discrimination, concluded that the Fourteenth Amendment does not limit permissible racial classifications to those that remedy past wrongs, but requires that race-based governmental decisions be evaluated primarily by studying their probable impact on the future.

(a) Disregarding the past history of racial injustice, there is not even an arguable basis for suggesting that the race of a subcontractor or contractor on city projects should have any relevance to his or her access to the market. Although race is not always irrelevant to sound governmental decision-making, the city makes no claim that the public interest in the efficient performance of its construction contracts will be served by granting a preference to minority business enterprises.

(b) Legislative bodies such as the city council, which are primarily policymaking entities that promulgate rules to govern future conduct, raise valid constitutional concerns when they use the political process to punish or characterize past conduct of private citizens. Courts, on the other hand, are well equipped to identify past wrongdoers and to fashion remedies that will create the conditions that presumably would have existed had no wrong been committed, and should have the same broad discretion in racial discrimination cases that chancellors enjoy in other areas of the law to fashion remedies against persons who have been proved guilty of violations of law.

(c) Rather than engaging in debate over the proper standard of review to apply in affirmative action litigation, it is more constructive to try to identify the characteristics of the advantaged and disadvantaged classes that may justify their disparate treatment. Here, instead of carefully identifying those characteristics, the city has merely engaged in the type of stereotypical analysis that is the hallmark of Equal Protection Clause violations. The class of persons benefited by the Plan is not limited to victims of past discrimination by white contractors in the city, but encompasses persons who have never been in business in the city, minority contractors who may have themselves been guilty of discrimination against other minority group members, and firms that have prospered notwithstanding discriminatory treatment. Similarly, although the Plan unquestionably disadvantages some white contractors who are guilty of past discrimination against blacks, it also punishes some who discriminated only before it was forbidden by law, and some who have never discriminated against anyone.

METRO BROADCASTING, INC.
V. FCC (1990)

Metro Broadcasting v. FCC (1990) concerned the constitutionality of the Federal Communication Commission's (FCC) policies designed to increase the percentage of minority-owned radio and television stations; the Court found that the FCC's policies were in fact constitutional.

SYLLABUS

Certiorari to the United States Court of Appeals for the District of Columbia Circuit No. 89453. Argued March 28, 1990 Decided June 27, 1990.

These cases consider the constitutionality of two minority preference policies adopted by the Federal Communications Commission (FCC). First, the FCC awards an enhancement for minority ownership and participation in management, which is weighed together with all other relevant factors, in comparing mutually exclusive applications for licenses for new radio or television broadcast stations. Second, the FCC's so-called "distress sale" policy allows a radio or television broadcaster whose qualifications to hold a license have come into question to transfer that license before the FCC resolves the matter in a noncomparative hearing, but only if the transferee is a minority enterprise that meets certain requirements. The FCC adopted these policies in an attempt to satisfy its obligation under the Communications Act of 1934 to promote diversification of programming, taking the position that its past efforts to encourage minority participation in the broadcast industry had not resulted in sufficient broadcast diversity, and that this situation was detrimental not only to the minority audience but to all of the viewing and listening public. Metro Broadcasting, Inc., the petitioner in No.89453, sought review in the Court of Appeals of an FCC order awarding a new television license to Rainbow Broadcasting in a comparative proceeding, which action was based on the ruling that the substantial enhancement granted Rainbow because of its minority ownership outweighed factors favoring Metro. The court remanded the appeal for further consideration in light of the FCC's separate, ongoing Docket 86484 inquiry into the validity of its minority ownership policies. Prior to completion of that inquiry, however, Congress enacted the FCC appropriations legislation for fiscal year 1988, which prohibited the FCC from spending any appropriated funds to examine or change its minority policies. Thus, the FCC closed its Docket 86484 inquiry and reaffirmed its grant of the license to Rainbow, and the Court of Appeals affirmed. Shurberg Broadcasting of Hartford, Inc., one of the respondents in No.89700, sought review in the Court of Appeals of an FCC order approving Faith Center, Inc.'s distress sale of its television license to Astroline Communications Company Limited Partnership, a minority enterprise. Disposition of the appeal was delayed pending resolution of the Docket 86484 inquiry by the FCC, which, upon closing that inquiry as discussed *supra*, reaffirmed its order allowing the distress sale to Astroline. The court then invalidated the distress sale policy, ruling that it deprived Shurberg, a nonminority applicant for a license in the relevant market, of its right to equal protection under the Fifth Amendment.

Held: The FCC policies do not violate equal protection, since they bear the imprimatur of longstanding congressional support and direction and are substantially related to the achievement of the important governmental objective of broadcast diversity.

(a) It is of overriding significance in these cases that the minority ownership programs have been specifically approved—indeed, mandated—by Congress. In light of that fact, this Court owes appropriate deference to Congress' judgment, see *Fullilove* v. *Klutznick,* 448 U.S. 448, 472478, 490, 491 (opinion of Burger, C.J.); *id.,* at 500510, 515516, n. 14 (Powell, J., concurring); *id.,* at 517520 (*Marshall, J.,* concurring in judgment), and need not apply strict scrutiny analysis, see *id.,* at 474 (opinion of Burger, C.J.); *id.,* at 519 (*Marshall, J.,* concurring in judgment). Benign race-conscious measures mandated by Congress—even if those measures are not "remedial" in the sense of being designed to compensate victims of past governmental or societal discrimination—are constitutionally permissible to the extent that they serve important governmental objectives within the power of Congress and are substantially related to the achievement of those objectives. *Richmond* v. *J.A. Croson Co.,* 489 U.S. 469, distinguished and reconciled.

(b) The minority ownership policies serve an important governmental objective. Congress and the FCC do not justify the policies strictly as remedies for victims of demonstrable discrimination in the communications media, but rather have selected them primarily to promote broadcast diversity. This Court has long recognized as axiomatic that broadcasting may be regulated in light of the rights of the viewing and listening audience, and that the widest possible dissemination of information from diverse and antagonistic sources is essential to the public welfare. *Associated Press* v. *United States,* 326 U.S. 1, 20. Safeguarding the public's right to receive a diversity of views and information over the airwaves is therefore an integral component of the FCC's mission, serves important First Amendment values, and is, at the very least, an important governmental objective that is a sufficient basis for the policies in question.

(c) The minority ownership policies are substantially related to the achievement of the Government's interest in broadcast diversity. First, the FCC's conclusion that there is an empirical nexus between minority ownership and greater diversity, which is consistent with its longstanding view that ownership is a prime determinant of the range of programming available, is a product of its expertise and is entitled to deference. Second, by means of the recent appropriations legislation and by virtue of a long history of support for minority participation in the broadcasting industry, Congress has also made clear its view that the minority ownership policies advance the goal of diverse programming. Great weight must be given to the joint determination of the FCC and Congress.

(d) The judgment that there is a link between expanded minority ownership and broadcast diversity does not rest on impermissible stereotyping. Neither Congress nor the FCC assumes that in every case minority ownership and management will lead to more minority-oriented programming or to the expression of a discrete "minority viewpoint" on the airwaves. Nor do they pretend that all programming that appeals to minorities can be labeled "minority" or that programming that might be so described does not appeal to nonminorities. Rather, they maintain simply that expanded minority ownership of broadcast outlets will, in the aggregate, result in greater broadcast diversity. This judgment is corroborated by a host of empirical evidence suggesting that an owner's minority status influences the selection of topics for news coverage and the presentation of editorial viewpoint, especially on matters of particular concern to minorities, and has a special impact on the way in which images of minorities are presented. In addition, studies show that a minority owner is more likely to employ minorities in managerial and other important roles where they can have an impact on station policies. The FCC's policies are thus a product of analysis rather than a stereotyped reaction based on habit. Cf. *Fullilove, supra,* at 524, n.4. The type of reasoning employed by the FCC and Congress is not novel, but is utilized in many areas of the law, including the selection of jury venires on the basis of a fair cross section, and the reapportionment of electoral districts to preserve minority voting strength.

(e) The minority ownership policies are in other relevant respects substantially related to the goal of promoting broadcast diversity. The

Appendix B

FCC adopted and Congress endorsed minority ownership preferences only after long study, painstaking consideration of all available alternatives, and the emergence of evidence demonstrating that race-neutral means had not produced adequate broadcasting diversity. Moreover, the FCC did not act precipitately in devising the policies, having undertaken thorough evaluations in 1960, 1971, and 1978 before adopting them. Furthermore, the considered nature of the FCC's judgment in selecting these particular policies is illustrated by the fact that it has rejected other, more expansive types of minority preferences, *e.g.*, set-asides of certain frequencies for minority broadcasters. In addition, the minority ownership policies are aimed directly at the barriers that minorities face in entering the broadcasting industry. Thus, the FCC assigned a preference to minority status in the comparative licensing proceeding in order to compensate for a dearth of minority broadcasting experience. Similarly, the distress sale policy addresses the problem of inadequate access to capital by effectively lowering the sale price of existing stations and the problem of lack of information regarding license availability by providing existing licensees with an incentive to seek out minority buyers. The policies are also appropriately limited in extent and duration and subject to reassessment and reevaluation before renewal, since Congress has manifested its support for them through a series of appropriations acts of finite duration and has continued to hold hearings on the subject of minority ownership. Provisions for administrative and judicial review also guarantee that the policies are applied correctly in individual cases and that there will be frequent opportunities to revisit their merits. Finally, the policies impose only slight burdens on nonminorities. Award of a preference contravenes no legitimate, firmly rooted expectation of competing applicants, since the limited number of frequencies available means that no one has First Amendment right to a license and the granting of licenses requires consideration of public interest factors. Nor does the distress sale policy impose an undue burden on nonminorities, since it may be invoked only with respect to a small fraction of broadcast licenses, only when the licensee chooses to sell out at a low price rather than risk a hearing, and only when no competing application has been filed. It is not a quota or fixed quantity set-aside, and nonminorities are free to compete for the vast remainder of other available license opportunities.

No.89453, 277 U.S. App. D.C. 134, 873 F. 2d 347, affirmed and remanded; No.89700, 278 U.S. App. D.C. 24, 876 F. 2d 902, reversed and remanded.

Brennan, J., delivered the opinion of the Court, in which White, *Marshall, Blackmun*, and *Stevens, JJ.*, joined. *Stevens, J.*, filed a concurring opinion. *O'-*

Connor, J., filed a dissenting opinion, in which Rehn*quist, C.J.*, and *Scalia* and *Kennedy, JJ.*, joined. *Kennedy, J.*, filed a dissenting opinion, in which *Scalia, J.*, joined.

ADARAND CONSTRUCTORS, INC. V. PENA, SECRETARY OF TRANSPORTATION, ET AL. (1995)

Adarand Constructors v. Pena (1995) was an extraordinarily complicated case that resurfaced in 2001 as *Adarand Constructors v. Mineta*; in its 1995 form it was extremely influential in its ruling against set-asides for minority businesses by the U.S. Department of Transportation, and, by extension, to all federal agencies.

SYLLABUS

Argued January 17, 1995—Decided June 12, 1995.

Most federal agency contracts must contain a subcontractor compensation clause, which gives a prime contractor a financial incentive to hire subcontractors certified as small businesses controlled by socially and economically disadvantaged individuals, and requires the contractor to presume that such individuals include minorities or any other individuals found to be disadvantaged by the Small Business Administration (SBA). The prime contractor under a federal highway construction contract containing such a clause awarded a subcontract to a company that was certified as a small disadvantaged business. The record does not reveal how the company obtained its certification, but it could have been by any one of three routes: under one of two SBA programs—known as the 8(a) and 8(d) programs—or by a state agency under relevant Department of Transportation regulations. Petitioner Adarand Constructors, Inc., which submitted the low bid on the subcontract but was not a certified business, filed suit against respondent federal officials, claiming that the race based presumptions used in subcontractor compensation clauses violate the equal protection component of the Fifth Amendment's Due Process Clause. The District Court granted respondents summary judgment. In affirming, the Court of Appeals assessed the constitutionality of the federal race based action under a lenient standard, resembling intermediate scrutiny, which it determined was required by *Fullilove* v. *Klutznick*, 448 U.S. 448, and *Metro Broadcasting, Inc. v. FCC*.

Held: The judgment is vacated, and the case is remanded.

Appendix B

Justice O'Connor delivered an opinion with respect to Parts I, II, III-A, III-B, III-D, and IV, which was for the Court except insofar as it might be inconsistent with the views expressed in Justice Scalia's concurrence, concluding that:

1. Adarand has standing to seek forward looking relief. It has met the requirements necessary to maintain its claim by alleging an invasion of a legally protected interest in a particularized manner, and by showing that it is very likely to bid, in the relatively near future, on another Government contract offering financial incentives to a prime contractor for hiring disadvantaged subcontractors. See *Lujan v. Defenders of Wildlife*, 504 U.S. 555, 560.

2. All racial classifications, imposed by whatever federal, state, or local governmental actor, must be analyzed by a reviewing court under strict scrutiny.

(a) In *Richmond v. J. A. Croson Co.*, 488 U.S. 469, a majority of the Court held that the Fourteenth Amendment requires strict scrutiny of all race based action by state and local governments. While *Croson* did not consider what standard of review the Fifth Amendment requires for such action taken by the Federal Government, the Court's cases through *Croson* had established three general propositions with respect to governmental racial classifications. First, skepticism: "'[a]ny preference based on racial or ethnic criteria must necessarily receive a most searching examination,'" *Wygant v. Jackson Board of Ed.*, 476 U.S. 267, 273–274. Second, consistency: "the standard of review under the Equal Protection Clause is not dependent on the race of those burdened or benefited by a particular classification," *Croson, supra*, at 494. And third, congruence: "[e]qual protection analysis in the Fifth Amendment area is the same as that under the Fourteenth Amendment," *Buckley v. Valeo*, 424 U.S. 1, 93. Taken together, these propositions lead to the conclusion that any person, of whatever race, has the right to demand that any governmental actor subject to the Constitution justify any racial classification subjecting that person to unequal treatment under the strictest judicial scrutiny.

(b) However, a year after *Croson*, the Court, in *Metro Broadcasting*, upheld two federal race based policies against a Fifth Amendment challenge. The Court repudiated the long held notion that "it would be unthinkable that the same Constitution would impose a lesser duty on the Federal Government" than it does on a State to afford equal protection of the laws, *Bolling v. Sharpe*, 347 U.S. 497, 500, by holding that congressionally mandated "benign" racial classifications need only satisfy intermediate scrutiny. By adopting that standard, *Metro Broadcasting* departed from prior cases in two significant respects. First, it turned its back on *Croson*'s explanation that strict scrutiny of

267

governmental racial classifications is essential because it may not always be clear that a so called preference is in fact benign. Second, it squarely rejected one of the three propositions established by this Court's earlier cases, namely, congruence between the standards applicable to federal and state race based action, and in doing so also undermined the other two.

(c) The propositions undermined by *Metro Broadcasting* all derive from the basic principle that the Fifth and Fourteenth Amendments protect persons, not groups. It follows from that principle that all governmental action based on race—a group classification long recognized as in most circumstances irrelevant and therefore prohibited—should be subjected to detailed judicial inquiry to ensure that the personal right to equal protection has not been infringed. Thus, strict scrutiny is the proper standard for analysis of all racial classifications, whether imposed by a federal, state, or local actor. To the extent that *Metro Broadcasting* is inconsistent with that holding, it is overruled.

(d) The decision here makes explicit that federal racial classifications, like those of a State, must serve a compelling governmental interest, and must be narrowly tailored to further that interest. Thus, to the extent that *Fullilove* held federal racial classifications to be subject to a less rigorous standard, it is no longer controlling. Requiring strict scrutiny is the best way to ensure that courts will consistently give racial classifications a detailed examination, as to both ends and means. It is not true that strict scrutiny is strict in theory, but fatal in fact. Government is not disqualified from acting in response to the unhappy persistence of both the practice and the lingering effects of racial discrimination against minority groups in this country. When race based action is necessary to further a compelling interest, such action is within constitutional constraints if it satisfies the "narrow tailoring" test set out in this Court's previous cases.

3. Because this decision alters the playing field in some important respects, the case is remanded to the lower courts for further consideration. The Court of Appeals did not decide whether the interests served by the use of subcontractor compensation clauses are properly described as "compelling." Nor did it address the question of narrow tailoring in terms of this Court's strict scrutiny cases. Unresolved questions also remain concerning the details of the complex regulatory regimes implicated by the use of such clauses.

Justice Scalia agreed that strict scrutiny must be applied to racial classifications imposed by all governmental actors, but concluded that government can never have a "compelling interest" in discriminating on the basis of race in order to "make up" for past racial discrimination in the opposite direction. Under the Constitution there can be no such thing as either a creditor or a debtor race. We are just one race in the eyes of government.

Appendix B

O'Connor, J., announced the judgment of the Court and delivered an opinion with respect to Parts I, II, III-A, III-B, III-D, and IV, which was for the Court except insofar as it might be inconsistent with the views expressed in the concurrence of Scalia, J., and an opinion with respect to Part III-C. Parts I, II, III-A, III-B, III-D, and IV of that opinion were joined by Rehnquist, C. J., and Kennedy and Thomas, JJ., and by Scalia, J., to the extent heretofore indicated; and Part III-C was joined by Kennedy, J. Scalia, J., and Thomas, J., filed opinions concurring in part and concurring in the judgment. Stevens, J., filed a dissenting opinion, in which Ginsburg, J., joined. Souter, J., filed a dissenting opinion, in which Ginsburg and Breyer, JJ., joined. Ginsburg, J., filed a dissenting opinion, in which Breyer, J., joined.

UNITED STATES V. VIRGINIA ET AL. (1996)

United States v. Virginia concerned the constitutionality of single-sex education at Virginia Military Institute, an all-male military school; the Court ruled that single-sex education was discriminatory if women did not have a comparable public institution to attend, and ordered VMI to admit women.

SYLLABUS

Argued January 17, 1996—Decided June 26, 1996.

Virginia Military Institute (VMI) is the sole single sex school among Virginia's public institutions of higher learning. VMI's distinctive mission is to produce "citizen soldiers," men prepared for leadership in civilian life and in military service. Using an "adversative method" of training not available elsewhere in Virginia, VMI endeavors to instill physical and mental discipline in its cadets and impart to them a strong moral code. Reflecting the high value alumni place on their VMI training, VMI has the largest per student endowment of all undergraduate institutions in the Nation. The United States sued Virginia and VMI, alleging that VMI's exclusively male admission policy violated the Fourteenth Amendment's Equal Protection Clause. The District Court ruled in VMI's favor. The Fourth Circuit reversed and ordered Virginia to remedy the constitutional violation. In response, Virginia proposed a parallel program for women: Virginia Women's Institute for Leadership (VWIL), located at Mary Baldwin College, a private liberal arts school for women. The District Court found that Virginia's proposal satisfied the Constitution's equal protection requirement, and the

Affirmative Action

Fourth Circuit affirmed. The appeals court deferentially reviewed Virginia's plan and determined that provision of single gender educational options was a legitimate objective. Maintenance of single sex programs, the court concluded, was essential to that objective. The court recognized, however, that its analysis risked bypassing equal protection scrutiny, so it fashioned an additional test, asking whether VMI and VWIL students would receive "substantively comparable" benefits. Although the Court of Appeals acknowledged that the VWIL degree lacked the historical benefit and prestige of a VMI degree, the court nevertheless found the educational opportunities at the two schools sufficiently comparable.
Held:

1. Parties who seek to defend gender based government action must demonstrate an "exceedingly persuasive justification" for that action. *E.g., Mississippi Univ. for Women v. Hogan,* 458 U.S. 718, 724. Neither federal nor state government acts compatibly with equal protection when a law or official policy denies to women, simply because they are women, full citizenship stature—equal opportunity to aspire, achieve, participate in and contribute to society based on their individual talents and capacities. To meet the burden of justification, a State must show "at least that the [challenged] classification serves 'important governmental objectives and that the discriminatory means employed' are substantially related to the achievement of those objectives.'" *Ibid.,* quoting *Wengler v. Druggists Mutual Ins. Co.,* 446 U.S. 142, 150. The justification must be genuine, not hypothesized or invented *post hoc* in response to litigation. And it must not rely on overbroad generalizations about the different talents, capacities, or preferences of males and females. See, *e.g., Weinberger v. Wiesenfeld,* 420 U.S. 636, 643, 648. The heightened review standard applicable to sex based classifications does not make sex a proscribed classification, but it does mean that categorization by sex may not be used to created or perpetuate the legal, social, and economic inferiority of women.

2. Virginia's categorical exclusion of women from the educational opportunities VMI provides denies equal protection to women.

(a) Virginia contends that single sex education yields important educational benefits and that provision of an option for such education fosters diversity in educational approaches. Benign justifications proffered in defense of categorical exclusions, however, must describe actual state purposes, not rationalizations for actions in fact differently grounded. Virginia has not shown that VMI was established, or has been maintained, with a view to diversifying, by its categorical exclusion of women, educational opportunities within the State. A purpose genuinely to advance an array of educational options is not served by VMI's historic and constant plan to afford a unique

270

educational benefit only to males. However well this plan serves Virginia's sons, it makes no provision whatever for her daughters.

(b) Virginia also argues that VMI's adversative method of training provides educational benefits that cannot be made available, unmodified, to women, and that alterations to accommodate women would necessarily be so drastic as to destroy VMI's program. It is uncontested that women's admission to VMI would require accommodations, primarily in arranging housing assignments and physical training programs for female cadets. It is also undisputed, however, that neither the goal of producing citizen soldiers, VMI's *raison d'être*, nor VMI's implementing methodology is inherently unsuitable to women. The District Court made "findings" on "gender based developmental differences" that restate the opinions of Virginia's expert witnesses about typically male or typically female "tendencies." Courts, however, must take "a hard look" at generalizations or tendencies of the kind Virginia pressed, for state actors controlling gates to opportunity have no warrant to exclude qualified individuals based on "fixed notions concerning the roles and abilities of males and females." *Mississippi Univ. for Women*, 458 U.S., at 725. The notion that admission of women would downgrade VMI's stature, destroy the adversative system and, with it, even the school, is a judgment hardly proved, a prediction hardly different from other "self fulfilling prophec[ies]," *see id.*, at 730, once routinely used to deny rights or opportunities. Women's successful entry into the federal military academies, and their participation in the Nation's military forces, indicate that Virginia's fears for VMI's future may not be solidly grounded. The State's justification for excluding all women from "citizen soldier" training for which some are qualified, in any event, does not rank as "exceedingly persuasive."

3. The remedy proffered by Virginia—maintain VMI as a male only college and create VWIL as a separate program for women—does not cure the constitutional violation.

(a) A remedial decree must closely fit the constitutional violation; it must be shaped to place persons unconstitutionally denied an opportunity or advantage in the position they would have occupied in the absence of discrimination. See *Milliken* v. *Bradley*, 433 U.S. 267, 280. The constitutional violation in this case is the categorical exclusion of women, in disregard of their individual merit, from an extraordinary educational opportunity afforded men. Virginia chose to leave untouched VMI's exclusionary policy, and proposed for women only a separate program, different in kind from VMI and unequal in tangible and intangible facilities. VWIL affords women no opportunity to experience the rigorous military training for which VMI is famed. Kept away from the pressures, hazards, and psychological bonding characteristic of VMI's adversative training,

VWIL students will not know the feeling of tremendous accomplishment commonly experienced by VMI's successful cadets. Virginia maintains that methodological differences are justified by the important differences between men and women in learning and development needs, but generalizations about "the way women are," estimates of what is appropriate for *most women*, no longer justify denying opportunity to women whose talent and capacity place them outside the average description. In myriad respects other than military training, VWIL does not qualify as VMI's equal. The VWIL program is a pale shadow of VMI in terms of the range of curricular choices and faculty stature, funding, prestige, alumni support and influence. Virginia has not shown substantial equality in the separate educational opportunities the State supports at VWIL and VMI. Cf. *Sweatt* v. *Painter*, 339 U.S. 629.

(b) The Fourth Circuit failed to inquire whether the proposed remedy placed women denied the VMI advantage in the position they would have occupied in the absence of discrimination, *Milliken*, 433 U.S., at 280, and considered instead whether the State could provide, with fidelity to equal protection, separate and unequal educational programs for men and women. In declaring the substantially different and significantly unequal VWIL program satisfactory, the appeals court displaced the exacting standard developed by this Court with a deferential standard, and added an inquiry of its own invention, the "substantive comparability" test. The Fourth Circuit plainly erred in exposing Virginia's VWIL plan to such a deferential analysis, for "all gender based classifications today" warrant "heightened scrutiny." See *J. E. B.* v. *Alabama ex rel. T.B.*, 511 U.S. 127, 136. Women seeking and fit for a VMI quality education cannot be offered anything less, under the State's obligation to afford them genuinely equal protection.

976 F. 2d 890, affirmed; 44 F. 3d 1229, reversed and remanded.

Ginsburg, J., delivered the opinion of the Court, in which Stevens, O'-Connor, Kennedy, Souter, and Breyer, JJ., joined. Rehnquist, C.J., filed an opinion concurring in the judgment. Scalia, J., filed a dissenting opinion. Thomas, J., took no part in the consideration or decision of the case.

APPENDIX C

INITIATIVES AND REFERENDUMS

Initiatives—citizen-initiated ballot measures—were a popular form of activism in the 1990s, and they proved to be especially influential in the field of affirmative action. Proposition 209 was placed on the California ballot in 1995; it passed the same year, outlawing affirmative action in the state in 1996. Initiative 200 was placed on the Washington State ballot in 1998; it passed in 1998 and outlawed affirmative action in the state in 1999.

PROPOSITION 209

This initiative measure is submitted to the people in accordance with the provisions of Article II, Section 8 of the Constitution.

This initiative measure expressly amends the Constitution by adding a section thereto; therefore, new provisions proposed to be added are printed in *italic type* to indicate that they are new.

PROPOSED AMENDMENT TO ARTICLE I

Section 31 is added to Article I of the California Constitution as follows:

SEC. 31. (a) The state shall not discriminate against, or grant preferential treatment to, any individual or group on the basis of race, sex, color, ethnicity, or national origin in the operation of public employment, public education, or public contracting.

(b) This section shall apply only to action taken after the section's effective date.

(c) Nothing in this section shall be interpreted as prohibiting bona fide qualifications based on sex which are reasonably necessary to the normal operation of public employment, public education, or public contracting.

(d) Nothing in this section shall be interpreted as invalidating any court order or consent decree which is in force as of the effective date of this section.

(e) *Nothing in this section shall be interpreted as prohibiting action which must be taken to establish or maintain eligibility for any federal program, where ineligibility would result in a loss of federal funds to the state.*

(f) *For the purposes of this section, "state" shall include, but not necessarily be limited to, the state itself, any city, county, city and county, public university system, including the University of California, community college district, school district, special district, or any other political subdivision or governmental instrumentality of or within the state.*

(g) *The remedies available for violations of this section shall be the same, regardless of the injured party's race, sex, color, ethnicity, or national origin, as are otherwise available for violations of then-existing California antidiscrimination law.*

(h) *This section shall be self-executing. If any part or parts of this section are found to be in conflict with federal law or the United States Constitution, the section shall be implemented to the maximum extent that federal law and the United States Constitution permit. Any provision held invalid shall be severable from the remaining portions of this section.*

INITIATIVE 200 PROPOSED WASHINGTON STATE CIVIL RIGHTS INITIATIVE

PROPOSED BALLOT TITLE

Shall government entities be prohibited from discriminating against or granting preferential treatment to individuals or groups based on race, sex, color, ethnicity, or national origin?

PROPOSED BALLOT SUMMARY

This initiative prohibits government from discriminating against or granting preferential treatment to individuals or groups based on race, sex, color, ethnicity, or national origin in public employment, public education, or public contracting. Government includes all public entities, including the state, cities, counties, public schools, public colleges, public universities, and other governmental instrumentalities. This initiative does not repeal or modify any law or governmental action that does not discriminate or grant preferential treatment.

274

Appendix C

CO-SPONSORS & CO-CHAIRS

Representative Scott Smith
19311 – 110th Ave Ct E
Graham, WA 98338-8140
(206) 846-8947

Tim Eyman
7721 Corliss Ave N
Seattle, WA 98103-4934
(206) 528-1685

An ACT Relating to prohibiting government entities from discriminating or granting preferential treatment based on race, sex, color, ethnicity, or national origin; and adding new sections to chapter 49.60 RCW.

BE IT ENACTED BY THE PEOPLE OF THE STATE OF WASHINGTON:

{+ NEW SECTION. +} Sec. 1. (1) The state shall not discriminate against, or grant preferential treatment to, any individual or group on the basis of race, sex, color, ethnicity, or national origin in the operation of public employment, public education, or public contracting.

(2) This section applies only to action taken after the effective date of this section.

(3) This section does not affect any law or governmental action that does not discriminate against, or grant preferential treatment to, any individual or group on the basis of race, sex, color, ethnicity, or national origin.

(4) This section does not affect any otherwise lawful classification that:

(a) Is based on sex, and is necessary for sexual privacy or medical or psychological treatment; or

(b) Is necessary for undercover law enforcement or for film, video, audio, or theatrical casting; or

(c) Provides for separate athletic teams for each sex.

(5) This section does not invalidate any court order or consent decree that is in force as of the effective date of this section.

(6) This section does not prohibit action that must be taken to establish or maintain eligibility for any federal program, if ineligibility would result in a loss of federal funds to the state.

(7) For the purposes of this section, "state" includes, but is not necessarily limited to, the state itself, any city, county, public college or university, community college, school district, special district, or other political subdivision or governmental instrumentality of or within the state.

(8) The remedies available for violations of this section shall be the same, regardless of the injured party's race, sex, color, ethnicity, or national origin, as are otherwise available for violations of Washington anti-discrimination law.

(9) This section shall be self-executing. If any part or parts of this section are found to be in conflict with federal law, the United States Constitution, or the Washington state Constitution, the section shall be implemented to the maximum extent that federal law, the United States Constitution, and the Washington state Constitution permit. Any provision held invalid shall be severable from the remaining portions of this section.

Sec. 2. This act shall be known and cited as the Washington State Civil Rights Act.

Sec. 3. Sections 1 and 2 of this act are each added to chapter 49.60 RCW.

INDEX

Locators in **boldface** indicate main topics. Locators followed by *g* indicate glossary entries.

277

Affirmative Action

Index

279

Affirmative Action

Index

281

Affirmative Action

Index

Affirmative Action

Index

Affirmative Action

Affirmative Action

Index

Index

Affirmative Action

Index

Stone, Lucy 8–9
strict scrutiny 154g
  and *Adarand Constructors,
    Inc. v. Pena* 84, 86,
    120–121
  *City of Richmond v. J. A.
    Croson Co.* 71
  conservative justices and
    21
  Hopwood v. Texas 99
  *Metro Broadcasting, Inc. v.
    Federal Communications
    Commission* 76, 77
  Podberesky v. Kirwan
    88–89
  *Regents of the University of
    California v. Bakke* 19,
    45, 47
  *United States v. Paradise et
    al.* 66, 67
  *Wygant et al. v. Jackson
    Board of Education et al.*
    58–59
structural inequality 154g
Sturm, Susan 144
suffrage. *See* voting rights
suit 154g
Summers, Lawrence H. 137,
  139
Supreme Court, U. S. *See also
  specific cases*
  accusations of
    discrimination against
    130
  affirmative action rulings
    by **18–20**
  appointment by George
    H. W. Bush to 21
  cases brought before
    34–88
  cases declined by 128
  changed balance on 78
  and Civil Rights Act of
    1875 7, 110
  Bill Clinton's
    appointments to 21
  conservative justices
    appointed to 20–21
  consolidation of similar
    cases 14
  current justices on 23
  dissenting opinions from
    159
  Dred Scott ruling by 6
  and educational policy
    157
  highway construction
    program challenge
    135

and *Hopwood v. Texas* 122,
  136
Thurgood Marshall and
  145–146
and Proposition 209
  challenge 124
Public Information
  Officer web site **232**
race discrimination cases
  9–10
Ronald Reagan's
  appointments to
  20–21, 116
Clarence Thomas and
  146
web sites for cases of
  160, 161
Sweatt v. Painter (1950) 11,
  12, 98, 112
syllabi of cases 159

T

Tarlton Law Library **232**
taverns 30
television
  broadcasting licenses for
    4, 75–78
  women/minorities in
    127
Terenzini, Patrick T. 24–25
tests
  college entrance exams
    139
  employee. *See* employee
    testing
  literacy 111
  standardized 130, 134
Texaco 95
Texas
  admissions requirements
    in 122–123
  anti–affirmative action
    drive in 124
  bilingual debates in 139
  and Federal Educational
    Rights and Privacy Act
    132
  higher education in 22
  Hopwood v. Texas **98–102**
  poll tax in 29
  professional schools in
    117
  public university
    affirmative action
    admissions in 122
  and race in higher
    education admissions/
    scholarships 121
  Sweatt v. Painter 112

Texas A & M University 121
Texas Southern University law
  school 136
textile mills 12
Thirteenth Amendment 6,
  28
  ratification of 109
  text of **238**
Thomas, Clarence 78, **146**
  *Adarand Constructors, Inc.
    v. Pena* 85, 121
  anti–affirmative action
    rulings by 23
  appointment of 116,
    118
  George H. W. Bush and
    142
  Anita Hill and 144
  opposition to affirmative
    action by 20, 21
Thompson, Tommy 22–23,
  142
Tien, Chang-lin 123
Tilden, Samuel 110
Time 162
title 154g
Title II of Civil Rights Act of
  1964 31, 113
Title VI of Civil Rights Act of
  1964 31, 33, 113, **154**
  guidelines for 119
  Health, Education and
    Welfare interpretation
    of 116
  and Native Americans/
    Asian Americans 119
  *Regents of the University of
    California v. Bakke*
    46–47
Title VII of Civil Rights Act
  of 1964 33, 113, **154**
  EEOC established under
    31
  Firefighters v. Cleveland
    60–62
  *Franks v. Bowman
    Transportation Co.*
    40–42
  Griggs v. Duke Power Co
    34
  *Hazelwood School District
    v. United States*
    42–43
  interstate commerce and
    discrimination under
    31
  *Johnson v. Transportation
    Agency, Santa Clara
    County* 117

293

Affirmative Action

Index